Caleb S. Henry

Considerations on Some of the Elements and Conditions of Social

Welfare and Human Progress

Caleb S. Henry

Considerations on Some of the Elements and Conditions of Social Welfare and Human Progress

ISBN/EAN: 9783337371449

Printed in Europe, USA, Canada, Australia, Japan

Cover: Foto ©Suzi / pixelio.de

More available books at **www.hansebooks.com**

CONSIDERATIONS

ON SOME OF

THE ELEMENTS AND CONDITIONS

OF

SOCIAL WELFARE

AND

HUMAN PROGRESS.

BEING

ACADEMIC AND OCCASIONAL DISCOURSES AND OTHER PIECES

BY

C. S. HENRY, D. D.

NEW YORK:
D. APPLETON AND COMPANY.
443 BROADWAY.
LONDON: 16 LITTLE BRITAIN
1861.

TO

MY FRIEND

EDWARD BECH.

PREFACE.

THE pieces contained in this volume are now collected and published at the request of many of my friends, particularly among my former pupils, attendants on my lectures in the New York University. The title under which they appear, has been given them as being a sufficiently appropriate indication of their general scope and purport. The reader will find some repetitions—naturally enough occurring in pieces written at intervals during so long a period on topics so nearly related. I have not thought it worth while to attempt retrenching them, because in most cases it could scarcely be done without detriment to the context where they

occur. I have therefore let them stand as they
were.

This volume contains some things not quite
in unison with the tone of popular opinion—particularly in relation to the working of our political
institutions and to our future fortunes as a nation.
On these topics the utterance of honest censure
and prophetic warning is not only unacceptable,
but quite likely to subject one to odium, as wanting in patriotism. But who is the better lover of
his country, he who lulls the people with soft strains
of pleasing adulation, and kindles their fancy with
bright pictures of future greatness and glory ; or
he who tells them of the rocks and dangers that
are around them, and of the conditions on which
their safety depends ? I profess to love my country as much as any man that breathes ; but I do
not think the best way to show it is by perpetual
eulogies on our superiority as a nation. I desire
for my country a glorious future ; no man can more
fervently pray for it ; but I do not think the best
way to make it sure is to be forever casting brilliant
horoscopes, without a single suggestion of the possibilities of disaster and defeat. At all events

there are enough to flatter our self-love ; let one faithful friend be permitted to point out our faults. There are enough to cry peace and safety ; let one voice of warning be tolerated. If there is any thing unsound in the principles and doctrines I have propounded ; any thing erroneous in the conditions of social and political salvation I have laid down as indispensable ; any thing false or over-drawn in the evils I have sketched ; any thing unreal in the dangers I have pointed out, let it be shown and no man can be more ready to acknowledge it than I shall be.

As to the rest, these discussions touch upon the greatest problems of human thought, and embrace questions of the highest scientific and practical interest ; and I cannot but hope they will be regarded as worthy of the candid consideration of cultivated and thoughtful persons, whether or not they may agree with every opinion advanced.

NEWBURGH, on the Hudson,
August, 1860.

CONTENTS.

THE IMPORTANCE OF ELEVATING THE INTELLECTUAL SPIRIT OF THE NATION.

1

"——While the employment of the mind upon things purely intellectual is to most men irksome, whereas the sensitive powers by our constant use of them acquire strength—the objects of sense are too often counted the chief good. For these things men fight, and cheat, and scramble.

"Therefore in order to tame mankind and introduce a sense of virtue, the best human means is to exercise their reason, to give them a glimpse of a world superior to the sensible; and while they take pains to cherish and maintain the animal life, to teach them not to neglect the intellectual."

THE IMPORTANCE OF ELEVATING THE IN-
TELLECTUAL SPIRIT OF THE NATION.

I FEEL myself honored by the invitation that
has drawn me here to-day. It is the first time in
my life that I visit these seats of learning ; but I
am glad there are other associations than those of
sight, which banish the sense of strangeness and
pleasantly awaken the feeling of home. The Society at whose request I come is itself a portion of a
much larger community—the great Brotherhood of
Scholars—composed of all those who are animated
by a common love of good letters ; and these Academic seats are, if I may be allowed the expression,
one of the fair Chapters of our Order, where the
humblest of its members may be sure of a Brother's
welcome. Festivals like this we hold to-day have a
natural influence to quicken the scholarly spirit,
and to brighten the golden chain that unites the dis-

ciples of Letters. Laying aside the cares of ordinary
life, we meet together as scholars, to indulge in the
free communication of those sympathies that are
common to the lovers of good learning. The occasion has naturally suggested to me as a subject of
remark—the importance of drawing closer together
the bonds of brotherhood among the lovers of letters, and of more earnest exertions to exalt the intellectual spirit of the nation.

It seems to me there are some peculiar considerations, connected with the condition of our country, that render it exceedingly desirable and important, no less for the welfare of the country generally, than for the more immediate interests of
truth and learning, that a loftier tone, and a livelier sympathy, should pervade and connect the
whole body of those who either are themselves engaged in the higher pursuits of science and letters,
or appreciate the worth and value of such pursuits.
In this country, while intellectual activity, in its
higher departments, is, on the one hand, not favored by some causes that exist elsewhere, it is, on
the other hand, positively repressed by many un-
friendly influences, that are either peculiar to our
country, or work in a peculiar degree. It seems
needful, then, to cast about for something to sup-

ply what is wanting, and to counteract what is injurious ;—to give a quickened impulse, a higher flight, and a wider reach to intellectual exertion ; —and to work such a change in the state of opinion and direction of the public resources, as shall secure to the loftier pursuits of truth, beauty, and letters, those fostering influences of which they are now so sadly destitute.

Whether or not these results, in any sufficient degree, can be fairly hoped for, they are still objects attractive to the imagination and to the wishes ; and at all events we shall find it interesting to survey the present state of cultivation in our country, and the influences that affect it.

We have among us no LEARNED ORDER of men. I use the expression for its convenient brevity, not meaning by it merely those who are devoted to the pursuits of learning in the strict sense of the word, but also all those who give their lives to intellectual inquiry and production in any of the higher departments of science and letters. We have a most respectable body of educated men, some of them engaged in the applications of science to the arts of life, but most of them exercising the different public professions. Whether or not they are

all adequately appreciated and rewarded, still we
have such a class, employed in working with, com-
bining and applying—in explaining, communicating, and diffusing, the knowledge already possessed.
But in addition to these we want an order of men
devoted to original inquiry and production, who
without reference to the more palpable uses of
knowledge shall pursue truth for its own sake.
We need a class of men whose lives and powers
shall be exclusively given to exploring the higher
spheres of knowledge, opening new sources of truth
and beauty, increasing the amount and extending
the domain of science. We need an order of men
who may be free to leave the mists and the vapors
that settle upon the low grounds of the earth, and
getting themselves up into the mountain-tops, may
dwell there in a serene and lofty seclusion alike
from the goading of life's cares and from the fe-
verish stir and strife of its coarse and beggarly elements, and in the clear air beholding with pure
and tranquil heart "the bright countenance of
Truth," may catch and reflect its divine spirit to
all times. In short, we want an order of men, surrounded with all needful appliances, and left with
a free mind to follow the impulses of their nature
in the highest spheres of science and letters.

Such an order of men is a component part of every sound and perfect body politic. It is indispensable to its highest welfare. " Man liveth not by bread alone," any more as a nation than as an individual.

> We live by Admiration, Hope, and Love,
> And even as these are well and wisely fixed,
> In dignity of being we ascend.
>   WORDSWORTH.

National well-being consists in the development of the proper humanity of a nation—in the cultivation and exercise of the reason and moral nature, and in the subordination to these of all the lower principles. It is found in the wisdom, the intellectual elevation, and the virtuous energy of a people ; and of these, the light of pure and lofty science is the quickening impulse and the genial nutriment. All pure and elevated truth is in itself good, and it does good. It is of God, and it leads to God again. Without its noble inspiration we may indeed serve the turn of this world's lowest uses ;—we can gain money, grow fat and die ;— but we are not fit for the better ends even of this world. " He," says Bishop Berkeley, " who hath not meditated much upon God, the human soul, and its chief good, may possibly make a shrewd and thriving earth-worm, but he will indubitably make a blundering patriot and a sorry statesman." As the well-being of individuals is in proportion to the culture and right exertion of those rational and moral faculties which mark and distinguish our humanity, so the welfare of a nation requires that the select number of those who are endowed with preeminent gifts of intellectual power, should be left free, with all observance and respect attending them, to follow those inward promptings of their nature which mark their true vocation—their mission on the earth—the promotion of God's glory by seeking and exploring the highest sources of truth and beauty, for the honor and instruction of their country. Such minds should, in the noble language of Milton, " have liberty in the spacious circuits of their musing, to propose to themselves whatever is of highest hope and hardest attempting"—whether in " beholding the bright countenance of Truth, in the quiet and still air of delightful studies," or as " poets soaring high in the region of their fancies, with their garlands and singing robes about them." " These abilities," he goes on, " wheresoever they be found, are the inspired gifts of God, rarely bestowed, but yet to some in every nation, and are of power, beside the office of a pulpit, to imbreed and cherish in a great people the seeds of virtue and public civility, to allay the perturbations of the mind, and set the affections in a right tune."

A learned order is, moreover, one of the *conservative powers* of a nation, necessary in order to check the undue predominance of the more gross and material elements.   In this country it is peculiarly necessary to counteract the overgrowth and dangerous tendencies of the commercial and political spirit. The overgrowth of these influences in other countries is checked not only by venerable institutions both of religion and of learning, but also by ancient dignities, more imposing forms of government, and various other causes which have no place in this country.   The only counteracting influences that can be brought to bear in this country against the undue love of wealth and politics, are RELIGION and LETTERS ; and religion, left as it is to take care of itself, will be entirely inadequate, unless the intellectual spirit of the nation be elevated by high and pure letters.

There is no theme so much a favorite amongst us as the glorious career and magnificent destiny of our country.   Our presses teem with gorgeous visions of the future.   It is the subject of popular dec-

1*

lamation through the length and breadth of the
land.   The public mind has been too much dazzled
by these brilliant pictures.   It is comparatively a
small thing that we have drawn upon ourselves the
sneers of other nations, who from a distance are
more camly watching the progress of our history.
Nor is it the chief evil that comes of indulging these
self-pleasing fancies, that they foster an overweening national pride.   The greatest danger is, that we
shall fall into the habit of looking upon it as a settled and inevitable thing that we are to become not
only the largest and richest, but the freest, wisest,
and happiest nation on the globe, while we entirely
forget the *conditions* on which, after all, our national
prosperity is suspended.   In the confident tone of
these predictions, it seems to be forgotten that the
true interests and permanent welfare of our nation
can be secured only by maintaining ourselves in
harmony with the universal and invariable laws of
the moral world.   It seems to be forgotten that
there are causes, in active operation at this moment,
quite as powerful to work our downfall as to secure
our greatness.

I have alluded to the dangerous predominance
of two elements in our country.

The one is the *love of money*.   Our national

character is eminently distinguished, and in the view of other nations disgraced, by this trait.   The whole mass of society, from the top to the bottom, is heaving with the restless struggle for gain.   It takes, indeed, in many of its manifestations, a cast of grandeur, from the energy it calls forth, and the vastness of the schemes it employs itself upon. The boundless physical resources of the country are unfolding with unparalleled rapidity.   The din and bustle of internal improvement is ringing from one end of the land to the other.   The country is growing rich beyond all computation ; and almost every man in the country is hastening to be rich.   Now it is not necessary to quarrel with this development of the physical resources of our land.   But it is necessary to be aware of the corresponding dangers it brings, and to guard against them.   It is needful to feel that national wealth is by no means necessarily national well-being ; that merely to be rich no more makes the proper well-being of a nation, than of an individual.   On the contrary, the natural tendency of excessive wealth is to luxury, and private and public corruption.   It contains the germ of every evil, and, unless checked and sanctified by higher and happier influences, is sure to degrade a nation —to blast its prosperity, and work its ruin.   This is a truth, of which all history is an impressive demonstration. It is not necessary to quarrel with the natural desire of acquisition ; but it is necessary to guard against its excess, and to keep it subordinate to its proper ends. In this country it is excessive. It is restless, insatiable, boundless—unhallowed and unredeemed by better influences, by a superior and pervading respect and love for higher and nobler objects. For along with this increase of wealth has come a prodigious growth of luxury—an infinite multiplication of the means and refinements of physical enjoyment ; and we are hurrying on with prodigious strides to a state of excessive *civilization* without due *cultivation*—of luxurious indulgence and the refinements of pleasure, without a proportionate growth of intellectual and moral culture, without a lively and respectful regard for the less material and less vulgar interests of life.

In such a state of things, the morals of a nation, and the tone of society, cannot but be injuriously affected. Unhappily these evils are but too visible. The use of a single word sometimes tells much in regard to the moral tone of a nation. Is not a sad state of moral feeling betrayed in a country where *wealth*—that good old-English word, designed to express the total sum of the elements of well-being,

including all that relates to man's higher nature
and wants—has come to mean nothing but *money;*
and where *worth* is used to tell *how much* a man
has ? Yet so it is. Mr. Wilkins hath a hundred
thousand dollars, and he is *worth* five times as much
as Mr. Johnson, who hath but twenty thousand,
while Mr. Thompson hath none, and is *worth nothing.* Throughout the country the great majority
of the mass of the people have a profound reverence
for nothing but money. Public office is a partial
exception. And why should it be otherwise ? They
see nothing else so powerful. Riches not only secure the material ends of life—its pleasures and luxuries ; but they open the way to all the less material
objects of man's desire—respect and observance,
authority and influence.

In the mean time the tone of society is de-
based.

The *luxury* of mere riches is always a vulgar
luxury. It is external, and devoid of good taste.
It always goeth about feeling its purse. It counteth
the fitness and propriety of its appointments by the
sum they cost. It calleth your attention to its glittering equipage, and saith it ought to be of the first
style, for it cost the highest price. It receiveth you
to its grand saloons, and wisheth you to mark its

furniture.   It inviteth you to its table, and biddeth
you note the richness of its plate, and telleth you
the price of its wines.

The *fashion* of mere riches is also a vulgar fashion.   The butterfly insignificance of its life is not
even adorned by the graceful fluttering of its golden
wings.   It is quite possible to have the extrava-
gance and frivolity of fashionable life, without the
ease and grace, the charms of wit and spirit, and
the elegance of mind and manners, that in other
countries often adorn its real nothingness, or cover
up the coarse workings of jealousy and pretension.

Such must always be the tendency of things
where the commercial spirit acquires an undue predominance—where the excessive and exclusive respect for money is not repressed by appropriate
counter-checks.   In some countries these checks to
the overgrowth of the commercial spirit are sought
for in venerable institutions of religion and letters,
in habits of respect for established rank, and above
all by throwing a considerable portion of the property into such a train of transmission, as that it becomes the appendage and ornament of something
that appeals to the higher sentiments, something
that is held in greater respect than mere riches, and
with the possession of which is connected high and

dignified trusts—a high education, and the culture and habit of all lofty and generous sentiments. This is unquestionably the *idea* lying at the ground of the English aristocracy, in the theory of the English constitution.   Hence inalienable estates, belonging not to the man, but to the dignity ; where the wealth is designed to be only the means of sustaining and adorning the dignity—of fulfilling its proper trusts—and of upholding those high interests of the country, of which the possessor of the dignity is but the representative ; and where habits of education from generation to generation are designed to teach and impress the value of many other things above mere wealth, and to connect with the possession and use of riches, honorable sentiments, liberal culture, and the disposition to respect and promote the cultivation of high science and letters, and all the more spiritual elements of social well-being.   And strong as are our prejudices in this country, it may at least be questioned, whether a fair estimate of the evils on both sides would not show that such an aristocracy is in many respects preferable to that which otherwise will and must predominate—the aristocracy of new riches, where the elements of society are in perpetual fluctuation, where the coarse pretensions of lucky speculators, and the vulgar struggles of all to get up, leave little room for the feeling of repose and respect.*

The other principal element of danger to our country is the *strife of party politics*. The structure of our government, with all its advantages, is attended with some peculiar perils. We are apt, however, to be deluded by an extravagant opinion of the efficacy of our form of government in securing the welfare of the nation. But there is no charm in a form of government. Government is but the condition under which the destiny of a people is wrought out for good or for evil by the peo-

---

* I was struck with the following passage in a recent well-written and agreeable book entitled "*Sketches of Switzerland.*" Speaking of the society at Paris, the writer had introduced an anecdote illustrating the simplicity of manners that characterized the celebrated Duke de Valmy; he then adds, "But I could fill volumes with anecdotes of a similar nature; for in these countries, in which men of illustrious deeds abound, one is never disturbed in society by the fussy pretension and swagger that is apt to mark the presence of a lucky speculator in the stocks.

"I have already told you how little sensation is produced in Paris by the presence of a celebrity, though in no part of the world is more delicate respect paid to those who have earned renown, whether in letters, arts, or arms. Like causes, however, notoriously produce like effects; and I think, under the new *regime*, which is purely a money-power system, directed by a mind whose ambition is wealth, that one really meets here more of that swagger of stocks and lucky speculations in the world, than was formerly the case. Society is decidedly less graceful, more care-worn, and of a worse tone to-day, than it was previously to the revolution of 1830."

ple themselves. The freest government is the one that is exposed to the greatest perils ; if it does not work well, it must work worse than others. Our form of government presupposes that the capacity of self-government is commensurate with the right ; consequently it is fit for us no longer than we are fit for it. Universal suffrage in the hands of an unenlightened and corrupt people is like deadly weapons in the hands of a madman. You can give the people the right of ruling only on supposition that they will rule well. But it is not a thing to be taken for granted that a majority can do no wrong or foolish things. The doings of a majority will never be a whit wiser or better than the wisdom and virtue of the individuals that compose it. The great question then obviously is : Whether the people at large are so enlightened and virtuous, that the present will of a majority, will, in the long run, always be an expression of what is wisest and best for the nation,—or at least, a truer expression of it than can be had in any other way ? It is no acceptable doctrine now-a-days to deny this. But taking human nature as it is given in history and experience, I must be permitted to doubt whether it is safe to assume it. Speaking abstractly, and without reference to any party, I must be permitted to avow the conviction that the majority of the wisdom and virtue of any country, which, for the good of the country, ought to rule, will always be most likely to have its proper influence, where the present will of a mere numerical majority is restrained and limited. Such is the theory of our constitution, and such the design of many of its provisions. But the democratic element of our government has acquired a predominating force never dreamed of by its framers. The constitutional checks upon the popular will have proved inadequate to preserve the intended balance, at least they have lost their hold upon the acquiescence of the people. It is an odious thing at the present day for any one to speak of the right or the necessity of checking the popular will. The President's constitutional right of veto—the independence of the Senate—and the inviolability of the Supreme Court, have all by turns been the objects of popular hatred and popular threats. Add to this the shape which the doctrine of the " right of instruction " is coming daily more and more to assume in the popular feeling—a feeling that goes nigh to strip the members of the national legislature of the character of trusted legislators for the people, whose duty it is to act according to their best judgment and discretion, for the good of the nation, and to make them a mere formal board to register the determinations that come up from the primary assemblies of a thousand local districts. It is not necessary here to draw the line exactly between what is right and what is wrong in this feeling ; it is adverted to only to show the increasing tendency of the people to hold exaggerated and exclusive views on every subject involving the question of popular power.*

---

* It is impossible to lay down any proposition in absolute terms on this point. It is certainly the theory of our constitution that the people are wise enough to choose men to be their legislators and statesmen; but it does not follow that they are wise enough to be legislators and statesmen themselves. Nobody is born a legislator or statesman, and it is equally absurd to suppose the mass of the people can ever become such. Besides, the absolute and unqualified assertion of the right of instruction would involve the greatest inconveniences and absurdities. For the right which is exerted in one case, may be exerted in every other case ; and the *consequences* would be such as were certainly never contemplated by the constitution. On the other hand, it seems implied in the spirit of our government, that the deliberate sense of the community on great and general questions should be regarded by their representatives ; and there seems no particular objection to its being expressed in the shape of instructions. This is probably all that moderate and enlightened holders of the right of instruction care to maintain. But it is none the less true that the tendency of popular feeling goes far beyond this, exaggerating it to an absolute and unqualified right. The root of this and every other instance of the undue predominance of the democratic spirit, is in radically false and absurd notions of the grounding principles of government, and particularly in the prevalent confusion of *civil* with *nat-*

Whatever dangers grow out of this, are a thousand-fold increased by the unlimited extension of suffrage. Not contented with giving the right to all the native born of our own land, without any provision to exclude those whose ignorance unfits them, or whose necessities expose them to corruption,—we extend it to all the vagabonds that come to us from other lands. The oppressed and degraded, the idle and ignorant, the broken in fortune and fame, the outcasts of Europe, throng to our shores by hundreds of thousands yearly—to find here not merely asylum and protection, but to find themselves enrolled side by side with the sons of the land, and possessed of equal right to control the destinies of the nation. Without property or other stake in the welfare of the country ; without wisdom to exercise their new rights ; without sufficient time and opportunity given to acquire the knowledge and instruction that would fit them for the wise exercise of such rights, and without a serious conviction of the duties those rights impose —they become fit dupes for the party demagogue, bartering often their venal vote for the means of an hour's intoxication !

ural rights. In fact, the people of this country are politically educated in nothing but a false and overweening sense of *rights.*

With the progress of all these changes the *spirit of party* has progressively increased. Our country in some respects offers the finest arena in the world for the political demagogue. It was long ago apprehended by wise men as a possible thing, that a knot of party demagogues, under the name of "friends of the people," might have it all their own way, and rule and ruin the people with the people's own consent. It remains to be seen. Be the event what it may, certainly the licentiousness of the party press has risen to a tremendous height. Nothing is sacred or secure. The strongest stimulants are constantly administered to the worst passions of the people, and particularly to the prejudices and passions of that portion of the people who rarely read but one side, who commonly believe all that is told them by the accredited organs of their respective parties, and always believe what flatters their self-love. " It is the iniquity of men," says Jeremy Taylor, " that they suck in opinion as the wild asses do the wind, without distinguishing the wholesome from the corrupted air, and then live upon it at a venture." These dangers are a hundred-fold increased from the mode and the frequency of filling the highest office in the nation The country has no rest from one four years' end to

another, in preparing for these so frequently recurring struggles.   Its remotest corners are agitated ;
its quietest nooks are disturbed with the harsh conflict of opinions ;—while all over the land, pesti-
lent hordes of hungry office-seekers are stirring up
the strife, ringing changes upon popular watchwords, and exciting the passions of the people.
Why is all this ?   Because the patronage and
power of the President of the United States is far
greater than that of most kings.   I do not advert
to this, in order to quarrel with the fact : my only
object here is to ask if it would not be far better if
some mode of filling the office were fallen upon,
that should leave it more to the action of Providential agency ; render the man who fills it less dependent upon a party ; surround him in a greater
degree with less material, and more moral responsibilities ; and thus leave him more free to be the
head of the nation, and not of a party.*

* Hereditary succession is not here intended ; but some mode of
filling the executive office that may avoid the evils of frequent
popular elections.   In this country an astonishing prejudice prevails
among the mass of the people on the whole subject of government
—as if freedom of government were essentially and exclusively
connected with certain names and forms.   It needs, however, but
little knowledge of history to show that freedom may exist under
the names and forms of monarchy : while with all the names and
forms of a republic, a nation may be enslaved.   In regard to filling

Not only is there an undue predominance of the democratic element, subject to all the corrupting influences of a virulent party press ; but can any sober mind fail to see many proofs and indications that the popular spirit is tending towards the licentious anarchy of mob domination ? of Liberty without Law and Public Order ? Whenever, in any country, it fully comes to this, it is no matter

the executive, the problem—like every other problem in the general theory of government—is to fix upon the best mode where no mode is perfectly unexceptionable, that is, to fix upon the mode which is attended with the fewest evils. Where the executive is *elective for life*—as was the case in Poland—the evils of frequent elections—continual struggle and agitation—are avoided; but the conflict is fiercer and more dangerous when it does occur. To avoid altogether the evils of elections, the executive office in some constitutional governments—as in England—is made hereditary. In this case reliance is placed upon education and various other influences, to secure the requisite fitness for office; yet this mode, though in the opinion of the writer less exceptionable than frequent popular elections, is attended with obvious liabilities to evil. Is it allowable to suggest a mode that might perhaps be found to combine more advantages and fewer evils for our country than any other? Suppose there were a given term of Senatorial office longer, say, than the present; upon the expiration of which, those who had served through it, should fall into a grade of *Senatores Emeriti*—out of whom, one should be taken every four or six years, by lot or by rotation, or by some similar mode of designation, to be the President of the United States. In this way, the evils of popular election would be avoided; private ambition, and rival competition in a great degree excluded; while, on the other hand, the individual upon whom the office might fall, would be likely to be every way as suitable a person as can be secured by the present mode.

of mere speculation that a people can inflict upon
themselves a thousand-fold more curses than the
most iron despotism. History has set its seal to
this truth forever. That such will never be our
fate is devoutly to be hoped ; and there are some
grounds of good hope. They are found in the degree in which knowledge and virtue do actually
prevail in the nation ; in the wide extent of the
country ; the want of a great controlling metropolis, and in the distinction of State governments
and State rights. Moreover, there is reason to
hope that the influence of an ever-watchful minority in opposition, may be sufficient to counteract
the destructive tendencies of unrestrained democracy. Giving all weight, however, to these considerations, it still remains beyond a doubt that the
increasing love of office, the spirit of party, and
the profligacy of the party press, furnish ground of
reasonable alarm ; and every good man and lover
of his country must desire to see these evils diminished.

I have spoken with freedom upon this great
subject. The intention of this discourse might
perhaps have been sufficiently attained, by simply
adverting to the overgrowth of certain mercantile
and political elements, as affecting the cause of

letters and the welfare of the country.   But in following the train of my own thoughts I have been led to speak also incidentally—though I confess more at large than I intended—upon some points in the theory and working of our government, and to intimate opinions from which I am aware that many enlightened men dissent.   As to this, I can only say, that without reference to any particular party, and without any disrespect for the opinions of others, I have frankly expressed my own honest convictions.   Whether the particular views that have been intimated concerning the theory and working of our government are right or wrong ; and whether the tendencies to evil are, or are not, as great as have been supposed ; still every enlightened man must admit, that there is no form of human government but is incident to some peculiar class of evils ; that the dangerous tendencies of every democratic government are such as have been spoken of ; and that where the love of wealth and of party politics is advancing, as with us, to such a prodigious overgrowth—there, to secure the conservation of the State—the higher and more spiritual elements of national well-being ought to be proportionably powerful and active.   It is not, then, in the idle and arrogant spirit of mere fault-finding, that I have

2

spoken things so little likely to be gratifying to our self-love. The evils to which we are exposed have been pointed out, in order that we may more earnestly look for the means of conservation.

What then are the means of conservation? What are the counter-checks that will secure the safety of an intensely commercial and democratic State? They are RELIGION AND LETTERS. It is not my intention here to speak particularly of what religion can do as a conservative power in a nation. It may be observed however, in passing, that while religion influences the character of a people, it is itself likewise always modified by the people—by the institutions and spirit of the country. In a country intensely democratic, where religion has no fixed and settled institutions, but is left, like every thing else, to the determination of the popular will, may we not suppose it will receive a peculiar cast and direction? Where the intellectual energies of the people are not at all meditative—turned within, but all projected outward, concentrated upon the palpable objects of material utility; where all is excitement and conflict, agitation and intensity; will not religion be likewise subject to a corresponding form of development and action? Will not its tone and the direction of its influence be in continual fluctuation ? Will there not be a restless craving for religious novelty and excitement ? Will not its teachers find it hard to preserve the independence of their sacred functions ? Will they not be exposed to the alternative of losing their influence, or of becoming passive weathercocks to obey and indicate the ever-shifting direction of the popular gale ? Will not the people everywhere call out for preaching " suited to the spirit of the age " ?—not meaning by it preaching suited to correct and amend the spirit of the age, but agreeable to the taste of the age ; for this mighty " spirit of the age," like every thing else belonging to the supreme people, never thinks itself capable of being in the wrong, or needing correction. It demands an applauding echo, not a rebuke. Is there no danger that this " spirit of the times," so enlightened in its own esteem, and so wanting in reverence for every thing but itself, instead of submitting to be met, checked, and corrected, by the whole, undivided, old-fashioned gospel, will lay sacrilegious hands upon it, and— tearing a portion of its more external truths and applications live asunder from the living whole and from their inward and spiritual grounds—will mould and narrow and concentrate the whole of religion upon an everchanging succession of objects of external and material reform—hurrying forever onward in a restless career of fierce fanaticism ?

Before you answer these questions, look to that part of the country from whence have sprung and spread some of the most remarkable religious developments of the age ; and where too, it is to be noted, have been shown the most remarkable spectacles the world has ever seen of intense activity on the grandest scale, exerted for the physical ends of life—rooting out forests, building up city after city, carrying forth roads and canals, and growing rich, as by the magic ministry of Aladdin's lamp.

In a country like ours then, where the democratic and commercial elements are so intense, it cannot be expected that religion will exert an adequate conservative influence ; *unless the intellectual tone of the people can be exalted.* It is the office of Religion to diminish, by her views of eternal things, a too intense and absorbing devotion to the gross and material objects of life ; but she will battle it unequally, unless she is aided by causes that shall excite and cherish a taste and respect for the higher and more intellectual objects and enjoyments of the present life.

Let us then turn to LETTERS, as the other conser-

vative element of the state—and the necessary com-
plement of the former. In this aspect of our country, we find, in some parts, public schools, a press
teeming with popular works, and a body of teachers
and writers actively engaged in communicating and
diffusing existing knowledge. I will not stop to
dwell at length upon defects in all this. It might
be shown how the system of education, established
among us, tends, in some important respects, not
so much to quicken intellectual power and to form
decided intellectual tastes, as to furnish the modi-
cum of knowledge necessary to enable our youth to
rush upon the arena of life and play their part in
the great struggle for wealth or office. It might
be shown how the continual multiplication of works
like most of our popular productions tends to create
a vague and superficial knowledge, which serves
rather as a substitute for thinking than to invigorate
the powers of thought ; and how the mind even of
the commonest reader gets more good from grap-
pling with one master-mind, and by patient,
strenuous self-exertion, fathoming the depth of one
master-work, than by skimming forty volumes of
" Familiar Elements," and similar fourth-rate productions that are continually coming forth.* I

* " What the youth of a nation needs," says Cousin, " are

might point out some indications of a morbid taste in the present reading public, which require a higher tone of literature to correct. . But let whatever there is of letters among us be accepted as good ; and surely it is very good in comparison with having nothing of the kind, or even—some exceptions being made—with having less of it; for it tends to the diffusion of knowledge—a thing essential to the welfare of the country, so it be sound and wholesome knowledge ; still it is obvious to remark that the diffusion of knowledge is not its advancement. Carrying the streams all over the land is not keeping the fountains fresh and full. The teachers—those engaged in simplifying and communicating existing knowledge—can have but little time for increasing its amount. They can have but little time, even if they have the intellectual power, to explore the fountain heads, to enlarge them, to open new and fresh springs. Yet this is needed ; otherwise the streams are likely to get dry and stale.

thorough and profound works, such even as are something abstruse and difficult; in order that they may get the habit of encountering and overcoming difficulties, and serve as it were an apprenticeship to fit them for life and its labor. It is a sad thing to deal out to them only slight general notions in such a form that a child of five years old may learn to recite the whole book in a day from beginning to end, and imagine it knows something of human nature and the world. Not so should it be. Strong minds are made by strong studies," etc. Cours de la Phil. V. I. Lec. 11.

We need then an order of men—of lofty intellectual endowment, of original creative power, exclusively devoted to the highest departments of truth, beauty, and letters; an intellectual High Priesthood, standing within the inner veil of the Temple of Truth, reverently watching before the Holy of Holies for its divine revelations, and giving them out to the lower ministers at the altar;—thus teaching the teachers, enlarging their intellectual treasures, exalting their intellectual spirit, and through them instructing and elevating the whole body of the people. This lofty style of letters, as we have said, is good in itself. It is good as a component part of the common weal. It is good too—it is indispensably necessary—as a counteracting power to the predominant evils that have been displayed.

But how shall a learned order be created ? The very state of things that renders it most needful, not only fails to create it, but is adverse to it. Politics and business, public life and commercial enterprise, absorb the greatest portion of the best energies of the nation. The public will never create it. The public will pay for a cheap and inferior style of letters. The public will pay only for what it comprehends the value of ; it cannot comprehend the value of a Plato, a Bacon, a Michael Angelo, a Newton, a La Place ; it will not support them. It will not even respect and honor them while alive, unless it sees them surrounded with other titles to their reverence than those which come from the nature and value of their labors—unless it sees them honored by the State. Centuries after they are dead, from the tardy prevalence of right opinion in the higher quarters, the multitude may come to have a vague impression that they are great names, not to be mentioned without respect.

It is a sad reflection, how comparatively solitary and uncheered by sympathy and respect, even in the best condition of society, is the path of a truly great and original mind—especially when devoted to the more profound and spiritual investigations of truth. As Coleridge says of some such one, they stride so far ahead of their age that they are dwarfed by the distance. It is perhaps one of the penalties of greatness—one of the abatements, in the equal orderings of Providence, from the enviableness of such high gifts. The fate of BACON is an impressive case in point. The name of BACON is now a word of reverence in the mouths of tens of thousands of the multitude, who have never indeed read a line of his philosophical works, and know nothing of their contents, unless perhaps they have skimmed the outlines of his great work in the " Library of Useful Knowledge," or gleaned some crude notions from more casual sources. Few are aware, however, that in his own days, and among his own countrymen, his philosophical labors were not only not understood and esteemed, but depreciated and ridiculed —and that not merely by the courtiers and men of the world, but by the men of genius who ought to have comprehended the new sources opened to them. The shallow witticism of the " pedant king " on his great work—"*that like the peace of God it passed all understanding*"—was but the key-note of the whole symphony of the times. Well was it for Bacon that he could sustain his mighty spirit by keeping the " times succeeding " ever before his mind ; and in his last legacy " leave his name and his memory to foreign nations and to his own countrymen *after some time be passed over.*"* This is not a solitary instance. The history of literature is full of similar cases ; but we cannot stop to signalize them. A most eminent instance, in our own age, might be pointed out, in the " myriad-minded "

* See D'Israeli's Curiosities of Literature, 2d Series.

2*

Coleridge—a man of most surpassing intellectual greatness, wonderful alike for every kind of learning and for every kind of creative power. He was indeed valued and revered by a few—the elect spirits of the age—and among them some of the highest and brightest names of our times, whose verdict is prophecy, whose applause is fame ; but by the great body of his cotemporaries he lived neglected and depreciated. But neither have I time, nor dare I attempt, to make his fitting eulogy. Succeeding times will do him justice, and vindicate his titles to the reverential homage of his country and mankind.

In a country where commercial enterprise and public life absorbs such a disproportionate share of the strongest energies of mind, it is rare to find the men of the world, even the best of them, adequately appreciating the value, and respecting the labors of men of genius. " These men of strong minds, but limited capacities," as D'Israeli says, are rather inclined " to hold in contempt all studies alien to their own habits." This, which has ever been to a great extent the tendency, even in the most favorable condition of things, is, from the peculiar state of our country, eminently the tendency with us. Where shall we look in our political and commercial world at the present day, for such men as CICERO, uniting literary and philosophical tastes and labors with public affairs ; or the magnificent LORENZO DE MEDICI, distinguished at once as poet, and lover and cultivator of philosophy and art, as well as the great merchant and head of the State—gathering around him the choicest literary spirits of the age ; loving them ; cheering and quickening their zeal by public honors and rewards ; and in his intervals of leisure from affairs, living with them in genial communication on the highest themes of truth and beauty :

> ——Non de villis, domibusve alienis,
> Nec, male, nec ne, lepus saltet.   Sed quod magis ad nos
> Pertinet, et nescire malum est :

> ————Utrumne

> Divitiis homines, an sint virtute beati ?
> Et quo sit natura boni ; summum que ejus.
> HORACE Sat. L. II. 6, 71.

Neither by the public then, nor by individuals, in the present state of things, can we expect that a body of high and original cultivators of truth and letters, will be adequately sustained or respected.

But it may be thought that men of genius should be sustained by the sentiment of duty, and

the consciousness of their high vocation ;—by a
calm and lofty confidence in the verdict of " succeeding times ; " and, above all, by the ever fresh impulse of that love of truth and letters *for their own
sake*, without which no external motives will avail
to call forth great and noble works.   It is indeed
true that no one is worthy the name of philosopher,
poet, or artist, who regards the pursuit of truth and
beauty, as mere means to earthly and private ends.
Such a feeling would of itself sufficiently betray
that the genial power of high production—the true
mens divinior—had never stirred within them.   It
is the remark of FUSELI, that no great and genuine
work of art was ever produced where the artist did
not love his art for its own sake ; and the remark
applies to every branch of science and letters.*   All
the master-works of the mind must be the genial

* I cannot resist the inclination to mention the circumstances in
which I first saw this remark of Fuseli.   It was in the studio of my
friend ALLSTON, to which I had been invited—a privilege rarely
extended to any one—to see a picture he had just finished.   The
sentence from Fuseli was written in pencil on the door of a cabinet,
and beneath it was another exquisite thought by Allston himself:
"He who loves his art for its own sake, will be delighted with excellence wherever he sees it, as well in the work of another as in
his own.   This is the test of true love."   This is beautiful, and
beautifully expressed,—and what is pleasanter still, it is just an expression of the true disposition of that most amiable man and ornament of our country's art.

production of those who find their labors their own "exceeding great reward." External motives can never bestow inward power. True love alone quickens creative energy. He who can be drawn to labor in the cause of truth and letters only by the earthly rewards of money and honor, will never do any thing worthy of reward.

All this, however, by no means proves that such rewards are not needed, in order to give free and unrestrained scope to the action of more genial impulses. The man of genius must have a livelihood. However sincere his love of the true and beautiful and good in science, art and letters, for their own sake ; however glorious his energies ; however strong the inward impulse to high and noble production ; he may be pressed down by the force of external circumstances. The necessity of providing for the wants of to-morrow by the cares of to-day, may forbid his giving himself up to the objects of his love. The votary of high truth and letters should be so provided for, that that he may abide in the "quiet and still air of his delightful studies," and not be dragged forth to struggle in the work-house of the world for his daily bread. Then as to the respectful appreciation of his labors by his fellow-men. The man of genius is a man ; and therefore feels

the want of human sympathy. He may glow with
a pure and fervent love of truth and beauty ; he
may have a calm and self-sustained conviction that
he is not living in vain, nor for himself alone, but
is working in a high vocation to which he is called
of God ; he may have a serene and lofty confidence
in the sentence of succeeding times ;—yet he will
often feel a discouraging sense of loneliness, if he
sees himself the object of disregard or depreciation
among his fellow-men ; and on the other hand, he
will be cheered and quickened by knowing that the
respectful thoughts and kind feelings of his contemporaries are with him in his labors.   Thus we see
that genius may be repressed, and rendered fruitless to the world, if it is left a prey to the cares of
life, or the sense of disregard.   Here then lies the
value of State endowments—places of dignified
labor and ample provision for a body of men devoted to the highest interests of science and letters.

The State is the proper power to form and sustain such an order of men.   The State is the power
that can most adequately cherish the cause of lofty
science and learning.   It does this, not by creating genius, not by communicating a love of
truth and letters for their own sake ; but by making such provision that these impulses may have

free scope.   Government can supply a place for a learned order to work in ; and can put honor on their work in the eyes of the multitude.   The multitude honors what it sees honored by the State. In this country, above all others on the globe, men of science and letters have no place, no position, in the social system.   The respect paid to wealth and public office engrosses all the respect that in other countries is awarded to high letters.   The multitude in this country, so far from favoring and honoring high learning and science, is rather prone to suspect and dislike it.   It feareth that genius savoreth of aristocracy !   Besides, the multitude calleth itself a *practical* man.   It asketh : *what is the use ?*   It seeth no use but in that which leads to money, or to the material ends of life.   It hath no opinion of having dreamers and drones in society. It believeth indeed in rail-roads ; it thinketh well of steam ; and owneth that the new art of bleaching by chlorine is a prodigious improvement ;—but it laughs at the profound researches into the laws of nature, out of which those very inventions grew ; and with still greater scorn it laughs at the votaries of the more spiritual forms of truth and beauty, which have no application to the palpable uses of life.   Then, again, the influence of our reading pub-

lic is not favorable to high letters. It demands, it
pays for, and respects, almost exclusively, a lower
style of production ; and hence a natural influence
to discourage higher labors. As old SPENSER sang,
two hundred years ago :

> If that any buds of poesy
> Yet of the old stock, 'gin shoot again,
> 'Tis or self-lost the worldling's meed to gain,
> And with the rest to breathe its ribauldry,—
> Or, as it sprung, it wither must again ;
> *Tom Piper makes them better melody !*

The State then ought to cherish high science
and letters by endowments, for two reasons : first,
in order to supply to a superior order of men such
a competent provision as will leave them free to devote their powers exclusively to lofty study and
production ; secondly, in order to develop in the
people a proper feeling of respect for the importance
of such labors, by the honor it puts upon them.*
Something of this is done in other countries. A
learned order is, to some extent, recognized and
sustained as one of the integral elements of the commonwealth. In the theory, at least, of the British
constitution—which, taken all in all, is wonderfully

* This is illustrated at considerable length, and set in various
lights, in Bulwer's " England and the English."

adapted to human nature as it is, and to the wants of the social condition ; the working of whose machinery may, in the progress of time and change, have become disordered, and need rectifying, but whose dissolution or organic change should be dreaded—in the theory of this constitution, the State charges itself with the duty of providing for the good of the people what the people will never provide for themselves. Hence the Cathedral, University, and other Endowments for learning, science and art—places of high honor and trust—designed, in the IDEAL of them, to be filled by the best minds of the land ; where, with a modest but dignified provision for life and its wants, surrounded with rich and ample libraries, it becomes their duty to devote themselves to the highest departments of truth and letters ; working not with immediate reference to the bulk of the people, but for the teachers of the people—guarding the fountain heads of learning, and opening new springs ; promoting thus the good of all—honored and respected by all, not because all can fully comprehend the meaning and value of their pursuits, but because all see them honored by the State.

Would that we could hope for some support of a like kind for the intellectual interests of our country. But what has government ever done to cherish these interests ?   Next to nothing in comparison with their importance and its own means. It has occasionally ordered a picture or a statue ; it has subscribed for a few books.   Oh, if a portion of those superfluous millions, whose distribution has created so keen an excitement, could have been devoted to founding and cherishing a great and noble institution for the cultivation of lofty science and letters, what occasion of joy to every lover of the cause, and to every enlightened lover of our country !   Little, however, can at present be expected from government.   The action of our government is but the reflection of the popular will ; it has but little power to form and direct the public mind. It will be yet a long time before the country at large is adequately awake to the importance even of primary education.   It is pleasant to perceive a growing sense of this ; but the importance of a generous provision for the cultivation of the higher departments of science and letters is scarcely at all felt.   So far, indeed, is the mutual connection and harmony of the two from being discerned, that there is a disposition on the part of the friends of popular education—even among those who ought to know better—to dislike and oppose the claims of high science and letters.   A great change must be wrought in public feeling, before the ample resources of the country will be applied to this great object.

What then remains ?   Shall the lovers of good letters despair of the cause ?   Oh no !   Let them stir themselves up to a loftier zeal in proportion to the adverse influences that press upon them.   Let them mutually quicken in each other those genial impulses which the chill cold atmosphere of the country so tends to repress.   Let them brighten the golden chain that unites them.   Let a livelier sympathy pervade and animate the whole brotherhood of those who love and honor the cause of truth, of beautiful art, and of good letters.   Let them combine their exertions, and direct them to supplying those fostering influences which the Public and the State withhold.

It is greatly to be regretted that there is not a more intimate connection among our men of letters ; that they meet no more frequently as a class—have no more free communication—and make themselves no more felt as a distinct body and a positive element in the social system.   Perhaps in part it is owing to the want of some such point of common attraction as the capitals of Europe supply ; but more to the fact that those among us who are in any degree devoted to the cultivation of letters, give to its pursuits only the intervals of leisure snatched from the duties and cares of other professions, upon which they are dependent not only for subsistence, but for their social position and consequence. They are thus scattered abroad over the land—isolated, amidst the ungenial influences that surround them, with but little leisure or opportunity to indulge in the sympathies of brotherly communion, and to combine and strengthen their influence for the promotion of high letters.

Would, however, that the love of these great interests, and a sense of their value to the country, might lead to more vigorous and combined exertions to promote them. If I might suggest, in broken hints, the outline of a scheme that I should desire to see embodied—I would say: Let a great association be formed, embracing all who cultivate, and all who appreciate the value of good learning, high science, and noble art. The objects of such a union should be by mutual sympathy, to quicken in each other the love of these things and to excite to genial production ; to supply, as far as possible, the requisite *material conditions*—the means and appliances —that may give free scope to the impulses of genius;

and to act upon the intellectual spirit of the nation
—exalting its tone, developing the power and exciting the disposition to appreciate and cherish the
productions of genius.   In imitation of the German
Society of Naturalists, let there be an annual Congress of the disciples of good letters, held in different
places on successive years ; and let not the influence
of these meetings die away with the speeches that
are made.   Let suggestions concerning all the most
important *desiderata* in the highest departments
of Philosophy, Art, and Literature, be received,
carefully weighed by appropriate committees, and
discussed in the most catholic spirit.   Let prizes be
proposed, and works of pre-eminent merit be
crowned.   But above all, let the most strenuous
and unwearied exertions be directed to securing
those material provisions which are requisite to
call a portion of the highest talent and genius of
the country into the field of science and literature.
Here would be included the foundation of libraries,
containing the most perfect apparatus for the
thorough cultivation of every department of letters,
and complete collections in nature and art ;—and
last, but most essential, endowments for the dignified and honorable support of genius—where, free
from life's cares, it may follow the impulses of its

nature. Here let all those whom God hath formed
for great poets, great artists, and great philosophers,
find every condition and every influence to quicken,
unfold, and perfect in themselves the rare and
excellent gifts of God. Here " in the quiet and
still air of delightful studies," let the tenure and
obligations of their position and the sense of duty
unite with the inward promptings of their nature,
leading them to work, each in his high vocation, for
the glory of God and the honor and instruction of
their country and mankind.

If this be but an IDEA that can never be
realized, surely it is an idea beautiful to the imagination, and attractive to the wishes of every lover
of truth and letters. Even if it cannot be fully
realized, something may be done. A beginning
may be made by the union and combined influence
of those who have these interests at heart, and they
may at length so act upon the intellectual spirit of
the country as to secure the fostering influence of
the State. At all events, the duty of uniting in
the promotion of this great end, rests upon all who
love the cause of truth and human progress. It
rests upon all whom history and reflection have
taught to dread for our country the debasing and
deadly tendencies of a too intense and absorbing

devotion to the mere physical interests of life. It rests upon all who would elevate the intellectual tone of the nation—develop its true humanity—and raise it to the true freedom of virtuous energy. It rests upon all who would secure to our beloved country the permanent possession of its true dignity and proper well-being. There is no alternative. We must be rich and great. We cannot—like the mountain dwellers of Switzerland and the Alps, or the poor inhabitants of Iceland—find in our poverty, and in the influences of religion, those safeguards of our virtue and our welfare, which render the conservative influence of high intellectual culture comparatively unimportant. We must be rich and great ; and our riches and greatness will inevitably prove our ruin—spite of all that religion will effect—unless the intellectual spirit of the nation be elevated by the pervading influence of a spiritual Philosophy, a pure Literature and a noble Art.

REMARKS ON SOME OBJECTIONS TO THE FOREGOING VIEWS.

[NEARLY a quarter of a century has passed away since the foregoing address was delivered. In reading it over now, in 1860, I think it right to say that while I still regard the general principles and leading views of the discourse as just and important, I find some things expressed in somewhat stronger and less qualified terms than I should now use. But, particularly, I hold it due to truth and to my own convictions to say—and I am glad to have the opportunity to say—that there has been, I think, during the last twenty-five years, a very considerable improvement in the intellectual tone of the nation ; that if wealth and public office are still inordinately worshipped and pursued, yet not only the number of those who hold higher objects in higher esteem is greatly increased, but among the people at large there is much more a disposition to honor and respect high science and letters. In 1836 New York had an ASTOR HOUSE; in 1860 it has, and for a number of years has had, an IRVING HOUSE, a PRESCOTT HOUSE, an EVER-ETT HOUSE, a BANCROFT HOUSE, and, for aught I know, a BRYANT HOUSE, too; and the like thing is true in our other great towns.

The views advanced in my discourse met with some objections at the time. In particular they were strongly assailed—not directly in form, but with unmistakable directness in purport and inten-tion, and not over respectfully in terms—by the gentleman who followed me the next year, in ad-dressing the same literary societies.* I subjoin ex-tracts from some remarks made in reply in the NEW YORK REVIEW for April, 1838, a journal I had established, and which was at that time under my editorial charge. I do it not out of any per-sonal feeling—if I had any at that time (and I

---

* An address delivered before the Literary Societies of the Uni-versity of Vermont, August 2, 1837. By George G. Ingersoll. Burlington.

3

do not know that I had) it is long ago gone—but because they contain what seems to me a substantial answer to the objections most likely to be made against the leading views of my discourse, and particularly against endowments for the promotion of science and learning, letters and art, and may serve to fortify some of the positions there taken, which I hold to be sound and good.]

Instead of telling his audience wholesome truths, and inciting them to higher exertions in the cause of good letters than those which we have, in this country, been too contented with—the author of this address has chosen the easier task of administering to a self-satisfied vanity already inflated to an unhealthy degree. Nay, more ; *he seems to have had in his eye, some brother-orator who preceded him on a like occasion ;* and who, instead of laying on the altar the usual offering of fulsome eulogy, was wicked enough to intimate that some things might be better in this country than they are. He therefore comes forward to pour the precious balm of unction into the rankling wounds, to smooth down the ruffled plumage of self-love.

It seems to have been an opinion expressed by somebody, that there is in this country an excessive love of gain. The author of this address thinks this is not the fact ; *for* the same thing, he says, is true of England, of Europe, of the world ! Indeed, he rather inclines to the opinion that it is a tendency of human nature ! at least he quotes classical authority for the opinion : *Hominum sunt ista, non temporum; nulla ætas vacavit a culpa !*

On the whole, however, after some dubitation on the matter, he thinks it is but fair to admit that the spirit of money-getting is very strong—too strong, indeed ; yet it would be a pity if it were less so. This part of his subject, in truth, seems to have slightly perplexed the orator ; though the dexterity with which he has contrived to make one sentence neutralize the other, is only equalled by that of the renowned editor of the Little Pedlington Observer.

Of one thing, nevertheless, the orator is positive, and that is, that the love of money—which is not excessive, and is yet lamentably too strong, though it would be a pity if there were less of it—is by no means the *exclusive* passion of the people of this country. In proof of this, he triumphantly appeals to the fact, that on the " annual return " of the commencement of the University of Vermont, " the office, the counting-room, the shop, the **farm, the** home, are all forsaken ; and all ages, sexes, and conditions, throng to its observance ! " He intimates, also, that the like is true at other colleges. This conclusively shows not only that the people have a respect and love for learning, and a literary taste, but that nothing more need be wished for on this score ; and not only so, but that there is in this country abundant provision and encouragement of every sort and kind for the cultivation of all the highest and abstrusest departments of science and learning ; and therefore, to point out any defects or to suggest any improvements, evinces an equally unpatriotic and ridiculous spirit of fault-finding !

For ourselves, our simple creed on this subject is, that the love of gain is a very strong passion, and the pursuit of it a very engrossing pursuit, among the people of this nation. With the unfolding of the physical resources of the country, and the prodigious increase of commerce and manufactures, the tide of wealth has rolled over the land ; and the passion for getting greatly and rapidly rich has naturally kept pace with the facility of getting rich. Now, connected with all this there is but one single thing to be feared—namely, lest the love of gain become exclusive. There is but one thing to be desired—not that there should be less wealth, but—

that along with it there should be more of that high intellectual cultivation which is at least an equally indispensable element of national well-being.   According to our mode of thinking, we have already arrived at that point in our history, when we have so far fulfilled the first and more material part of the mission of a young nation, that it has become all-important to turn our attention to the higher and more intellectual part.   For as it would certainly be dangerous if the subordinate and material conditions of national well-being should acquire an undue predominance, so there is ground to fear it.

It is no matter how rich a people may be, provided there be at the same time a due proportion of love for intellectual and spiritual interests. Otherwise the love of riches will be excessive, debasing, dangerous.

" It is said, however," (observes the author,) " that the great evil is, we have no checks to this spirit—such, for instance, as do exist in the Old World.   These checks, I take it, are established rank, primogeniture, form of government, and so on, matters all very good for those who choose them.   But, without stopping to give any reasons, I shall merely say that, for one, I am very glad there are no such checks among us.   I should like, indeed, to stop to ask a definition of this same word check, thus used ; for when I turn to the mother country where such matters are found, I conclude check does not mean to suppress, hardly to control; if it does, why do we hear, in the very midst of such checks, lamentations over what is called ' an almost religious veneration for riches ? '   I cannot but stop, however, to admire the consistency of rejoicing in a state of high refinement and elegant leisure which wealth has brought about, and to sustain which wealth is absolutely indispensable, and at the same time condemning the pursuit of that which must be attained in order to the same state elsewhere.   It seems like the individual who has retired from a business long and actively engaged in, with his fortune and in his splendid mansion—with library, pictures, statues, garden—gravely chiding some young man who has just started into life, and comparing his own learned, dignified repose with the vulgar hurry and sordid views of this same money-getting youth."—Pp. 17, 18.

This is exceedingly *ad captandum;* we will not call it flippant and foolish, but it is destitute of any valid bearing whatever upon the point in question. It is a simple question of fact, whether, compared with the degree of wealth and physical refinement we have already attained, the higher departments of intellectual production are held in due respect, duly provided for, and rewarded.   It is a simple question of fact, whether the pursuit of wealth does not absorb an undue proportion of the national energies to the neglect of higher pursuits.   If so, it would seem quite easy to understand the desirableness of some influences that might operate—not "to suppress" the pursuit of wealth but—really to "check" the tendency to a too excessive and exclusive pursuit of it. "Established rank, primogeniture, and so on," might not work very well in this country. We, too, may be "very glad" we have no such things : they might work more evils here in other respects than they would prevent in the particular respect in question. They may, also, as the author intimates, be quite insufficient checks in England ; but that does not prove they are destitute of all salutary effect even there ; least of all does it prove that it is not desirable there should be some influences, of some kind, in this country, to diminish a too exclusive devotion to wealth, by presenting at least other, if not higher, objects of respect and pursuit. Then, as to the "inconsistency" which our critic "stops to admire," and the smart simile by which it is illustrated—all this is easily put in a just light by the simple inquiry, whether we have not already wealth enough in this country to justify and require a much higher style of cultivation than obtains, and a much better provision for the encouragement and reward of high intellectual exertion. There is a great deal of fallacy in the common-place talk about our youthfulness as a nation.   The truth is that the comparatively short period of our national existence is no measure of our advancement in civilization.   We are civilized enough and rich enough, not only to have, but for our permanent and continued well-being to stand in need of, some better provision for the cultivation of the higher departments of learning and science. Not only is there no such necessity, as the orator intimates, for the chief energies of the country being devoted to money-getting, but, unless a much larger proportion than the spirit of the nation now calls for, be turned to higher objects, we shall become a degenerate people.

It has been suggested by some, as highly desirable, that there should be created in this country special endowments, either by legislative or private munificence, for the support of a body of men devoted to the cultivation of those higher departments of science and learning, which—although of great intrinsic worth, and, rightly considered, of indispensable importance among the elements of national well-being—are not likely to be adequately cherished by the people at large.   The author of this address, however, is opposed to such a system.   It does not work as well in Europe as could be desired ; therefore it is not best to try it at all !   He quotes largely from English and continental authorities ; and seems to think the question is perfectly put at rest by them. Apart from the folly of totally condemning a system which, because insufficiently established, and fettered in its working by causes not necessary and inherent, does not produce all the results that might be produced by an adequate and unfettered system, the orator ought to have recollected that on a question where " doctors disagree," the disagreement really proves very little, except the disagreement ; certainly the opinions of the doctors on one side do not prove the opinions of doctors on the other side to be wrong. Speaking of the English Cathedral and University endowments, Dr. Chalmers recently said : "it is *the churches and colleges of England in which is fostered into maturity and strength almost all the massive learning of our nation.*" Now, we take leave to say, that in our apprehension Dr. Chalmers is right. What does it avail to say, with the Eclectic Review, as quoted by this orator, " that many of the most valuable and elaborate productions of the present day, as well as of former times, have been given to the public, not by men of leisure who had uninterrupted command of weeks, and months, and years ; but by men whose professional avoca-

tions seemed scarcely compatible with authorship ? "
This may be very true, particularly in the departments of History, Mathematics, and Physics—not
to mention those departments of literary production
which have no relation whatever to the question.
Yet it is still true, that even in the departments
mentioned, "many of the most valuable and elaborate productions" have been due to the fostering
influence of endowments, and would in all likelihood
never otherwise have been given to the world. But
the value of endowments, and the truth of Dr.
Chalmers' assertion, is seen in relation to other departments of production. In the Theological, Classical, Ecclesiastical, Biblical, and Oriental learning
of England, almost all the great works, the most·
valuable contributions have come from the learned
endowments of the Church and Universities. Now,
this is a province of intellectual inquiry in which
profound and massive learning is requisite ; and we
say the popular patronage will never demand and
adequately encourage the highest style of production. It is in vain also to expect that there will be
enough of love and leisure for these pursuits to secure an *adequate* supply of profound works, from
men absorbed in the cares of professional or public
life.

Brilliant exceptions there may occasionally be, no doubt ; still the general truth is as we have stated it. The fact is, and there is no controverting it, that there are many departments of production in which a profound and thorough learning is requisite ; such as can be acquired only by a life-long devotion ; which the popular patronage has never anywhere rewarded and never will reward ; which has been secured by the endowments of England. Popular favor will reward the exertions of a Scott, an Irving, a Dickens, whom we mention with all honor and respect—as well of some others, for whom we profess no respect ; but that popular patronage will ever give, not fortunes, but even a decent subsistence, in reward for the exertions of such men as More, and Cudworth, and Potter, and Lowth, and Lee, and hundreds of others, who, under the genial fostering of England's endowments, have spent their lives in learned labors for the " honor of their country and the glory of God "—any man must be very weak to expect. Now, we happen to be of opinion that the labors of such men are as valuable and necessary a part of a nation's best wealth, as those of a Scott or an Irving (and we value as much as anybody the labors of such as these) ; and believing, as we do, that in this country we are lamentably deficient, and that popular patronage will never secure us such labors, we should be exceedingly glad to see a wise and well-regulated system of endowments to encourage and reward them.

THE POSITION AND DUTIES OF THE EDUCATED MEN OF THE COUNTRY.

.

THE POSITION AND DUTIES OF THE EDU-
CATED MEN OF THE COUNTRY.

WE meet, on this your anniversary, as a Brotherhood of Scholars ; and perhaps I should best have
consulted the spirit of the occasion, if I had selected
some subject of purely literary interest, or endeav-
ored merely to promote the elegant enjoyment of
the hour. But I have taken the liberty to give
our thoughts a more practical direction. I remember that but few, if any of us, are *mere* scholars.
Those who have come here to-day from different
places, have come up from strenuous engagement
with the intense life that is heaving and struggling
all around us ; and when we go from here, it is to
return into the crowd and pressure of that life again.
And those who are about to be sent out at this

time from this seat of learning, must leave "the still air of delightful studies," in this quiet and beautiful retreat, and go forth to do honor to their Benignant Mother in the active service of their country and their God.

On this account I have thought it might be appropriate and profitable for us, as from this landing-place, to look out over the scene in which it is our destiny to live and work ; and to notice what it presents for warning and for guidance :—not forgetting indeed that we are scholars, but on the contrary, bearing in mind that our obligations are specially determined by the fact of our belonging to the educated class in the nation.—It is therefore of the Position and Duties of the Educated men of the country, that I wish at this time to speak.

It will not be questioned that the scholars of our country have a special vocation, which is determined by all that constitutes the peculiar characteristics of our country and of our age. It is incumbent on us, therefore, to comprehend the spirit of our country and of our age. We are to remember that we have fallen on the nineteenth century and not on the twelfth—that we live in America, and not in Austria.   I do not mean that we should not understand the Past.   Unless we understand the Past, we cannot understand the Present; for the Present is born of the Past.   Nor do I mean that we should not seek to understand the most general spirit of the world, as well as of the country in which we live ; for our country stands in manifold relations with other countries, and, rightly considered, moreover, there are, in every age, pulsations which throb throughout the heart of universal Humanity.   Still, it is to the actual mind and heart of our own country we must speak, if we mean to live and speak to any purpose in our own times, or even for the times that shall come after us.

Rarely in the history of mankind is there to be found any great work of genius, of permanent and enduring influence, which has not borne the form and pressure of its age.   Not always in sympathy, often indeed in resistance to the spirit of their times, yet ever, with few exceptions, as those who knew and felt what was the spirit of their times, have the great thinkers and teachers of the world uttered themselves.   And above all things is it requisite that the educated men of this country should understand the spirit of the country in which they are to live and work.

The educated class represent the liberal cultivation of the nation ; and to them chiefly belongs the
duty of sustaining and cherishing the higher and
more spiritual elements of social well-being.

The manifold elements which compose the well-
being of a nation may be comprehended under the
twofold division of material or physical, and moral
or spiritual.—In the MATERIAL are included the
means of physical support and comfort—food, cloth-
ing, and shelter ; the security of person and property ; the arts of life which serve to multiply and
refine the sources of material enjoyment ; in short,
every thing that relates to the useful or to the agreeable—every thing that is implied in the proper
meaning of the word CIVILIZATION.

On the other hand, the SPIRITUAL elements of
national well-being result from the unfolding and
activity of the principles of man's higher life, as
a being capable of the Idea and Love of the True,
the Beautiful, and the Good,—capable of discerning
that these words relate to objects which have a
reality and a worth beyond all material objects, a
value independent of all consequences of private
advantage.   Hence, among the spiritual elements
of social welfare are to be reckoned the pursuits of
pure science ; the productions of creative Art ; the

sense also of justice, honor, patriotism, loyalty, and reverence ; and the heroic spirit that can dare and endure for unselfish ends ; in short every thing that is implied in the CULTURE of a nation as distinguished from its mere civilization.

To the proper well-being of a nation it is essential that these elements should exist in a due and proportionable blending. It is indispensable that the material should be subordinated to the moral interests.   Wherever and in whatever degree the reason becomes enslaved to the senses, there and in that degree do the people sink below their proper life, and fail to realize the true idea of a commonwealth.—Yet it is of the infirmity of our corrupted nature that the sensual life, as in individuals so in nations, is ever tending to predominate over the spiritual.

In our country this tendency is prodigiously increased by causes connected with the physical growth of the country, and with the working of our political institutions.

Our country offers the most remarkable spectacle ever presented in the history of humanity. From three millions, in little more than half a century, we have grown to seventeen millions of people.   Inheriting an immense territory, teeming with boundless resources, we entered upon the first mission of every infant nation—that of subduing the rude yet rich nature that spread out everywhere around us. In this task we have not been compelled to proceed with the slow steps that have marked the progress of other nations. To the work of unfolding the wealth of the new world, we have brought all the facilities afforded by the mature civilization of the old world. The science, the skill, and the capital of Europe, which centuries have been slowly accumulating there, have been grasped and applied here with a boldness and energy that have wrought in a day the labors of an age. It is but a few years since we entered upon the conquest of a country wilder than Germany in the days of Cæsar, and ten times more extensive ; and yet in that short space we have reached a point of physical development which twenty centuries have not accomplished there. The forests have fallen down—the earth has been quarried—cities and towns have sprung up all over the immense extent of our land, thronged with life, and resounding with the multitudinous hum of traffic ; and from hundreds of ports the canvas of ten thousand sails whitens all the ocean and every sea, bearing the products of our soil and manufactures, and bringing back the wealth and luxuries of every

quarter of the globe.—Then, too, the tremendous
agencies of Nature—the awful forces evolved by
chemical and dynamic science—have been subdued
to man's dominion, and have become submissive
ministers to his will, more prompt and more powerful than the old fabled genii of the Arabian
Tales.   Little did our fathers, little did we ourselves,
even the youngest of us, dream—in the days of our
childhood, when we fed our wondering imaginations
with the prodigies wrought by those Elemental
Spirits evoked by the talismanic seal of Solomon—
that these were but faint foreshadowings of what
our eyes should see in the familiar goings on of the
everyday life around us.   Yet so it truly is.   Ha !
gentlemen, the STEAM ENGINE is your true Elemental Spirit ; it more than realizes the gorgeous ideas
of the old Oriental imagination ; *that* had its different orders of elemental spirits—genii of fire, of
water, of earth, and of air, whose everlasting hostility could never be subdued to unity of purpose ; *this*
combines the powers of all in one, and a child may
control them ! — Across the ocean, along our coast,
through the length of a hundred rivers, with the
speed of wind, we plough our way against currents,
wind, and tide ; while, on iron roads, through the
length and breadth of the land, innumerable trains,

3*

thronged with human life and freighted with the
wealth of the nation, are urging their way in every
direction—flying through the valleys ; thundering
across the rivers ; panting up the sides, or piercing
through the hearts of the mountains, with the resist-
less force of lightning and scarcely less swift !

All this is wonderful ! I look upon it with admiration, not unmixed with awe. The old limitations to human endeavor seem to be broken through
—the everlasting conditions of time and space seem
to be annulled ! Meanwhile the magnificent
achievements of to-day lead but to grander projects
for to-morrow. Success in the past serves but to
enlarge the purposes of the future ; and the people are rushing onward in a career of physical development, to which no bounds can be assigned.

Yet we must remember that all this is only the
spectacle of the energies of a great people intensely
directed to material ends. It is the unfolding of the
conditions of physical enjoyment. And however
great and important these are, they constitute but a
part, and that a subordinate part, of the elements
of social welfare and the true greatness of a nation.
Unless interpenetrated and sanctified by the pervading presence of the higher elements of spiritual

OF THE EDUCATED MEN OF THE COUNTRY. 71

culture, their tendency is to corrupt and degrade us. They can make us rich and highly civilized, though they can never give to civilization its highest charm of graceful refinement; for that is a spiritual quality, and can only come of moral culture. They may make us rich; but may leave us vulgar, purse-proud, ostentatious, and sensual; and never, in themselves and of their own tendency, can they make us a wise, a good, and truly happy people. Besides, it cannot be denied, in a profounder view, that the physical science of the nineteenth century; the mysterious forces of Nature which it has evolved; the tremendous powers which it has subjected to the will of man; and the immeasurably greater scope which he thereby gains, for rendering his outward life intense and diversified, have a tendency, not only to foster the spirit of absorbing worldliness, but also to engender a proud, irreverent, and godless spirit. I know that this is not its necessary result; God be thanked that it is not. To the right-hearted inquirer, every new disclosure of science may only serve to cherish a lowlier sense of the littleness of man's knowledge, and a profounder reverence for the Great Being, who, though pervading and upholding all Nature, yet, in his absolute glory and personal attributes, dwell-

ing above all Nature, can, by our mortal vision, be
only dimly seen in the glimpses of himself which
shine through the enveloping folds of the material
universe.   Still, wherever, among the mass of a
people, physical science is wholly or chiefly prized
as it ministers to wealth and enjoyment, the spirit
which it tends to engender is any thing but reverent.   Imagine a people destitute of spiritual culture ; where science is pursued merely for the sake
of compelling the powers of Nature to minister to
man's physical convenience ; where there are no
arts but arts of pleasure ; where the forms of honesty and justice are only outward forms, enacted
and observed as politic contrivances for individual
and general comfort ;—imagine such a people, and
you have before your minds a people without honor,
or magnanimity, without public spirit, loyalty, or
heroism, without reverence, morality, or religion.
They might be civilized in the highest degree ; they
might overflow with wealth ; the earth, the ocean,
and the air, might pour forth all their treasures ;
they might be surrounded with all the means and
refinements of material enjoyment, with not a crum-
pled rose leaf to disquiet the couch of luxurious
ease ; and yet they would be only a nation of refined animals, of civilized brutes.   We should belie

the instincts of our reason and conscience, if we should think otherwise of them.

Happily, such a picture is only imaginary.— Thanks to the benignant influences of Divine Grace diffused throughout the world, the reason and conscience, the spiritual life of man, though overmastered, can never be wholly crushed out ; and the social and domestic instincts are ever evolving moral affections—love, self-denial, sacrifice, heroism—which serve to exalt and purify the earthly life of man. None the less, however, is it true, that whenever the material greatly predominate over the moral elements in the life of any people, then the spirit of the nation begins to *approximate* to the corrupt, unhallowed, godless state we have imagined.

Now looking at the condition of our country at this moment, have we nothing to fear ? I do not quarrel with the prodigious growth of the elements of physical prosperity. I only ask, whether we have not reason to dread an *overgrowth ?* Is not our danger on this side ? I know there are many who have no other idea of national well-being than riches and greatness. So that a people can subdue the earth to serve the turn of their worldly uses ; so

4

that they can accumulate wealth and the means of
enjoyment—that is the extent of their solicitude.
They laugh at all this talk about the higher and
more spiritual elements of social welfare. I thank
God I am not of the number of such persons. " Contempt is ever the growth of a thin soil ; " * and
contempt of high moral and religious considerations
is eminently the mark of a poor and shallow intel-
lect. For myself, I must profess my conviction
that we are very far from growing wise and good and
truly happy as a nation, in the proportion that we
are growing rich and great. I believe there is a
prodigious and increasing overgrowth of the corrupting spirit of worldliness. I had rather we
should be poor as Iceland, yet with its pure faith
and morals and its love of letters, than we should go
on increasing in wealth and greatness without a corresponding increase in spiritual culture and moral
worth. I had rather—if this must be the alternative. But it need not be. If God has planted us
in a richer land, I do not see but we may unfold
and appropriate its manifold resources, without neg-
lecting the culture of our higher life. We may
dwell on the earth, and thrive ; yet we need not be

---

* Richard II. Dana ; unpublished Lectures.

mere thriving earth-worms.   We may follow worldly callings, and yet not be worldly-minded.   We may possess and enjoy wealth, without sinking into the life of mere material enjoyment.   The danger is great, it is true ; but corruption is not the necessary result of physical prosperity.—I cannot doubt that it is in the intentions of God, in the progress of our race, that the material world shall be still more perfectly subjugated, and its resources of material enjoyment be still more fully unfolded ; and yet the whole physical life of humanity be subordinated to its moral life—pervaded by it—yea, made to subserve its growth and perfection.   If this be so, the problem is not to arrest the physical growth of the country, but to make it the means of more perfectly unfolding our proper humanity, by the culture of the elements of spiritual life.   To contribute to the solution of this problem is eminently the vocation of the scholars of our country—of all who have been trained in liberal studies—of all who work in the liberal professions.

Let us now for a moment advert to the working of our *political* institutions ; for in this aspect our country presents a spectacle no less remarkable than in its physical growth.   I beg however a candid construction of what I am about to say. I am of no political party; and I shall not speak of party questions; but of *principles* and of the *tendencies* of principles, common to all parties; and perhaps I may say some things which to neither party will be entirely acceptable. Yet I cannot think that in a survey of the moral condition of our country, we should be justified in leaving out of view the most pervading and the most powerful of all the influences that affect the character of a nation—its political institutions. Nor can I think that courtesy, or the proprieties of an occasion like the present, should exclude all political views, except such as are known to be held in common by all. It seems to me that we should rather suffer every man freely to utter the thought that is in him—whether it be an echo of our own or not—if so it be uttered with deep conviction, with an earnest spirit, and with an honest purpose. Without any party bias, then, and with the highest respect for all those whose opinions may not coincide with my own, I shall proceed to express myself in my own fashion of thinking and speaking, relying on a kind and candid construction.

Theoretically perfect as is the frame of our government, it implies conditions of virtue and wisdom on the part of the people, which if they do not adequately exist, renders ours the most dangerous of all forms of government ; and I must avow my conviction that in its practical working, or rather in its abuses, our system is tending with prodigious power to corrupt and demoralize the nation.

It is the fundamental maxim of all political ethics, that political Rights imply political Obligations : so much the more Liberty a people enjoys, and so many the more Rights they possess, so many the more are their Duties.—Yet at the present moment, notions of popular rights appear to me to have sprung up and spread over the country, which are false, absurd, and dangerous.   We have got the habit of taking for granted that the people have a *right* to do, whatever they *please* to do ; and that whatever they please to do *is* therefore *right*.   Political RIGHT has thus become separated from DUTY ; and has practically come to mean nothing but mere POPULAR WILL.

We are continually told that the sovereign power resides in the people.   This is in its naked form but a *half-truth :* and, as has been well said, a half-truth is often the greatest of lies.   It is unquestionably true that the sovereign power, in a certain sense, resides in the people ; but in the sense in

which it is commonly understood, it is a great and
pernicious error.—It is God's ordinance, and the
necessity of man's nature, that man should exist in
SOCIETY.   To do this he must exist as a STATE—
that is, a community in which justice and social
order are maintained.   GOVERNMENT is the powers
of the State organized, embodied, and put in action ;
and the FORM of Government, is the particular mode
in which the powers of the State are embodied and
put in action.

Now undoubtedly the sovereign power resides in
the People, in the sense that the People have the
right of determining the form of their Government.
This is indeed a NATURAL right, but it is so no further than as men have a natural right to choose in
which way among several possible ways, they will
fulfil a duty ; and it is absurd to lay undue stress
upon the term.   It is not, however, an ABSOLUTE
right ; but a right growing out of a duty, and limited
by duty.   Society has the right of choosing the
form of its Government, because it is the duty of
Society to exist as a State for the maintenance of
social justice, and must have *some* form of government ; and it may choose any particular form it
prefers, provided it fulfils the duty of the State—
maintains the relations of justice—without which

Society cannot exist. In this sense, unquestionably, and in so far as relates to the form of government, the sovereign power resides in the People ; still it is not precisely an accurate statement of this truth to say, that the people have the right to choose whatever form of government they please, without regard to anything but their own mere will ; for, unless the various forms of government are assumed to be equally adapted to the great ends of society, it is more true to say that the people OUGHT to choose—not that form of government which they may simply prefer, but—that form which they conscientiously believe to be the best adapted under all the circumstances to secure the true ends of all government.

Hence it is clear, that the foundation of government is not in the mere unlimited will of the people ; and that the sovereignty of the people is not in mere natural right, but in duty. We are too prone in general to forget the great comprehensive truth, that rights and obligations ever go together. There is scarcely such a thing in all the empire of God, as the absolute right of doing what one merely WILLS to do. The only absolute right in the universe, is the right of *not being wronged.* And in political affairs, neither the mere will of a majority,

nor even of the whole people, can itself make a
thing right, or justify their action. Nothing can be
made right by mere willing to do it.—Still, as a
right which is to be *dutifully* exercised, I maintain
the doctrine that the sovereignty is vested in the
people. And in the exercise of the sovereign power residing in them, the people of this country have
organized our form of government—and have defined
and distributed the powers of the State. They
have done this in our CONSTITUTION. Practically
therefore to all intents and purposes, the sovereignty,
at this moment, and so long as the Constitution
stands unrepealed, is lodged in the Constitution.
That is the SUPREME LAW of the land ; there resides
the sovereign power of the nation ; and it resides
there out of the reach of the present will of a mere
numerical majority. The Constitution can be
changed only under particular circumstances, and by
three fourths of the states.

To this Constitution the people of the United
States at this moment owe an allegiance as loyal
and profound, as was ever claimed for the divine
right of kings, and much more sacred and ennobling. To all practical purposes the political rights
and duties of the people are just what they are defined and prescribed to be by the Constitution.

They have no other political rights than are therein allowed ; and are bound to all the duties therein enjoined.—The IDEA of the STATE in our country is : all the people acting under and according to the Constitution. This is what we mean by a free, Constitutional government, in distinction from a pure Democracy, like that of Athens, where all the people act without a Constitution. Such is the State in theory.—In regard to the *practical* exercise of Sovereign powers, it takes three fourths of the people to constitute the State. A mere majority is therefore no more the State, than Louis XIV. was the State ; and it is sheer absolutism, in our country, for the majority to set itself up as the State, just as much as it was in France for Louis XIV. to set himself up as the State. The Supreme Power of the nation no more resides in a mere numerical majority than in the minority. The majority possess just those rights and powers which are given by the Constitution, and no others. What are they ? As to their *personal* rights—though these are not strictly in the question, yet they may here be stated —in common with all the inhabitants of the land, strangers or citizens, voters or not voters, the majority have the right of being protected as individuals in their persons and property, provided they do no wrong ; and if they do wrong, of being fairly tried according to law by the judgment of their peers.—As to their *political* rights ; in common with all voters, they have in certain cases, in reference to the appointment of certain public agents, the right of suffrage ; and in regard to the questions thus submitted to the whole body of voters, the majority have the right of deciding. The amount of the political rights of the majority, then is this : that their will, when *legally* expressed, is decisive in regard to a certain number of questions submitted by the Constitution to a popular vote.—So far therefore from constituting the State, a numerical majority of the people, in their political action, is simply an organic part of the State, just as the Legislative, Judiciary, and Executive, are organic parts of the Government ; and its rights and powers, like theirs, are conferred, defined, and limited by the Constitution ; and finally these rights and powers are inseparably linked with duties—the majority are bound to act within their limits, and to act conscientiously there.

These are the simplest elements of our political ethics. They belong to the very primer of our political science.—Yet how well are they understood ; how much are they felt ; how much are they practically regarded ?—Alas, gentlemen, I know not how it may appear to you ; but to me it seems that in comparison with their indispensable necessity to our political salvation, these truths are scarcely at all felt. Unless I greatly mistake the spirit of the country, there is a blind feeling, widely prevalent and rapidly increasing, as if the mere present will of a majority, however expressed, and on all subjects, as well without as within its legal limits, is, and of right ought to be, the SUPREME POWER of the nation. Whenever the people are told that there is any thing which they cannot rightfully do, their impulse is to feel indignant, as if some monstrous outrage were perpetrated against the sacred principles of eternal justice, which they were called upon to avenge. To differ from the popular opinion seems to them a crime—a thing to be punished. They cannot understand that you have as good a right to your opinion, as they to theirs—that they differ from you, as much as you do from them.—In proof that this is so, go and address the popular political assemblages of our country. Tell them that you honestly believe it to be a possible thing that there shall not be wisdom and virtue enough in the nation to make the experiment of self-government successful ; and in nine cases out of ten you provoke their displeasure, not merely for being bold enough to utter an unpopular doctrine, but as being guilty of treason against the sacred principles of freedom. Tell them that you think it best for the popular good, and therefore right, that the popular will should be checked by constitutional restraints ; and ten to one you will be hustled from the stand as an aristocrat, a monarchist, an enemy to the people. Or, if they allow you to remain there long enough, tell them that the original framers of our Constitution were true and genuine lovers of rational freedom, and yet that they have framed the Constitution so as to be a check upon a present numerical majority ; that our frame of government in various respects is full of restraints upon the popular will ;—and there are thousands and tens of thousands to whom such doctrine would be entirely strange and revolting. They would not even believe you. Yet you would tell them nothing but the truth—nothing which our public men do not know to be true. Why is it, then, that our public men rarely or never tell the people these truths, comment, explain, and urge them? It is because these truths, however important and vital, are odious to the people ; and they will not bear them.

From this erroneous and exaggerated notion of Rights, and this feeble sense of Duties, it is easy to see to what dangers we are exposed. When the people feel as if the cause of popular rights, as they understand them—that is, the right of the majority to do just what it pleases—is not only their own cause, but the cause of every thing most sacred, of Truth, of Freedom, and of God ; what protection has society against licentious abuses of power ?   In private life the man who does every thing he has a right to do, in the sense of the word now in question—that is, every thing which the Law will not punish him for doing—is a villain. That we are not cursed with such villains at every turn in life, we owe to the influence of conscience and the power of public opinion. But what protection is there in conscience, or in public opinion, against the unjust acting of a people firmly believing in the Divine Right of a majority to have its own way at all events ?   How much is the responsibility of a multitude felt by the individuals that compose it ?   Is it not practically as if it were a question concerning the seventeen millionth part of the national conscience ?—In the name of Liberty the Jacobins of France cut off the heads of poor decrepit old women for complaining of the national bread ; for not crying out lustily enough the watchwords of revolutionary frenzy ; and even for the singular crime of being " *suspected of incivism.*" Hundreds of similar atrocities you may find in the records of their Revolutionary Tribunals. I do not say that we shall ever witness any such abominable excesses among us. I do not believe we shall. None the less however are we bound to be aware of the dangers to which we are exposed from exaggerated notions of the rights of majorities. The tendency is to make the popular will overbear all moral considerations, and all constitutional limitations. Popular majorities may come to feel themselves justified in reaching their ends by almost any and every means. In the strife of party politics the people may come to feel as if it were allowable to secure a victory in any way, right or wrong ; and political corruption, if not openly justified, will be condemned only in the opposite party, while in reality its heinousness will be lightly thought of, if only it be coupled with the Spartan virtues of dexterity and success.

In such a state of things all honorable and upright freedom of political opinion and action in public men is in danger of becoming next to impossible ; and the truly enlightened patriot, the true friend of the people—who, because he is their true friend,

will not flatter their passions and echo all their notions, be they right or wrong—is likely to be deprived of all scope for public action. The demagogue
will carry it over him by a thousand to one. There
never was a country in the world, from the days of
Pericles to the present time, which furnished such
unbounded scope for the demagogue as ours ; and
never was a country so cursed with demagogues.
The demagogue and the courtier are but opposite
poles of the same character. The demagogue perpetually tells the people that they are sovereign—
that there is no higher law than their will. Like
the courtier he flatters and cajoles the sovereign, in
order to mislead and rule him. What chance for a
fair hearing has the honest friend of the people ? It
certainly cannot be said to be unnatural for men to
confide in and yield themselves to the guidance of
those who bow to their will, flatter their vanity, or
minister to their passions. In point of fact what
public man dares resist the current of party opinion, and the demands of party discipline ? What
truths unpalatable to the popular taste, however vitally important to the public welfare, do the politicians of either party dare to tell the people ? What
popular errors, however dangerous, do they dare
expose and denounce ? From the political and

party presses, controlled by demagogues, the people almost never hear the truth. Morning, noon and night, they are fed on falsehoods ; and nursed in prejudices, hatreds and animosities. All considerations of truth, decency and reverence, give way before the violence of party spirit ; and the blind and bitter spirit of party is continually stimulated by provocatives addressed to the ignorance, the prejudices and violent passions of the people ; and in the midst of all their professed homage, love and respect for the people, the demagogues show clearly enough to the discerning eye in what real contempt they hold the knowledge, the wisdom and the virtue of the people, by the boundless impudence of the lies, flatteries and quackeries with which they seek to cajole and lead them.

And which way tends the political destiny of the nation under these influences of the party presses and of political demagogues ? It tends to throw the absolute power of the nation into whatever party of demagogues, calling themselves friends of the people, can most successfully cajole and corrupt the people. It tends, in short, to a democratic absolutism—the worst of all forms of absolutism, the most pervading and the least conscientious. Any party supported by a popular majority, can at any time overbear the Constitution, and absorb into itself all the powers of the State.—Thus with all the forms of the Constitution remaining, the Constitution itself may be effectually subverted. And which way tends this state of things ? Is not nearly every thing in the country now decided by party majorities, procured fairly and legally, if possible, but procured at all events ? And what is the great absorbing party question ? Every one knows. Not a petty municipal officer in the obscurest village in the country, whose election does not turn on the Presidential question. To what does this tend but to an absorption of all the powers of the State into the Executive ? I do not say this as belonging to either party. I go with neither ; and all that I have said is freely applicable by all parties. I speak only of the direction in which, unless we shut our eyes to all the lights of past history and to all the facts of present observation, we must believe we are at this moment tending. Significant tokens have already displayed themselves, which he who has eyes to read them, cannot fail to interpret. Is not the legislation of the country, at present and to a prodigious extent, originated and controlled by Executive influence ? Has not the existence of the Senate, one of the august and inviolable branches of our constitutional government, been openly threatened ? Has not the independence, and therefore the constitutional existence, of the Judiciary been invaded by the proposals to render its judges removable at executive pleasure ? Have we not come within a few years past to hear the Executive spoken of as THE Government ; to hear of the obligations of office-holders to regard themselves as servants of the Executive, instead of being holders of public trusts for the Nation ; with various other expressions of the like kind—expressions never dreamed of in the days of Washington— expressions which would have been heard with horror in those days, but which are now such familiar terms in our political vocabulary that we use them without thinking the changes they imply ?

Now can any one fail to see that these influences of party demagogism, supported upon the false and exaggerated notion of the rightful supremacy of a popular majority, tend to the virtual overthrow of the Constitution ? The forms of the Roman Republic—its senate, its tribunes, and its consuls—remained for ages after all the powers of the state had passed into the hands of an absolute executive supported by prætorian guards. This may never be our destiny. But how much better off are we likely to be with an absolute executive supported by the unconstitutional powers of a popular majority?

Many look for salvation in a change of men— in the party tables being turned. I look for no such thing. The danger lies not in any particular party, but in principles held by all parties, or at least in the necessity which all parties will, I fear, ever be under of echoing, and supporting themselves upon, the erroneous popular doctrine which now lies practically at the ground of our system. I look for no permanent political salvation in a mere change of parties and men. I look for political salvation only in a return of the people to true notions of liberty—to sound constitutional political opinions, to the spirit of loyalty, of reverence for law and order, and to public virtue.

It is not, however, gentlemen, chiefly with reference to its bearing upon the integrity of our Constitution, nor with reference to any changes which may hereafter be wrought in our mere political existence, that I have dwelt upon the popular notion respecting the rights of majorities, and upon the spirit and tendencies which have their root in this prevalent notion. For after all, in an abstract view, it matters comparatively little what form of gov-

ernment we have, provided it be well administered,
and provided the people be truly cultivated, wise
and good.   It is in the virtue, the moral worth, of
the people, that the well-being of a nation essentially consists.   But I have dwelt upon it, because
political   institutions,   government   and   laws,   are
everywhere the most powerful of the causes that
form   the   moral   character   of   a   people ;   because
every free government can do more to exalt or corrupt the morals of a nation than all other causes ;
and because I cannot resist the conviction that the
actual political influences which are at work in our
country, are tending to corrupt the moral spirit of
the nation.

Look at the working of parties among us.   Is it
not a grand political GAME—the possession of the
powers and patronage of the government being the
stake ; demagogues the players ; and the people the
pawns ? Is not every thing decided by a hot conflict
of party tactics ? Is it not considered and called a
battle, a war ; and by an easy association has not
the old corrupt adage, " all is fair in war," come
to be a practical maxim ?   Hence in our elections
what scenes of violence ; what licentiousness of the
party press ; what misrepresentation of facts for
political effect ; what slander, calumny and abuse

heaped in turn upon every eminent person in the nation ! Latterly the temper of people, in these respects, has passed into their great legislative body ; and the scenes of vulgar and indecent violence which have been recently enacted in Congress, are fitter for a bear garden than for the dignified assemblage of the representatives of a great people. What must be the effect of this, reacting again upon the spirit of the nation ? Does it not tend to eat out of the heart of the people all loyalty—all reverence for justice, law and public order ? Persons may think lightly of this ; but I ask them to tell us how there can be a great heroic people with- out REVERENCE. It is impossible. And in order to maintain in the heart of a people reverence for Justice, Law and Public Order, the people must reverence also the Forms, the Institutions, in which those great Ideas are embodied and represented. FORM is throughout the Universe the necessary condition of every spiritual manifestation. The moral life of a nation is displayed and seen and felt only in its forms, just as the life of the vegetable and animal world is seen and felt only in its appropriate forms. When the people cease to reverence the institutions and persons which embody and represent the ideas of Justice, Law and Public Order, it is but a short step to cease to reverence the ideas themselves. With the decay of reverence for the forms, dies out also the reverence for the substance. Like the besotted Africans they may indeed continue to set up the *Fetisch* gods of their self-will, and to dash them down at every caprice of passion ; but all sense of loyalty, all profound feeling of the allegiance which they owe to the sacred majesty of justice, law and order, will be merged in a wilful determination to have their own way at all events.

Then, again, consider more directly the influence which the popular feeling that politics is a war, and that all is fair in war, must have upon the private morals of a nation. How long will it be before that people who stick at nothing in politics will come to stick at nothing in morals ? It is impossible that political profligacy should not in the long run lead to corruption in private morals. All history proves this truth ; and, gentlemen, our own observation may suffice to give us more than one token of the direction in which we are moving. Within the last five or six years, there have been more government defaulters, and more breaches of other high pecuniary public trusts—ten times more in number and amount, than in the whole former period of our national existence. Will any one say that these and many other instances of moral dereliction ; as well as the scenes of lawless violence that so frequently occur, and the comparative apathy with which they are looked upon and forgotten ; cannot be traced to the working of political influences ? To me it seems there is no cause so obvious ; no solution so adequate.   Let political corruption once become an organized element in the political action of a nation, and it cannot fail to corrupt the private morals of the people.   I do not say that corruption has become an organized element in the political action of this nation ; but I do say that within the last few years there have been developments enough in this direction, to overwhelm us with shame, and to become the ground of serious apprehension for the future.

Thus, gentlemen, I have rapidly glanced at some aspects of our country, connected with its physical growth, and with the working of its political institutions.   It may perhaps be thought that the representation is overdrawn and falsely colored.   I do not admit that it is so.   It will not be denied that sources of danger and tendencies to evil exist in all nations.   Those which exist in our case are certainly not those which result from poverty—desti-

tution of physical resources, skill, enterprise and
energy ; nor from political restraint or oppression.
They are precisely those to which a rich and free
people—an intensely enterprising and intensely
democratic people—are exposed.   Besides, it is
chiefly of principles and tendencies I have spoken ;
and as to what I have said respecting the evils
actually existing among us—the party press, demagogues, unconstitutional notions of popular rights,
political corruption—I maintain that it falls below
the truth of facts.   I do not say that these evil
influences will soon or ever work the actual downfall
of the nation ; but I do say that such is the inevitable result of their unchecked working.   I do not say
that there exist no checks.   I freely and gladly
admit that there are manifold conservative powers
in action amongst us.   But notwithstanding these
better influences, the dangers to which we are
peculiarly exposed are of such sort and so great as
to beget reasonable apprehension ; at all events
they show the immense importance of specially
cultivating the higher moral elements of national
welfare, by which alone the dangerous tendencies to
undue worldliness and to political and social corruption can be effectually counteracted.

   It is in this connection that I urge the duty

which rests upon the educated men of the country of striving to exalt and purify the intellectual and moral spirit of the nation. Not that I would make an invidious distinction; not that the duty does not rest upon all classes, upon every true patriot and good man. But it is a body of young scholars whom I address : it is upon the body of the educated men of the country that the duty in question eminently rests. Of the culture of the nation they are the proper representatives, and the special guardians. If they are indifferent and negligent, what other class will be earnest and faithful ? What other class could discharge their special obligations ?

Eminently then upon the educated class rests the obligation of cherishing the higher intellectual and moral interests of the commonwealth. It is a duty which in this country is not only immensely important, but surrounded with peculiar difficulties. Amidst special tendencies in the spirit of the nation to a predominating worldliness, it is the vocation of our scholars to cherish in themselves and diffuse around them a love of science, of letters, of art—of all that is liberal. Unaided, and even counteracted, by the working of our political institutions, they are to strive to extend the spirit of political virtue—public spirit, heroism, reverence

,5

for law and order.   In their endeavors to exalt and fortify the private morals of the nation, they find their exertions counteracted not only by the ordinary temptations which surround mankind, but also by the strongly demoralizing tendency of our party politics.   Thrown so early, too, as our young scholars are into the struggles of professional exertion ; isolated from each other in the midst of the intense practical and material life that is around them, they are greatly exposed to the danger of losing the love of good letters, the liberal and cultivated tastes, which they may have gained ; and of surrendering themselves to the very influences which they should strive to counteract.

But if we cannot expect that the body of our educated men will go forward and perfect themselves in a high and refined cultivation, there is yet one part of their vocation to which it is right to expect them to be faithful.   This is to preserve the spirit of the LIBERAL callings.   The liberal Professions have indeed utility, and not beauty, for their end ; and in this respect they differ from the liberal Arts. But still they are liberal professions ; because they are, according to the idea of them, free from the necessity of seeking private gain or advantage as their end.   They have utility for their end ; but it is the public utility, and not the private advantage of those who pursue them. In other callings, important as they are in their results to society, and respectable as they are in themselves, the end for which they are pursued is wealth or a livelihood. This is in general the idea of them, and the reason why they are followed. On this ground rests the expectation that the callings of the merchant, the banker, the farmer, the artisan, will be followed to any extent required by the public interests. But, in the *idea*, at least, of the liberal professions, although their members must have a livelihood in order to practise them, yet they are not to practise them merely for the sake of the livelihood. Herein lies the ground of the more dignified position and more respectful estimation which society has accorded to the liberal professions. The clergyman, the physician, the teacher, the lawyer, are supposed to engage in their several callings for the sake of the public welfare ; and in proportion as they make their professions mere means to private ends—even their own livelihood, they degrade their callings, and forfeit their title to public respect.

In the olden times, this idea of the liberal professions was more distinctly recognized than at present : on the one hand, the members of the

liberal professions were expected to perform the
duties of their callings without pecuniary charge ;
and on the other hand, the people were supposed
to be under obligation to provide freely for their
modest yet dignified support ; and to hold them in
honorable estimation, all the higher for the worldly
advantages or chances of advantage they surrendered.   At the present day also we see the recognition of this idea in the sentiment of the incongruity
of a clergyman being devoted to mere worldly pursuits ; in the indignation which would be felt against
the physician who should refuse the gratuitous suc-
cors of his art to the sick and dying poor ; in the
disgrace, and probable expulsion from the society
of his brethren, with which a lawyer would be visited
who for the guerdon of pecuniary reward should lend
himself to pervert the course of justice and become
a villain's tool.   Yet it is to be deeply lamented that
there is too little of the true spirit of the liberal
callings, both among those who follow them and in
the community at large.   Let it be cherished, and
kept alive and quick in the minds of our educated
men, and incredibly great and salutary will be its
influence in exalting and refining the spirit of the
whole nation.

Again : let our educated men shun the politician's trade. I do not say they should never accept of public offices of trust and honor, nor that they should never seek them ; but they should never seek them for private ends, and they should only accept them when they believe they can fill them honorably and independently for the public good. Our scholars and professional men should take a deep interest in politics ; should indeed study them profoundly ; but never should they become mere politicians, partisan aspirants for popular favor and applause, greedy seekers of office and the gains of office. They should aim to be independent, free-spoken teachers of political truth and political duty. They should strive to make themselves understood as a body of honest counsellors, seeking by pen and tongue and personal influence to make the people truly enlightened on all political doctrines and measures ; to whom the people may look for fair discussion, true information, and sound advice. Let them tell the people the truth—the truth which the demagogues will never tell them.

Were it not that a wisdom in the manner, and a blamelessness of character almost more than human, might seem requisite in order not to impair the peculiar spiritual influence of their office, I

would say that the ministers of religion should become political teachers of the people from the pulpit. I do not mean that they should meddle with
party politics, nor that they should treat political
subjects—whether general principles or special
measures—as politicians. Let them leave that to
others. But that it should be inexpedient (when
done without impropriety of language or manner)
for them to urge distinctly upon the minds and
consciences of their flocks the sense of Christian
responsibility in the exercise of their political rights,
is the fault of the people. To "honor the king"
is a sacred injunction which in Holy Scripture stands
in immediate connection with the precept to "fear
God;" that is to say, a Christian people are as
much bound to discharge Christianly their political
as their other social duties; and it is the business
of the ministers of religion to enforce every branch
of moral duty. I can conceive that the clergy
might, with such simplicity and affectionate spiritual
earnestness, so manifestly free from all selfishness
or worldiness of tone or purpose, unite in the habit-
ual practice of urging the obligations of Christian
morality in the exercise of political rights, as not
to impair, but rather to increase the salutary influence of their office. If it must be admitted that

this can scarcely be expected in fact—that the pulpit must carefully abstain from coming into contact with the actual beating heart and life of the nation ; then it is an admission which it seems to me a sad necessity to be obliged to make.*

Again : upon the educated men rests especially the duty of sustaining the cause of sound popular education, as well as all higher cultivation of letters, science and art. We must beware of leaving this great cause in the hands of mere politicians. The system of public instruction indispensable to the welfare of every nation, and eminently of ours, requires that moral and religious culture should never be separated from a wholesome and wisely adapted intellectual training. I have no faith in the mere Lord Brougham "schoolmaster." He may be ever so much "abroad among the people," and yet do the people as much harm as good. I have no faith in the mere diffusion of popular knowledge, as an adequate culture of the people. The minds of the young should be trained, strengthened, formed into right habits, imbued with right principles, with the elements of future self-culture and self-guidance,—not merely

* The present view (1860) on this point, to which the author has been led, is given at large in the subsequent piece on Politics and the Pulpit.

stuffed with a crude mass of superficial facts, mis-
called "useful knowledge."

Above all I have no faith in the merely negative
religious character of popular instruction. I regard
it as one of the most monstrous solecisms that the
popular education of a Christian nation should be
organized—if not with an atheistic forgetfulness
that there is a God, yet—with such a studied avoid-
ance of almost every thing distinctively Christian.
The political welfare of this country can be secured
by no diffusion of mere knowledge. Edu cation—
the education of the mass—must be thoroughly
Christian. There is no country on the globe where
the social virtue and political prosperity of the nation so entirely depend upon the intelligence of the
people being pervaded by a deep sense of the old-
fashioned Christianity which recognizes the Gracious
Influences of God's most Holy Spirit, conferred
upon the human race through Christ, as the only
source of goodness in man, and the only sure safe-
guard and support of pure morals and true national
well-being.

I have now, gentlemen, given (and very imperfectly, I am sensible) some brief suggestions as to
the position and duties of our educated class, in

relation to some of the evils of our times, and more especially to some dangerous tendencies to which we are exposed.   If these dangers exist, surely we shall neither diminish nor avoid them by shutting our eyes to the fact.   Nor ought the full and frank statement of them to be stigmatized as the croaking notes of feeble alarmists despairing of the republic. Against all such reproaches I only stand up the more stoutly.   I plant myself on the ground established by philosophy and by history ; and I deny that there is any thing in the human nature of the nineteenth century, or any charm in the frame of our government, which can ensure us against the fate that has fallen upon other nations.   If, then, there are dangers to which we are exposed, the true practical wisdom is, neither to despise nor to exaggerate them ; but to see, to admit—and to guard against them ; neither to rest in a vain confidence, nor to abandon the cause of our country as hopeless ; but to extend and quicken all those influences which we know assuredly CAN and WILL secure the permanent welfare and true glory of the nation.

Let us not shrink, then, from our position.   Let us manfully stand up for the truth.   Democratic institutions have no intrinsic power to make us a wise and good, a truly and permanently happy peo-

5*

ple. Riches cannot do it. Diffusion of knowledge cannot do it. All these together cannot do it; they cannot even ensure us against downfall and ruin. But there are things that can do it. Let the influence of Christianity really and practically control the political as well as the social life of the nation ; let the people exercise their rights from a pure sense of duty ; let there be a proportionable diffusion of the spiritual elements of national welfare ; in a word, with CIVILIZATION let there be combined a proportionable CULTURE founded upon CHRISTIANITY ; and we shall certainly be not only a rich and great, but a wise, a good, and truly prosperous nation.

Here then, in the promotion of these great objects, is the vocation of all good citizens, and eminently of the educated men of the country. Let those who belong to this class be true to their high calling, and by the favor of Almighty God we may indulge the noblest hopes for our country and for the great cause of Human Advancement.

THE TRUE IDEA OF THE UNIVERSITY, AND ITS RELATION TO A COMPLETE SYSTEM OF PUBLIC INSTRUCTION.

THE TRUE IDEA OF THE UNIVERSITY, AND ITS RELATION TO A COMPLETE SYSTEM OF PUBLIC INSTRUCTION.

Your Association, young gentlemen, is that of a Brotherhood of Scholars : but not a Brotherhood of Scholars united solely by the common bond of liberal culture and the love of good letters, but also by the finer and tenderer bond of your common relationship to the institution in which you received your intellectual nurture. It recognizes that as your ALMA MATER—the benignant mother of your minds. The idea is a beautiful one ; and the sentiment it inspires is not less beautiful. It is at once a filial as well as a fraternal sentiment that brings you together at this festival season of our Academic year. You come here as brothers, because nurslings of the same fair mother. And though she is but a young mother,—scarce twenty years old,—she can already count by hundreds the children she has borne. Year by year, during nearly every year of her own existence, she has dismissed into the "wide, wide world" a goodly band of sons brought forth and brought up by her. Some of them have not been long away from her fostering care—the younger brothers among you, the purple light of youth, the *purpureum lumen juventutis*, still fresh upon them ; but others have been a good while gone, doing manly work in the service of their country and of mankind, to their own honor and their mother's fair renown. She is about to send forth another band of her children, an accession to the ranks of your brotherhood. This is the occasion that brings you together now : and I hope the filial, no less than the fraternal sentiment, will be quickened and deepened by your reunion. For the strength of the parent's heart is in the children's duteous love. And your Alma Mater is that sort of mother that may live forever ; and however old in years she may become, and venerable for age, may yet flourish in perpetual youth, the fruitful mother of new bands of sons year by year to the end of time ; with a perpetual improvement, too, in the intellectual life and development and nurture which her children draw from her. That such may be her destiny is, I trust, with you, an object of earnest desire and of loving hope. But its accomplishment depends on certain conditions, and I know not from what quarter these can so well be expected to be supplied as from your influence and exertions. For this reason, gentlemen, I have thought fit to occupy the hour of your meeting here to-night in presenting some considerations on the state of Higher Public Instruction in our country—its defects and needs, and the obstacles which stand in the way of realizing what every lover of good learning, and every enlightened lover of his country, and his race too, must desire to see among us—considerations which, I hope, may serve in some degree to give incitement and direction to your efforts for the prosperity and fair fame of your own Alma Mater, and for the advancement of the interests of Higher Education throughout the land.

A complete and perfect system of Public Instruction implies institutions for Primary, Secondary, and Higher Education. The Common School is for Primary ; the Academy (as it is called among us) is for Secondary ; and the College and University for Higher Instruction. The Common Schools should exist in every town and district in sufficient numbers to give to all the children of the commonwealth, of both sexes, the rudiments of necessary learning, the first elements of a sound education. The Academies are institutions where all those of either sex, whose condition allows, whose inclination prompts, or whose destination in life demands a greater degree of intellectual culture and a larger amount of knowledge than the Common School can give, may find the means of acquiring it. They should provide for imparting every thing included in the idea of what is familiarly called a good thorough English education, and also the Classical learning necessary to prepare young men for college. With the Academies I would also connect *Normal* instruction, or the training of persons for the special vocation of Teachers in the Common Schools or elsewhere.

But of these institutions I shall not further speak. It is to the state of Higher Public Instruction that I wish specially to direct your thoughts.

And to put the subject immediately before you,

that you may see at once the scope and drift of my remarks, I will say at the outset, that we have in this country no Universities, and we need them : we have Colleges ; and they need to be reformed— subordinated to the Universities, and connected with the lower institutions in such a way as to form a complete and perfect SYSTEM of public Instruction. This, gentlemen, is what I wish to unfold and put in a clear light. I shall give you the results of reflections that have, naturally enough, occupied my mind, from time to time, for many years : but I have greatly to regret that broken health and the pressure of many cares have not allowed me time to put the expression of them in such form and method as I could desire for this occasion.

I have said, gentlemen, that in this country we have no Universities. We have not. We have the name, but not the thing. A University, in its proper notion, is an institution which affords every possible advantage for the perfect acquisition of every branch of science and learning included within the circle of liberal studies. It implies an assemblage together in one place of all the conditions and means requisite for pursuing these studies to the utmost possible extent. It implies that any one

competent to enjoy its advantages, may find himself surrounded at the University with all the aids
and appliances needful or desirable for carrying out
his studies to the highest point of perfection, in
any direction throughout the whole sphere of science
and letters.

The University, gentlemen, is an organic whole ;
and so, like every other organic whole, it must have
its organizing principle, its determining idea : in
virtue of which all the constituent parts find their
title to admission, their place and their form ; from
which they grow ; around which they group themselves, and by which they are held together as one
perfect whole.   What is this constituent principle,
this central idea ?   It is a well organized body of
learned and able men dispensing the highest instruction in every branch of science and letters—not the
meagre and superficial instruction which alone can
possibly be given by one person undertaking all
branches, or many branches, and who having of
necessity only a smattering himself, can of course
impart no more than a smattering to others ; but
the profound and thorough instruction which can
be given only by the members of a learned society
numerous enough to carry the division of labor to
the greatest desirable extent ; thus allowing each

one, and making it each one's duty, to devote his best energies to the cultivation and perfectionment of his own department, and to the communication of the fruits of his studies in the clearest and best methods of exposition.   Out of this well organized division and connection of labor, comes that perfection in every part, and that completeness and unity of the whole, which makes the University what its name should import—a place where the universe of liberal studies is unfolded to the ingenuous mind in all the fulness and richness of its infinitely diversified forms, and yet as one great harmonious whole of Truth, Beauty and Goodness.

But there are also certain *material* conditions included in the notion of a University, because they are necessary to enable the members of the learned society to discharge their functions.   These are buildings, lecture rooms, and especially libraries, apparatus, laboratories, and collections in nature and art—so ample and complete as to leave nothing wanting for the investigation and illustration of every department of science and letters, whether for the use of those who dispense or those who receive instruction.

Such, gentlemen, is the University in its true idea ; and I say again, that while we have the name

among us, we have not the thing. We have many
Colleges, and several institutions with the name of
Universities, but which are in reality only Colleges.
But a College neither is a University, nor can fulfil
the function of a University. This is true, whether
you look at the matter in a theoretical or a practical way ; whether you consider what a College
ought to be and to accomplish, or whether you
consider what our Colleges, as they at present stand,
actually do or are able to accomplish. In a theoretical view, a College is an institution designed to
form the generally well educated man without reference to any particular destination in life ; to carry
on the culture and discipline of the faculties generally, already begun in the lower institutions—to
carry it on to such an extent, and also to impart
such an amount of liberal knowledge and accomplishment, as will prepare the young man either for
a dignified and useful position in cultivated social
life, or for professional studies, or for that further,
more extensive and profound study of the liberal
arts and sciences in any special direction, for which
it is the business of the University to provide.
And so in theory a College is not and ought not to
be a University. In the next place, in a practical
view, our Colleges cannot, if they would, accomplish

the proper functions of a University. They are none of them adequately provided, and most of them very slenderly provided, with the *material* conditions requisite for the profound and thorough study of all branches of science and letters—I mean libraries, apparatus, collections in nature and art. Nor less deficient in the *personal* conditions. In most of our Colleges there is only the Faculty of Science and Letters; and the body of Professors is so small that it would not be possible for each Professor to give those extensive, complete and thorough courses of instruction which the idea of a University implies, in any one, much less in all, of the subjects which it is made his duty to teach. This, I say, would not be possible, even if he had nothing else to do. But he has something else to do. His time is fully employed in imparting comparatively elementary instruction to immature young minds but partially prepared perhaps for the course of college studies. What advantages, then, do such institutions afford for carrying out the study of the whole circle of liberal arts and sciences to the utmost possible limit ? None at all. In some of our Colleges there are Faculties of Medicine, Law and Theology. But this does not make them Universities. For the courses of instruction are organized in respect of

extent, time, division and other particulars, to meet
the special and practical demands of professional
preparation, rather than as parts of a University
system : and even if this were not the case, what
has been shown in regard to the Faculties of Science
and Letters would still hold.   And so it is obvious
that our Colleges do not and cannot accomplish the
functions of a University.

That Universities are a need for this country, is
a point, gentlemen, which I should feel ashamed to
think it necessary to argue before you.   We do not
need a great many of them : but a certain number—
amply supplied with all the material and personal
conditions for realizing the true and noble idea of such
institutions—we do need. Who·can doubt they would
have an influence that can be brought into action in no
other way, in advancing the great interests of science
and good letters—interests with which, I need not
tell you, gentlemen, not only the intellectual and
moral well-being, but even the material prosperity of
the nation, are indissolubly bound up ? They would.
Such institutions would be a glory and a blessing to
the land.

Supposing, then, Universities to be established,

what shall be done with the Colleges ? Let them exist : let them, if need be, be multiplied. For the College holds an indispensable and most important place in a perfect system of Public Instruction. It is the place for the liberal education of those who do not go to the University, and by means of the liberal education it imparts, it also prepares for the University those who wish to advance to the highest degrees of learning and science. No student should come to the University who is not prepared to profit by its advantages : and no one *is* prepared who has not already acquired the amount of mental discipline and of liberal knowledge which form the well-educated man. This it is the proper function of the College to impart. The College does not and cannot form men of profound science and learning in every department of liberal studies. It does not make masters and doctors, competent to fill the Academic chairs of Universities or of Colleges, or to be in any sphere the great teachers of the world. This is not its function. It is the function of the University to do this. And on the other hand, it is not the special function of the University to *form* the liberally educated young man—it takes him already formed. The University is not the place to *train* and prepare the young man to think and to study for himself : but to *take* the young man already prepared to think and to study ; and then to *help* him in thinking and studying for himself, and to carry him forward, by instructions more extended, profound and diversified than the College can give, to the greatest possible perfectness of knowledge, whether in science or in learning. And the proper place, in a perfect system of Public Instruction, for the young man to gain the knowledge and the power to think and study which fit him for the University, is the College. In this view, and for those who go to the University, the College is subordinate to the University. But the College, in its proper function, is not limited to preparing young men for the University. It is also to form well-educated men who do not go to the University. We need a certain number of profoundly learned men in every department of science and letters : eminent Masters and Doctors, great luminaries in the intellectual sphere. These the University is to make—that is to say, supply the best means, and all the means, for enabling them to make themselves. But we also need an immensely greater number of well-educated young men : men whose minds have been trained by a course of liberal studies sufficiently diversified, and carried to a sufficient extent, to ensure a vigorous and well-proportioned development of their faculties. These the College makes, or, as before, gives them the best help to making themselves ; and so does a work which the University cannot do ;—I will not say a more or a less important work than that which the University does ; for it is idle and foolish to draw a comparison between the importance of two things, both of which are indispensable to the Commonwealth.

Let there be Colleges, then ; and let them be sufficiently numerous to afford a place for all who seek a liberal education. But let them be reformed. Let them be made what they ought to be. Let them be conformed to their proper idea. Let them not attempt the functions of a University ; for, as we have seen, they cannot and ought not to fulfil them. Let them be places to give a really " liberal education " in the fine old scholarly meaning of the term. Let the course of studies be " liberal" studies. Let not the object be the acquisition of special knowledge for this or that particular destination in life. Let such special acquisitions come afterwards as any one may choose. Let the College course of undergraduate studies be mainly a discipline for the mind. Let it afford scope and means for the

6

freest, fullest and most harmonious development and culture of all the mental faculties, without reference to any particular destination in life ; and for those acquisitions of knowledge and accomplishments of taste which form the true liberally educat ed man.   And for this end, there is no conceivable organization of studies so well adapted as the good old-fashioned *curriculum* of classical, mathematical, logical, rhetorical and aesthetical studies.   These studies, properly proportioned and thoroughly pursued, involve and secure the very best possible training of the mind.

And this brings me to notice one of the great defects of our College system.   Both too much and too little is done : and the consequence is that almost nothing is done as it should be.   The four years of undergraduate study is short time enough, in all reason, for accomplishing to any really good purpose the course I have mentioned,—even if the student comes from the Academy or Grammar School with a thorough preparation in elementary classical and mathematical learning, and with a considerable degree of culture and discipline of mind.   And yet, into this four years, we have now crowded a multitude of additional studies—making a list almost as large and wonderful as that which lively young ladies accomplish in the fashionable schools, where all languages and learning, all sciences and arts are learned in three years, and all the accomplishments besides ! And while thus crowding the course, we have at the same time, on the other hand, instead of raising the terms of admission, in practice often lowered them to almost nothing. What is the consequence ? Multitudes of young persons enter our Colleges without sufficient preparation, and some of them too young to be able to get it. They are unfit to go with profit through the course of classical and mathematical learning, even if it were not compressed and hurried through with, in order to make some time for the modern additional courses, which, in their turn, of necessity often are compressed into mere meagre and fruitless compends. Some, the older, or more earnest and diligent students, make the best of it—work nobly, gain something, which enables them to educate themselves after they leave College : but the younger or more indolent drag heavily through the four years,—and leave College with "small Latin, less Greek," and no living insight into the principles of Science ; with diplomas in their hands which they could not, some of them, for their lives, bear a creditable examination upon. Such is a strong picture (but I am sad to say, and

sure as sad, it is not an untrue one) of the wretched
consequences that have come from attempting too
much, and doing nothing thoroughly. And the
remedy lies in a return to the proper idea and proper work of the College ; in discarding from the College *curriculum* those courses which properly belong to the University or to the professional and
practical schools ; and in establishing and adhering
inexorably to a far, far higher standard of preparation for admission ; in making a thorough mastery
of the old liberal course a possibility and a reality,
and so inspiring that true love for good learning
which thorough learning always does inspire, and
imparting that high discipline and fine culture
which will be through life a source of pleasure and
a source of power.

Understand me, gentlemen, on one point. I
have no objection to all sorts of courses of practical
instructions (as they are called) in the modern languages, in physics, in the applications of science to
the useful arts—in short, every thing which the spirit
of the age and the wants of the times are said to
demand ; I have no sort of objection to their being
connected with our Colleges—provided two things :
first, that such practical courses be, in their nature,
either literary or scientific ; and second, that they

be not crowded into the four years undergraduate
course, but come after it, or one side of it. As to
the first condition, there must be some limit : and
if this be not the principle of limitation, you cannot
have a limit unless an arbitrary one. There are
various vocations in practical life which not only
proceed upon scientific principles, but which also
imply and demand a *scientific knowledge* of those
principles on the part of those who follow them :
such as Civil Engineering, Navigation, and the like.
And to such studies you must limit these practical
courses in our Colleges, else you must also have
College lectures on the science of soap-making and
calico printing, and every other useful art. Within
this limit, such practical courses may well be admitted into our Colleges, for the benefit of those who
cannot go to the University to study the sciences
and their applications from a purely scientific interest, and in the connection and extent in which they
enter into the University system. But I insist on
the other condition—that they be not crowded into
the proper undergraduate course ; for that would
be a detriment to both. The proper College course,
the simply Academic course, is needful for the pure
interests of science and good letters, needful to
make scholars with the spirit of scholars, prepared

for the University, and for social and public life ; and nothing should be crowded into it to impair its proper function.

There is another point in which I would alter the practice of our Colleges. It is in the matter of degrees. I have said that the College does not and cannot form men of profound science and learning in every department of liberal studies. It is not the province of the College to make Masters and Doctors, competent to fill the Academic chairs of Universities and of Colleges, or to be in any sphere of science and learning the great teachers of the world. That is the province of the University—so far, that is, as it depends on any institution to do it. Our Colleges now confer the *title* of Master and Doctor. But they cannot form the thing. The thing itself, the true Master, the true Doctor, the competent man to fill Academic chairs, or in any way to set up to instruct his fellow-men with any title to their deference as having something of just authority to teach—this, I say, the thing itself, of Master and Doctor, if it gets made at all in our country, is not made by the Colleges : it is self-made after the College has been gone through with and left behind. The very practice of our Colleges in conferring these degrees is an admission of this fact.

They are mostly not given in course, but as honorary recognitions that men have made themselves what the College did not make them. This would be all very well, so long as we have no true University, provided these titular distinctions were conferred only where they are thoroughly deserved. But as it is, there is something laughable, and at the same time sadly degrading to high letters, in the way in which these honors are scattered broadcast over the land—and some of them without any regard to their special significance :—the title of Doctor of Laws, for instance, lighting on the surprised head of some eminent political, literary, or other distinguished personage who perhaps never in his life opened a book on the Canon or the Civil law ; who knows not, it may be, the distinction between them. He is made Doctor of Laws, because, being a layman, it would hardly do to make him a Doctor of Theology, or being a clergyman, the doctorate of Divinity is not thought quite sufficient for his years, his popular eminence, or the worldly importance of his parish.

But let true Universities be established : and then let the Colleges be restricted from conferring any other degree than the Baccalaureate. Let all the others be University degrees. And let them all, both in the College and in the University, be conferred only when fairly earned ; not as a matter of course after a certain attendance on the lecture room, as is too much the case now ; but only after a thorough and rigorous examination sustained in the special Faculty, be it Arts, Theology, Medicine, or Law, in which the degree is taken. Let the degrees be *taken*, or in the old Academic language be "proceeded to," not *given* as mere titles. Let· any man take them all, if he will study for them and earn them : but let no man have any of them upon any other condition. Let this be the rule— there may be occasions for special exceptions—but but let this be the rule : and then the title would be something more than an empty name. It would be a guarantee for the presence of the thing. It would have some weight, some authority. It would be a real honor, to be sought for and won and worn with honest pride, to the great benefit of all the interests of truth and good letters.

Before dismissing the topic of the proper idea of the University, I will take occasion here to say a word as to a Theological Faculty. The great number of distinct religious denominations that exist in our country, and the importance which each one naturally and justly attaches to the theological system by which it is distinguished, renders the establishment of a University Faculty of Theology a matter of great practical difficulty. To avoid this difficulty, the organization of a Theological Faculty was expressly excluded from the plan of the New-York University. My learned and accomplished friend and predecessor, in his recent excellent tract on University education, proposes to avoid the difficulty in the same way.* But I cannot agree with him. A Faculty of Theology is as indispensable as any other Faculty to the idea of a complete University. The Science of Theology—to say nothing of its importance in its higher religious and practical aspects—is, in the philosophical principles which underlie it, in its history, in its literature, in its relations with the civilization and

---

* *University Education*, by H. P. TAPPAN. At the time this discourse was delivered, Professor Tappan was elected to the Chair which my broken health compelled me to resign ; and it was to me a matter of great joy that my place would be filled by one so eminently qualified to do honor to the institution, and to promote all the interests of true learning and science. He has since then accepted the office of Chancellor of the University of Michigan. May all success attend him. I may mention here that I learn from him that he has changed the opinion expressed in his tract, to which reference is made above, and has, on further reflection, come to the same view as that I have taken.

social culture of mankind, one of the most profound
and profoundly interesting departments of human
thought and knowledge.   A University, in the
proper sense of the term, without a Faculty of Theology, is a thing that cannot be created.   And
rather than avoid the practical difficulty by mutilat-
ing the true idea, I would attempt to realize the
idea in the most comprehensive way :—by organizing the Theological Faculty in sections sufficiently
numerous to meet all reasonable desire of the different religious denominations, so that the Faculty of
Theology would in fact consist of several distinct
Faculties, each substantially complete—allowing,
if you please, each communion to have its special
system represented in the University by a body of
Professors of Theology, supported by its own endowment and appointed on its own nomination, subject
to such limitations and common regulations as the
University organization would make requisite.   Students might then attend the lectures of either of the
sections, or of several, or of all, according to their
choice—degrees in Theology, however, depending
only on passing the proper examinations in the
complete course of some one section of the Faculty,
whichever they should elect.   In this way all objections on the score of the University favoring one

religious system at the expense of the rest, would be avoided ; while the widest and freest scope would be given to the pursuit of Theological Science : and surely that man must have small confidence in his own creed who imagines the cause of truth would in any way suffer in the long run by such an organization.

Such, gentlemen, is my view of the needs of Higher Instruction among us : . the University created ; the Colleges reformed.   Let this be done in the way I have sketched ; and then with the Common Schools and Academies, we shall have, and not till then shall we have, a complete system of Public Instruction.

Now, gentlemen, to create and sustain such a system, we must, I think, look to the STATE.   I know this suggestion will strike you as burdened with great difficulties—immense obstacles in getting the State to undertake the matter, and immense liabilities, if she should undertake it, that the true and noble idea, especially of the Higher Institutions, will be violated, impaired, or imperfectly realized, not only from incompetent legislation in the organization of the system, but from the pernicious influence of party politics in its administration. In view of these liabilities of mischief, I should vastly prefer that the University should be entirely independent of the State ; that it should be established by the union of private individuals enlightened enough to conceive the true idea ; rich enough and liberal enough to provide the requisite material endowments ; and wise enough to leave the whole organization and administration in the hands of competent men versed in academic affairs, whose special profession and vocation it is to understand such matters.

But, gentlemen, I must say that I think there is less to hope for in looking in this direction than to the State. And so to the State, it seems to me we must look, if anywhere. Besides, in a theoretical view, the State is the proper power to do this work—under the obligation of doing it rightly and well. It is the obligation of the State to provide a complete and perfect system of Public Instruction. The obligation is already partially recognized in the practice of this Commonwealth, as well as of many other States in the Union. Besides, the State is the only power able, in some respects, to do the work as it should be done. To create the University ; to perfect the Colleges ; and to organize them in connection with the primary and secondary institutions into one great whole, such as the needs of the Commonwealth demand, such as the idea of a complete system of Public Instruction implies, is a PUBLIC work, and can be well done only by the public power.

These institutions, moreover, should be free. No charge for instruction should be made in any of them—no more in the University and in the College, than in the Common School. This is implied in the very idea of Public Instruction. To effect this, immense appropriations of money are needed. This is another point that must not be omitted in our view of the case. To create a great and true University in this Commonwealth; to perfect the organization of the Colleges and Academies; to increase their number, if need be; and to give free instruction in them all, would require millions of ex- ·penditure. To establish in this City a great University, such as ought to be established, requires a provision for the proper dignified support of at least fifty or sixty Professors. There are nearly a hundred and fifty in the University of Berlin. They must be supplied too with all the material conditions for their work :—buildings, libraries, apparatus, museums, and galleries of art, and the like.

I cannot put down the expenditure necessary to effect this at less than five millions. And several millions more would be required to perfect and complete the organization of the Colleges. In short, a complete system of Public Instruction requires an expenditure that can only be made by the State.

But the State can do it. Eminently of the Public Will is it true that "where there is a Will there is a Way." Let only the people of this State feel the importance of it to the glory and welfare of the Commonwealth, and what are ten millions ? what are twenty millions ? A tax so trifling as to press with scarcely a feather's weight on any one, would enable the State to command the amount, and in ten years repay it both principal and interest. Five millions to found a University in this City ! It sounds large : but in less than twice five years it might be saved from the needless and profligate expenditure of this most misgoverned town.

The thing can be done if only the people will it. To lead them to will it is the great point. They have willed great public works of material utility for the public health and convenience, and for the increase of the public wealth. They need be made see that there are spiritual utilities more important still to the best life and welfare of the Commonwealth. They need be made see that a great and perfect system of Public Instruction, though it do not reimburse its cost in the visible and tangible revenue of dollars, is a higher public interest than Croton Water Works and Erie Canals, which do ; that if it be a wise and politic thing in the public to create the one, it is even more so to create the other—and far more noble and honorable and fitting to the glory of a magnanimous Commonwealth.

To stir up the public mind in this matter, belongs eminently to the educated young men of the State. And you, gentlemen, if you enter at all into the greatness and nobleness of the idea ; if you appreciate its paramount importance to the interests of Science and Good Letters, to all the moral and all the material interests of the Commonwealth ; you will not be deterred by the difficulties that lie in the way from exerting the great influence which your liberal culture puts it in your power to wield, in forming the mind and guiding the will of the people of this great and rich State in a right direction on this point. This is the practical purpose I have in view in this discourse. This is the great mission which I conclude my Academic life by invoking you to undertake, and as far as in you lies, to accomplish.

You will have great obstacles to overcome. I admit it. With a vast multitude of the mass of the people, there are probably not so much false views and positive hostilities to contend with, as the absence of all views, and all sense of the importance of any system of higher Public Instruction.

But the greatest and worst obstacles lie in the prevalence of false views and strong prejudices of various sorts among other classes. Of these let me sketch a few types.

There is McCheese, the great provision dealer. He started in life scarcely more than able to write his name. He has made money. He is rapidly rolling up his plum. He turns up his nose in greasy contempt at the idea of taking his money to make learned men. What is the use of learning? He has got on without it. He is opposed—not from any hatred of it as something of superior value which *he* does not possess. For he knows of nothing of superior value to money. It has never entered his head that anybody else should be so foolish as to dream there was.   It is simply a useless whim : and he is opposed to having his money taken for what is useless.   All his brethren will equally oppose you for the same reason.

Then there is Gubbins, ex-Auctioneer, long enough retired upon his fortune to have, in the intervals of turtle and champagne, looked around him and found out that there are in society some men, particularly men of learning and science, who affect to think there are other things in the world entitled to deference besides the mere possessor of money.   He has, perhaps, a dim suspicion they may be right.   But, at all events, with the instinct of a proud but ignoble nature, he hates what he tries to despise.   He will oppose any thing that puts his title to supreme deference in question.   So will his brethren.

There is, again, Fitzroy Cunningham, Esq., shrewd, clear-headed, clever ; with immense activity and versatility of mind, he has all his life been engaged in extensive and complicated transactions of trade and commerce—has amassed a more than princely wealth, which is still growing to greater

and greater expansion. With but a slender education, though perhaps at the ripe age of eighteen
he took a college degree before he went into his
father's counting house, yet he has, since then,
made himself variously intelligent, acquired a vast
amount of information of facts, events, men and
things that have fallen under his observation in
life—the kind of knowledge therefore he naturally
holds in most respect. He lives in a splendid
palace up town ; his wife drives out in a gorgeous
equipage, and gives brilliant entertainments. But
Fitzroy still keeps in his busy sphere, because he
loves it and is proud of it, not merely for its wealth
and the social consequence it brings, but for the
various energies and keen activities it demands.
He has little respect for learning and science in
themselves. He has a certain respect for great law-
yers, great politicians, and eminent public functionaries. But both he and they were made at the
colleges (such as they are) in the slight degree in
which they owe any thing to the college. Such
institutions he is willing to " patronize "—perhaps
be a trustee, if it gratifies his egotism : in which
position he will regard the Faculty as in some sort
in his employment, much on the footing of his
upper clerks, (hardly that,) whom it is his office to

tell how to do their work, (landsmen teaching pilots how to steer,) and to get the *maximum* of work at the *minimum* of salary.   But as to creating a great University, a great Society of Learned Men, with an ample public provision for their independent and dignified support—a society to which he is to look up with deference, as the great ornament and glory of the city, a great light and benefaction to the nation—he has no idea of it.   It is a project for making a great nest of dreamers and drones, entirely out of place amidst the splendid material and practical activities of the age.   Be sure you cannot count on his help.   He will not oppose you with the vulgar hatred of Gubbins ; but he will dismiss you with a serene, contemptuous disregard of your plan.   So will his brethren.

There is, besides, Quintus Queerleigh, able editor of the *Daily Trumpet*—politician, philanthropist, social reformer, believer in social progress, in divinity of the people, (except those who differ from him,) believer in every thing more than in the wisdom of the Past.   Clever man.   Really able.   Of manifold abilities.   Can write.   Can think, too. Says many wise and good things.   Honest perhaps. So some think him.   Great believer in himself, no doubt ; perhaps an honest believer in truth—that which he thinks such.   But not a learned man.   A self-made man : with the one-sidedness that often belongs to such men.   He has already in advance opposed you.   He bloweth with his Trumpet to the people, to warn them against you.   He telleth them that Common Schools are for the people : Colleges and Universities are only to pamper the pride of the rich, the grinders of the faces of the people. He bloweth with his Trumpet against the legislators —warning them of the wrath of the people, if they take the people's money to build up or sustain aristocratic institutions, contrary to the Gospel of Progress which the Trumpet proclaimeth : "Peace on earth ; and every man's coat cut the same length with his neighbor's."   "Useless institutions, too," saith Queerleigh.   " Look at me.   Am not I an able editor, politician, social reformer, writer, think- er?   No college made me.   I made myself.   That is the way to make men."

Foolish Queerleigh ! Foolish able editor ! Know- est thou not that there was a stuff in thee, and a spirit that has made thee an exception to the gen- eral rule ?   Few men perhaps, with thy lack of ad- vantages, would make themselves as able as thou art.   But with the advantages thou lackedst, many might.   Besides, clever as thou art, able editor, writer, thinker, thou art not a learned man. No disgrace. How shouldst thou be ? The thing for thee to be ashamed of is, that thou shouldst decry what thou hast not. For, those who are both as *able* as thou art, and as learned as thou art *not*, have said and testified in many ways, from age to age, that learning, high learning and science, and the discipline that comes with them, are good things, and minister to the greater ability of the ablest of able men. Hadst thou started in thy career of life possessed of the manifold culture and accomplishment of a thoroughly educated man, thou mightest have beaten thy actual self as much as thou now beatest many a printer's apprentice with whom thou didst begin thy career.

There is, too, Ptolemy Tongue-end—patriot, democrat, demagogue orator. He blows with his noisy breath a blast very much in unison with the Daily Trumpet. He "stumpeth" at Ward meetings. Unlike editor Queerleigh, he has no faith in the people, except in their gullibleness—no faith in any thing except the wisdom of buttering his bread with the people's money. So he blows any blast that he thinks may help him to the favor of the sovereign people. He getteth into the legislature, and there opposes, with great .wrath and noise, all grants to Colleges—calling them anti-democratic ; though he knows in his heart all the while that it is, of all things in the world, the most democratic, that the people should be taxed for the endowment of the highest institutions of learning, free to all, as are the Common Schools—that so the children of the people, out of the pockets of the rich, may receive an education that shall enable them to take their share in the great prizes of life. For nothing is more true than that the great prizes of life (other things being equal) are grasped by those who have the highest, most thorough and liberal education ; and without a great and perfect system of free Public Instruction, including the University and the Colleges, as well as the Common Schools, the children of the poor are, as a general rule, condemned to a hopeless disadvantage, in competition with the sons of the rich, in all the higher careers of life. There may be exceptional cases : but such must be the rule. This is so patent and palpable, it seems to me, to every man of common sense and common candor, that I have little patience with the false and stupid twaddle which hollow-hearted demagogues, like Tongue-end, or hopelessly wrong-headed able editors, like Queerleigh, are perpetually pouring into the ears of the unenlightened masses : putting the Common Schools and Colleges in opposition to each other—as if there was any contradiction between them ; as if one was not as necessary as the other, as if every principle of that democracy they prate so about did not require that the State should provide, not only free primary instruction for all the children of the people, but also the highest instruction for all such of the children of the people as desire to go onward and upward into the higher spheres of useful and honorable exertion.   Gentlemen, you may boldly join issue with these praters.   Expose the foolishness of their hackneyed cant.   Keep on doing so : and in due time, if you persevere, you will certainly disabuse the public mind.   Tongue-end will oppose you—till the people begin to think as he in his heart now thinks.   Then you will have his noisy voice equally in favor of the Colleges, and of a great University endowed by the state.   Then he will find out that such institutions are exceedingly democratic.   As to Queerleigh, he will doubtless hold on blowing his Trumpet to the same tune he now does, until he comes of himself to a wiser mind.   Of which, small hope.

Such, gentlemen, are some types of the op-

position you will encounter.   Others might be
sketched did time allow.   Besides these there is
another class of hostile influences, not directly opposed to the creation of the University, but, in several respects, standing in the way of the full realization of its true idea.   Of this sort is the party spirit
of religious sectarianism—the *odium theologicum*—
that bitterest of all hatreds ; and the meddling
spirit of solemn incompetent mediocrity in high
political and social places, thinking it has a special
gift and vocation to busy itself in fostering the interests of learning and science, yet destitute of any
true academic ideas ; and so meddling but to mar,
and sure to oppose if not allowed to mar.   All these
things are against you.   A formidable array.   I admit it.

But, gentlemen, there is no reason to bate heart
or hope.   The work to which I invoke you is a great
and noble work.   Not without encouragement to resolute and patient labor.   Tongue-end, and Queerleigh,
and Cunningham, and Gubbins, and McCheese, are
not all the people of the land.   There are others—
numerous in every class, especially among the more
enlightened, whom your influence may hopefully
reach.   Truth and sound opinion need only zealous
and resolute, and, above all, patient propagandists,

and in time it will spread outward and downward—
as all sound opinion, the world over, must and always
does spread—through the great, honest, and well-
disposed masses, who are ever ready, in heart and
will, to give their support to whatsoever the glory
and welfare of the commonwealth demands

Supposing the University to be established on
the footing I have suggested, there are certain ideas
and principles relating to its administration—to
the organization of the courses of instruction ; the
constitution of the Faculties ; the filling of the
Academic Chairs ; the source of Academic Honors ;
the conferring of Degrees, and the principles, conditions, and modes of their bestowal—which are indispensable to the highest success and usefulness of such
institutions.   These I intended somewhat to have
considered.   There are certain notions and practices, certain ways of thinking and feeling prevalent amongst us on these points, which are utterly
at variance with the true theory of a University—
with all pure academic principles.   These I intended to have signalized.   But the just treatment of
these topics would require a discussion too protract-
ed for this time.   I had therefore better not now
enter upon them.   At some other time, and in

7

some other form, I may perhaps call your attention
to them.

I must now bring my remarks to a close.   The
circumstances in which I stand before you will, I
trust, through your kindness, be allowed to justify
a word of personal reference.   For more than twelve
years I have discharged the duties devolving upon
my Professorship in this institution ; and you who
have attended at my lecture room—as most of
you have—know with what earnestness and zeal I
have discharged them.   These labors have been
their own exceeding great reward.   I have loved the
work.   I have tried to do your minds good.   I believe you think so too.   I have enjoyed the good
will of my colleagues, and such a kindly appreciation of my services on their part as leaves me nothing to desire on that score.   These are convictions
which I cherish more than it is worth while for me
to attempt to express.

It is not a light thing, therefore, for me to resign
my place here.   I had hoped that in the groves of
Oakwood—in the beautiful retreat which, in the
intervals of academic labor, has been my home for
eighteen months, I might find such repose and in-
vigoration for my overworn nerves as would enable

me still to discharge the pleasant labors of my office. In that hope I am disappointed.   The sentence of entire "rustication" has been passed upon me— and that in a worse than the academic sense of the term : for it is without limit of time.   I bow to the decree of the doctors and, I will add, not irreverently, to the will of God.   And in taking leave of you and of my public labors, I beg you to accept the assurance of the lively interest I shall ever feel in your personal welfare and in the prosperity, enlargement, and fair renown of the institution which has been the scene of the labors of the best years of my life.   A University in name, I hope through your resolute and persevering efforts it will become a University in the fullest reality of the thing—a glory and blessing to this city, to the nation, to mankind.   God prosper the cause of science and good letters, of truth and human progress throughout the world.

NOTE.

Since the foregoing was delivered, I have further urged the need of a University, in an article contributed to the editorial columns of the New York *Daily Times*, June 22, 1854, in which I have said:

"The time has come when a great and true University

has become a necessity for the country.   .   .   .   .   .
Even if such an institution were not of incalculable importance to the material prosperity of the nation—which
it is—yet it is profoundly true, and a truth that should
be profoundly felt in the great mind and heart of the
people, that there are spiritual utilities derivable from the
culture of high science and learning, more important to
the best life and welfare of a great and rich commonwealth than all material utilities.

*We believe it to be within the scope of the constitu-
tional powers of the General Government to establish a
National University on the broadest foundations, and
with the amplest endowments.*   But if there be a doubt
about this, the people should remove the doubt by amend-
ment of the Constitution.   Such an institution would be
a glory and a blessing to the nation and to mankind.
.   .   .   .   .   The progress of our country in territory,
in population, in wealth, is already wonderful, and is destined to go on to a still more wonderful extent.   .   .   .
Thus great as we are, and pre-eminently great as we are
destined to be, in every element of material grandeur,
shall we not have the distinction and the glory, and
enjoy the exalting and conservative influences of possess-
ing the greatest University in the world ?   Why not ?
The money it would cost is but a trifle—large as the
amount would be and should be, yet but a trifle—compared with the honor and advantage it would bring."

The establishment of a National University was an

object to which WASHINGTON attached great importance. He seems to have had no doubt about the power of the General Government in the matter; and how greatly he had the object at heart may be seen in the numerous references to it in his official communications, and in his private correspondence. I am glad to perceive that IRVING has brought this point so clearly out in the last volume of his Life of Washington.

CALIFORNIA: THE HISTORICAL SIGNIFICANCE OF ITS ACQUISITION.

.

CALIFORNIA.

———•••———

AT a time when the golden treasures of California are attracting nearly all regards and absorbing nearly all interest, it is important not to neglect other aspects of the case which are even more remarkable and wonderful. We propose, therefore, to touch (and our space will allow us to do scarcely more than barely touch) upon some of those considerations which go to show the immense results that seem destined to follow from our new territorial acquisitions on the Pacific.

It is no ordinary position, that in which these acquisitions have placed us. It is a position of the deepest world-wide historical significance. It is so with reference to the peculiar relations which those new territories stand in to our nation and to the rest of the world. It is so with reference to all

7*

that constitutes the world's historical present, which, springing out of all the past, contains in itself the mighty, unevolved, undisclosed future. Its significance is not so much in what we actually see to-day, as in what we know must come to pass, as the stream of the world's history goes broadening and deepening on in the ages to come. Its significance is in the fact that it contains the elements, the principles, the forces of A NEW CENTRALIZATION OF THE NATIONS OF THE EARTH. It is the beginning of a great American epoch in the history of the world. Just as certainly as there was a period when Asia was historically the centre of the world; and subsequently a period when Europe became so; —just so certainly the acquisition of these territories on the Pacific, seems destined to make our country the world's historical centre. Over the two oceans that wash our eastern and our western shores, Europe and Asia seem destined to reach forth their arms, to meet and shake hands with each other across our continent. We do not say we can predict with absolute certainty when and how far this is to be; but we say that, in the present condition of the world, its civilization, its science, its arts, its commerce, its means of communication—there are the conditions, the forces, which have but to work naturally forward in the direction they are now working, and, in all human likelihood, this stupendous result must in due time come to be accomplished—a new historical centralization of the nations, and America the mediator between both sides of the old world.

Just consider how the case stands. In the sequel of a war, which it is not needful for us to characterize further than by saying that all unnecessary wars are unjust wars—in the sequel of this war, we have gained an immense accession to our territories on the Pacific Ocean.[*] Our government now stretches across the whole breadth of the continent from shore to shore, from the Atlantic connecting us with Europe on the one side, to the Pacific connecting us with Asia on the other side; and from the great chain of inland waters on the north, lying nearly on the furthest line of the temperate zone, to the tropical regions on the south—embracing an area nearly as large as all those states of Europe put together, which for more than a thousand years have been the centre of the civilization of the world.

---

[*] As this sentence was printed in the American Review, the acquisition of this territory is said to have been gained "by fair purchase." The words were an interpolation by the editor, and expressed an opinion I had carefully abstained from expressing.

And how stands it with our nation, considered as the possessors, the occupiers of this vast territory? In less than three-quarters of a century, within the memory of men now alive, we have grown from three millions of people to more than twenty millions ; and at the same rate of increase, many now alive may live to see us grown to a hundred and fifty millions. That immense region of our country which we have hitherto been accustomed to call the West—a term which has gone on constantly receding and extending in its application from the Ohio to the Missouri, and to the foot of the Rocky Mountains—that immense region has become full of life and of men ; innumerable steamboats swiftly meet and pass each other on the great rivers, where not long ago the solitary ark floated down the stream ; and all along their banks, where the hunter and the trapper but yesterday sought their game, great towns and cities have sprung up all astir with the multitudinous hum of men, and resounding with the din of labor and of traffic ; receiving and exchanging the products of a thousand millions of acres of those vast fertile plains, through which those mighty rivers flow— plains where the sturdy labor of ten thousand thousand strong-armed settlers has made the tall prairie grass give place to waving fields of corn and wheat.

But what has hitherto been our Great West, must cease to be so now. Our true West has passed over the Rocky Mountains, and lies along the shores of the Pacific from Oregon to California.

And the question now arises, whether those vast territories are to be filled up rapidly with people, and to remain an integral part of our nation, standing in a living social and political union with the States this side the Rocky Mountains? Of this, we think there can be no doubt. As to the rapid settlement of the country, this seems likely to be secured by the golden attractions that are drawing thousands and thousands thither from the Atlantic shores, from all parts of our country and from other quarters of the world.

But this alone, the mere filling up of the country by settlers, going, even the great majority of them, from among ourselves, and carrying the spirit and the love of our institutions, and the desire to remain in political union with us ; this will not of itself be enough to make those territories a permanent integral portion of the United States, and to secure those stupendous, world-embracing historical consequences of which we have spoken. For if communication is to be maintained between the Atlantic and Pacific shores only by long voyages around Cape Horn, or even by the shorter route through a foreign state, across the Isthmus by Chagres to Panama, it seems scarcely possible that a permanent political union can be preserved. The action of our central government can scarcely in this way stretch itself to embrace and keep the whole in a true political connection. The great Rocky Mountains, and the deserts said to lie between the two sides of the nation, will form a barrier to prevent the sense of oneness, the preservation of national feeling, and of true social and political union. But let the stupendous results of modern science be applied, let the great projected lines of railroad communication connect the two sides of the continent ; let the telegraphic wires electrically unite them ; and how different the case. Yet there is nothing impracticable in this ; nothing visionary ; nothing near so wonderful in the prospect of its speedy accomplishment as in what has already been actually accomplished in the recent past. And there are causes, commercial and political, which are as sure to work out its steady accomplishment, as the sun is sure to rise and set. And how easily then, under God, is the problem solved of binding and keeping together, in a living social and civil union, the eastern and the western shores of the continent. The Rocky Mountains, as to all practical effect, will sink down. The barriers of time and space will be annihilated. The tide of emigration, setting in from all parts of the country, can roll through the mountain passes ; and men can transport themselves from our eastern shores to settle on the Pacific in one-quarter of the time, and with one-tenth of the hardships that were involved in emigrating from New York to Ohio fifty years ago, or to the more western States even twenty years ago. Representatives from Oregon and California can reach their seats in the Capitol more quickly and more easily than representatives came from New Hampshire once. Add to this the communication of thought, passing literally with the speed of lightning to and fro across the continent, and from the central seat of government to the remotest points in the circuit of the nation ; and how different is the problem of binding together in a central union immense and remote states, from what it was in the time of the Roman Empire. It took more days, and we do not know but we may say more weeks, for the central government of Rome to communicate with its remote provinces, even along the great military roads, (those prodigious monuments of Roman grandeur,) than it will take minutes to carry the action of our central government to the shores of the Pacific, and to any other remotest point in the nation. Add again to this the sameness of language, institutions, and laws, which will prevail throughout the States; the effect of the reserved sovereign rights of the several States in securing all local interests and satisfying all local sense of importance; while, at the same time, membership in the Union secures innumerable advantages not otherwise attained, and gratifies the larger sense of national importance. Put these things together, and we do not see why, under God, we may not remain centrally united as a nation, though we grow to be fifty States and three hundred millions of people. The action of all historical causes, political, social, commercial, seems to tend more clearly to this than to any contrary result. We can see but one disturbing cause to cast the shadow of ill omen over these bright auguries, and that is in the institution of slavery in the Southern States, and in the hostile feelings it has engendered. But the smallness of the area where slavery exists, or ever can exist, as compared with the whole area of the country; the diminished relative political importance of the South in the future great growth of population in the free States ; the increasing conviction in the slave States that slavery makes them poor, (a conviction which the contrast between the growth of the slaveholding and of the adjacent non-slaveholding States forces more and more strongly home ;) the importance of the Union to the South, equal at least to that of the South to the Union ; and finally, the progress of moral convictions on the subject in the South, and the predominance of wise and conciliating counsels at the North, will, we trust, under God, solve this problem without rupture, by the gradual ultimate dying out of slavery at the South, in the same way that it has died out at the North ; a result which, we believe, would have already been substantially realized in the more northern slaveholding States, but for certain influences, coming partly from the lower South, and partly from the North, that have concurred to retard it.

But however this may be, the question of slavery will not retard the rapid filling up of the country on the Pacific Ocean. The great lines of railroad communication will be made, and the telegraphic wires will be set up along the track. This may be held for certain. And the accomplishment of this vast, yet simple and altogether outward and physical result, is of profounder importance, and must be so regarded by every one who knows how to estimate events in their true historical significance, than all the revolutions in the States of Europe, which have made the year 1848 a year of wonders in the chronicles of the world.

Its effect will not be limited to the binding together, in a true national union, the two sides of our continent.   It must work a change in the whole commercial relations of the globe.   The trade of China, and of a large portion of Asia, must find its way across the western ocean to our Pacific shores, building up great towns and cities there, and thence across the continent to the Atlantic coast, there to meet the trade of Europe coming over the Atlantic on its western route.   And thus for Europe the old problem of a western passage to the Indies will be solved in a way that Columbus never dreamed of, when he set out to find it across the trackless, unknown seas.   New York will thus lie within twenty-five days of China, and ten days of Europe ; and must become the great *entrepôt* of the world.   Thus we see how the connection between the eastern and western coasts of our continent, (which is certain, sooner or later, to be accomplished,) must change the commerce of the globe.

And this change involves other changes, affecting the whole course and character of the history of humanity, social, political, and moral. This is a point that needs not be argued to any one familiar with the history of the world, and competent to appreciate the working of historical causes. Always the stream of the world's history has been drawn into the course of the great lines of commercial communication ; and this must be more than ever the case in the present and coming age. America must become the centre of the world ; and that not in a merely physical or commercial way, but in a deeper, true historical sense—a sense not to gratify an overweening national pride and vain-gloriousness, whereof we have already more than enough, but a sense full of momentous responsibilities, involving infinite possibilities of evil as well as good.

Our country has entered on a new epoch in its history. From this year we take a new start in national development ; one that must, more than ever before, draw the world's history into the stream of ours. This enlargement of our own national sphere, takes place, too, remarkably enough, just at the time when the whole old-settled order of things in Europe is breaking up and passing forever away ; and the old world turns its eyes to the new with a sense never felt before, that its destiny is bound up with ours. The life of Europe seems destined also to pour itself upon our shores, as never in times past, and to help form that yet unformed national character which the coming age must determine for us.

Now, for what purpose has the providence of God conducted our nation unconsciously through the events of the last three years, to the edge and prospect of such a stupendous, startling future ?

We say the providence of God ; and we say this, not as mere words of course—a customary phrase, without meaning. For as certainly as Divine Providence is recognized for a truth at all, it must be recognized that there are two elements in history, a Divine element as well as a human element ; that a Divine idea is ever realizing itself in the historical life of humanity, as truly as in the life of nature ; in the events of human history, as in the phenomena of the material world ; an idea not realized, nor to be apprehended, in the developments of a day or a year, but in the flow of generations and ages. The disciplinary education of the human race—this, we believe, is the divine idea that underlies the whole history of the world. We have divine commentaries to this effect upon some of the most significant portions of the history of the ancient world.

Herein is the great and peculiar interest of the most ancient historical records. They contain not only the authentication of the idea, but its authentic application to the course of events. They enable us to see what otherwise we might not be able to see in any such determinate way. They disclose to us the providence of God, interposing with a special moral purpose in events which, to all outward appearance, were the mere results of the ordinary laws of nature and of the working of ordinary historical causes. Behind the series of outward events we are made to see the Supreme Disposer touching the springs of human action, permitting or thwarting the outward results of men's free determinations, and swaying with absolute grasp the agencies of nature. And, beyond question, the great purpose for which these historical records, enlightened by these divine commentaries, have come down to us, is to teach impressively, for all nations and for all times, the great truth that the Providence of God is the Genius of Human History. If we had similar commentaries on the world's whole history, the same great truth which is so impressively taught in those records would doubtless be seen with equal clearness on the face of all the history of the world. If the records of all nations, in all ages, were accompanied with like authentic interpretations, we should then see clearly the Divine as well as the human element in history.

But none the less is it necessary to a right conception of history that we should recognize the idea of Divine Providence, even where we lack the clear, authentic application of the idea to the interpretation of events. The mind and the hand of the Almighty, as well as the mind and the hand of man, have been in all the fates and fortunes of the nations —in the rise and fall of empires, the revolutions of dynasties, the wars and conquests, battles and sieges, negotiations and treaties, with which the pages of history are filled. Invisibly, in and behind the visible procession of events, the Supreme Disposer has presided over the course of events which have made the last year* memorable in the annals of the old world and of the new. And we say it is HE that has brought the course of history to one of those great epochs, when we cannot help looking both ways —backward on the past, and forward to the future. And though we may be quite unable to pronounce, in any determinate way, upon the Divine purpose

* Written in 1849.

in regard to the coming period, yet still the question is one we cannot well help framing to ourselves, and one which, in the way of reasonable conjecture, and probable interpretation, we cannot well help attempting to answer.

We have seen that all causes portend a new centralization of the nations ; and that our country seems destined in the coming age, to be the new historical centre of the earth—the mediator between both sides of the old world. And it seems no less clear that God intends to give here, on this continent, a scope for human energies of thought and will, such as has never yet been seen since the days before the flood ; to let here be seen the freest, widest, most diversified and powerful display of what man's science and skill can accomplish, in subduing the elements, in controlling and applying the tremendous forces of nature ; in overcoming and annihilating the old limitations of human endeavor ; in unfolding the physical resources of the earth ; in the creation of boundless wealth and a boundless sphere for action and enjoyment—a movement that shall draw the whole world around it and along with it in its gigantic march.

All this seems portended in the coming age, and to an extent of which we can now probably frame no adequate conception. Forty years ago he who should have predicted the results that man's science and man's energy have now brought to pass, and made so familiar to us that we cease to wonder at them, would have been laughed at for a madman. How do we know what new wonders man's science and man's energy are destined to bring to pass in the next forty years to come ? It is quite likely we should count him equally a fool who should describe to us what will be familiar matters of fact to our children.

But here the great and solemn question springs up, is this boundless physical development to subserve the moral and spiritual perfectionment of man and of society ; or is it, on the contrary, to lead to a godless, self-willed, gigantic wickedness ?

Of one thing we may be sure : no mere commercial and political centralization of the world, can accomplish the true fraternization of the nations of the earth. It is not in mere forms of government, not in the fullest, world-wide development of democratic institutions, to save and regenerate the world. Men must learn to reverence something higher than money and themselves ; they must learn that the spirit of self-will is not the genius of true freedom. It is not in popular education, as it

is called—mere intellectual culture and the diffusion of knowledge.   Men must be wise and good as
well as sharp and knowing.   No widest extension
of suffrage, and largest posssesion of political rights ;
no marvels of scientific discovery and application ;
no increase of wealth ; no multiplication of the
means and refinements of earthly enjoyment, can
work the regeneration and perfection of the social
state, and secure the permanent well-being of humanity.   A godless self-willed world, armed with
the more than gigantic powers over nature which
modern science gives, may rear heaven-climbing
towers, only in the end to be crushed in the fall of
their own toppling erections. Nothing in the long
run can save our country and the world from a fate
worse than that of the old Titans—nothing but the
living power embodied in the constitution of Christianity permeating and sanctifying this prodigious
material civilization.

We say this not merely as Christians ; it goes
upon a principle which no man can deny who is at
all competent to estimate the historical causes of
human progress, and upon a fact as undenied by any
one, as it is undeniable.   No competent historical
philosopher but admits the principle, that the fates
and fortunes of nations are determined, not merely

by material, but by moral causes—causes lying in the inmost mind and heart, in the character and spirit of the people ; and that, of all these causes the religious convictions and systems of a people, resting as they do upon one of the most deep-seated sentiments of human nature, are the most powerful. Equally undeniable and undenied is the fact that Christianity, considered as a special constitution of religion, not only has had an historical existence for near two thousand years, but in nearly all that time has been one of the most significant facts in the history of the world. At the present moment, it is the religious constitution prevailing throughout nearly the whole of the civilized portion of the earth. It is wrought more or less into the civil and social life, into the convictions and habits of our own nation, and of the nations of Europe, into the course of whose history the rest of the world is destined to be drawn ; and no sane man can for a moment believe that it is to be superseded in the ages to come by any other special religious constitution. If there is to be any religion in the coming age, it is to be the Christian religion.

Now what we have to say is, that if Christianity is to exist to any good purpose in the new and grand career of development on which the world is entering, it must exist not as a mere formula, not as a mere outward institute, but as a true moral power, an organic life power in the historical life of the world. It must exist as a counteracting power to the naturally destructive tendencies resulting from any prodigious, unchecked overgrowth of the mere intellectual and physical elements in the life of the people. Grandeur and wealth, luxury and corruption, dissolution and ruin, this is the brief but accurate summary of the history of the extinct, but once most powerful empires of the ancient world ; and he has read history to but little purpose, and has but little competency to read it to any good purpose, who does not know that without some adequate conservative moral power, our national history will sooner or later be summed up in the same words. And we may safely challenge any man to deny that Christianity, in the proper working of its spirit and principles, *is* that adequate conservative power. We may safely challenge any man to imagine any other power which, either in its own nature, or in the likelihood of its organic incorporation into modern civilization, can for one moment be regarded as equally adequate, or at all approaching to the solution of the problem of so permeating and sanctifying the elements of high physical civilization, as to secure the permanent welfare and true perfection of the social state.

We say Christianity, in the proper working of its spirit and principles ; for as a spiritual, a moral power, it can work only as it is let work ; it may be thwarted, resisted, perverted. Hence it is, that the history of Christianity enters into that which constitutes the deepest theme, the inmost sense of the world's whole history—the stuggle between good and evil. This we must bear in mind, or we cannot form a right historical appreciation of it. For eighteen hundred years it has been struggling with the powers of darkness and evil. And if it has not yet brought humanity to a state of social perfection, if it has not accomplished the social perfectionment of any nation where it has obtained a footing, one thing is undeniable : it has carried Christendom to a higher point of social and moral development than any nation of Pagan antiquity ever attained. To its power is due all that distinguishes modern civilization, all that makes it superior to the civilization of the Old World. This has been accomplished in spite of the resistance which pride and self-will, and selfishness, and passion, oppose to its proper influence.

And during this time we have had a memorable demonstration, in a true historical way, of the futility of all schemes for the perfection of the social state proceeding in a hostile repudiation of Christianity. In the eighteenth century human reason, (as it called itself,) having plundered from sacred tradition every point and particle of truth and wisdom, which made it wiser than human reason in the pagan ages of the world, saw fit to set up for itself, to proclaim its independence of divine instruction. At this stage it did not announce itself in atheistic or immoral hostility to Christianity. It only talked of separating philosophy from theology, of vindicating for the former its proper province and rightful independence. But it did not stop here. It began before long to deny and belie the very source of all the light it had, and to arrogate its stolen treasures as its own discoveries and possessions. And it went on philosophizing and philosophizing, until, in the end, it philosophized itself into the absolute denial of all spiritual truth ; till it announced, as the last and highest discoveries of human wisdom, that there was no God, no difference of right and wrong ; that man was a machine, and death an eternal sleep.

Then it set about the regeneration of humanity,

the perfecting of the social state, the bringing in the "age of reason." The French Revolution was the practical result, and the fitting exposition of its labors. It demolished all the past ; and on the basis of its grand negations—no God ; no right and wrong ; no spirit in man ; no life beyond the grave —it began re-constructing anew the social fabric, in which nothing was to be seen but universal brotherhood, equality and social bliss. The golden age was to be no longer a fable and poetic dream ; the bright ideal of a perfect social state was to be realized. Humanity, disenthralled from the yoke of priestcraft and superstition, (to which all social evils had before been owing,) was to come forth regenerated and ennobled in the pure light and free air of reason. Man was to realize a godlike and divine life by the very act of scouting and denying every thing godlike and divine !

We know with what success the preposterous experiment was wrought out. We know what loathsome abortions this French philosophy, after driving God (as it thought) out of the world, brought forth. With the cant words of "liberty," "equality," "fraternization," "age of reason," "human regeneration," "universal brotherhood," on its lips, it made man a terror to himself, made society worse than a cage of wild beasts, capable of inflicting a thousand-fold greater curses on itself than all the evils superstition ever wrought.

Now, we ask, if herein it was not the purpose of Divine Providence to teach mankind a lesson never to be forgotten ? Has not that atheistic immoral philosophy, with its insane, blasphemous babblings, made itself known by its fruits ? Has it not shown, on a grand scale, how much it could do for the regeneration of the world ? And has it not become a hissing and a by-word, a stench in the nostrils of all coming time ? Did not God thus lead humanity some steps onward in that wild and terrible night of anarchy and storms ? He did. He did. Never again, we may believe, will such a scene be enacted on this world's theatre. Never *such* a regeneration of humanity again. Never again such a destruction of the old spiritual and eternal foundations of social order, and such a re-construction of the social fabric on the basis of atheistic negations. The whole thing—the whole self-conceited, arrogant, jeering, profane, blasphemous thing—was first exposed in its infinite loathsome nakedness, and then exploded into infinite ineptitude and nothingness. But it has taught a great lesson. It has given an absolute demonstration of its futility and foolishness

—an historical demonstration on the widest national stage, with the whole world for spectators looking
on ; to the end that mankind may henceforward
forever point its finger and hiss at the stupid project of building up a perfect social state, by denying
God, and reducing man to the level of the brutes.
And that this lesson has been measurably learned,
the new French Revolution of the last year has
given proof—in the fact not only that it proceeded
upon no formal repudiation of Christian ideas, but
that all the political movements socially destructive in their nature, and having their root in a spirit
really hostile to Christianity, have been beaten and
put down, and their authors and abettors shown to
stand in a minority altogether insignificant and
powerless.   Doubtless there has been little enough
of the true religious spirit, in that series of rapid
and startling political changes ; doubtless, more
than enough of pride, self-will, selfish passion and
the exaggerated sense of rights, without the sense
of the duties they rest upon, imply, and impose ;
but still the national spirit has displayed itself in
no hostility to Christian ideas, in no insane attempt
to build up the new civil and social order upon the
destruction of Christian institutions.   This is one
of the most striking differences between this new

French Revolution and the first one. And it is a lesson which the present age has learned from the past.

But it is not enough for the coming age that this lesson be learned only in its negative side. Not enough that atheistic and immoral negations be no longer a fashionable creed. Not enough that Christianity be acknowledged as a formula, and exist as a visible institute, deferentially recognized while practically disregarded or resisted. Yet here precisely lies the danger to be apprehended. The spirit of the age is a spirit of hard worldliness and self-willed pride—not announcing itself in any theoretic rejection of the ideas of God and the divine constitution of religion, but in a disposition to resist and overbear the practical force of those ideas. The natural tendency of the prodigious multiplication of the material interests, of the prodigious extension of man's sphere of activity, and of the prodigious intensity of the outward life that is everywhere going on, is to increase this spirit more and more. It may be quite willing to allow the ideas of God and his Church, provided it may shape and bend them after its own way. It may be quite willing even to let them stand as they announce themselves in Christianity, provided a respectful acknowledgment

8*

of them will answer in place of practical submission to them. But if they become troublesome—they must stand aside.

Now, to this spirit Christianity must, of necessity, oppose itself; and in the collision it must conquer —if it is to save itself and to save the world. It must pervade and sanctify, master and control, the spirit of our nation, and of the nations drawn into its course in the career of boundless wealth and power, on which we have entered; or it cannot in any adequate way act as a countervailing, conservative power against the destructive tendencies of such a prodigious development of the mere material elements of civilization. It must gain the mastery, or be itself thrown off and crushed beneath the wheels of the mighty movement by which the world rushes on to destruction.

For, let merely worldly-wise statesmen and pseudo-philosophers dream as they may, no paper constitutions, no bills of rights, no universal suffrage ballot-boxes, no progress of science, no diffusion of useful knowledge, no schemes of social organization substituting checks and counter-checks of selfishness for the law of love, can work the regeneration of the social state, and make individual men live together as brethren ; and no political contrivances, no balance-of-power systems, no commercial relations, can effect the fraternization of the nations of the earth, and bring humanity up to a state of true social perfectionment, independently of those more purely moral influences which, if they come not from Christianity, cannot be looked for from any other source. We may get on after a sort ; we may get on for a long time to come ; but we cannot get well on in the best sense, and in the long run, unless Christianity becomes a true, living power, incorporated into the social organization, and permeating the historical life of the world.   Unless this, not only shall we never reach the true perfection of the social state, but we shall not continue to get on in the future as well as we are getting on now.   We shall fall, shattered, from the heights up which we are urging our tremendous way.

Our thoughts have carried us on to far conclusions ; but they are such as spring naturally from a consideration of the true historical significance of our new acquisitions on the Pacific—the immense consequences for our country and the world those acquisitions involve. And if our thoughts are at all just, the circumstances under which those territories are destined to be filled rapidly up, makes

the problem of our future fortunes as a nation infinitely momentous. The foundations of new states,
of a new social order, are being laid there   What
a hell upon earth, if the boundless lust of gold
be unrestrained, unsanctified by better influences !
Pandemonium was built of molten gold.   By the
immense significance, the world-embracing issues
that depend on the settlement of that land ; by
every pulse that beats for our country's true glory
and the world's true welfare, should we endeavor to
pour the highest and purest moral influences into
the new-forming life that is to spring up on those
shores.

THE PROVIDENCE OF GOD THE GENIUS OF HUMAN HISTORY.

THE PROVIDENCE OF GOD THE GENIUS OF HUMAN HISTORY.

EUROPE is again the theatre of war*—a war of which no one can foresee the end or the consequences. It may be a brief struggle, involving only the powers now standing in actual belligerent position, and ending in a substantial return to the previous state of things. It may be a prolonged contest, drawing into it all the powers of Europe, arousing a series of revolutionary struggles in Poland, Hungary, Italy, and Germany, and terminating in a vast reconstruction of the political map. It may lead to the overthrow of the Turkish Empire, to its absorption into the overgrown power of Russia, or to its partition among several powers. It may lead to the restora-

* Written during the Crimean campaign.

tion of the old Greek Empire, with consequences of momentous import to the Eastern Church and to the re-establishment of the old Unity of the Church Universal. The Almighty alone can see the end from the beginning. We shall not busy ourselves with political speculations and prophecies which time may make foolish. Our purpose is to improve this fitting occasion of recalling men's minds to the consideration of certain great principles much left out of view, but which, if the Bible be true, lie at the foundation of the philosophy of history, and which every genuine historical philosopher must recognize, not merely as a believer in the Bible, but because they are principles of historical philosophy.

A very considerable portion of the Old Sacred Books is taken up with records of civil and political events pertaining to the Jewish nation, and to other nations standing in historical relations with the Jews. But these sacred records are distinguished from all other historical documents in two respects : first, they were written under the divine direction and guidance—were traced as it were by the finger of the Most High ; and so we have a guaranty for the truth and accuracy of all the matters of fact re- corded in them, such as we have not in any other histories ; and secondly, they contain Divine Com-

mentaries on those matters of historical fact, such
as no other histories contain. On the first of these
points, it is not our design to dwell. For the purpose we have now in view, it may be conceded that
the records of profane history are sufficiently accurate in all the leading facts they relate. But the
second point, namely—that the sacred books give
us Divine Commentaries on the events they record
—this is the grand and most important peculiarity
by which the Holy Scriptures are distinguished from
all other historical documents.

Uninspired histories do not indeed limit themselves to a bare recital of those external events which
mark the rise and progress, the decline and fall of
nations. On the contrary, historical philosophy (as
it is called) attempts to give us commentaries—to
explain the interior causes and consequences by
which events are linked together in their outward
and visible procession—to give us, in short, the inner
spirit and life of history, that from which external
events derive their whole significance and worth.

But this historical philosophy is merely human,
not divine. And it is entirely incompetent to a
complete solution of the problem it attempts to solve.
The history of the world is the joint product of two
agencies: the one human, the other divine—the one
the will of man, the other the Providence of God.

Now when philosophical historians undertake to explain the course of national events by referring them merely to human agencies, their explanations must be not only defective but erroneous—*defective,* because they leave altogether out of view one great side of their subject, the Providence of God, namely, and its influence and purport; *erroneous,* because they cannot rightly explain the one without the other; they cannot interpret the human element in history without a recognition of the element that is divine. In point of truth, the idea of Divine Providence is the primal idea, the dominant or master idea, and contains in itself the key to the interpretation of the world's history, both in respect of its human element as well as of the element that is divine.

And even when historical philosophers recognize both elements; when they attempt to explain both the agency of man and the Providence of God in the course of events, we can never be sure their interpretation is correct. Human insight is limited and fallible. They may be mistaken in their appreciation of the human agencies by which the events of history are to be explained; and they are still more liable to be mistaken in their appreciation of the divine element, the Providence of God.

They may recognize the idea of Divine Providence as being even the primal idea for the solution of the world's history, and yet they may fail in the actual application of the idea. Attempts at a true explanation of events—reasonable conjectures—probable interpretations,—this seems to be nearly all that historical philosophy, mere human insight, unaided by divine instruction, can achieve.

This, then, is the pre-eminent distinction of the sacred historical records. They not only show us the visible procession of outward events, but they give us divinely inspired *commentaries* which correctly interpret to us the whole interior connection, the moral causes and consequences, the true character and purport of the events they record.

Look at the civil and political events recorded in the Holy Scriptures, and see what a different aspect they wear in the light of these divine commentaries, from what they would have to the view of mere human historical philosophy. What is it that stands out most clearly and impressively in these sacred disclosures ? It is, in the first place, the perpetual intervention of God in the course of events, and in the second place, a constant apportionment of national destiny according to national character and conduct. Of these two points the sacred books are full of illustrations ; and the time would fail for the barest reference to the tenth part of them. Sometimes the intervention of God was immediate and visible, miraculous and supernatural—as in the multitude of signs and wonders that marked the deliverance of the Israelites from Egypt, their guidance through the desert, and their establishment in Palestine. Sometimes it was in the control of the secondary agencies of nature, working, to all outward appearance, according to their ordinary and familiar laws, and in overruling the consequences and results of the free actions of men. And this is the kind of divine intervention which it is most to our purpose to observe. For here the inspired commentaries enable us to see what otherwise we could not see. Behind the series of external events, which in their mere outward and visible procession appear to be simply the result of ordinary historical causes, we see the hand of the Almighty Sovereign of the universe, now touching the springs of human action, now permitting or now thwarting the outward results of the *free will* of his creatures, and as to the mere physical agencies of *nature* swaying them with irresistible grasp.

To take an instance or two out of a multitude that go to illustrate what we mean. In the latter part of the reign of David, a pestilence broke out among the people, and in three days' time carried off seventy thousand men ; when it suddenly and entirely ceased. Now what could mere ordinary history-writers make out of this, except to record it as a very remarkable event ; or, at the utmost, try to make themselves wise by queries and speculations about the physical causes of such a fatal disease so suddenly springing up, and so suddenly dying out ? Yet in the light of the Divine Commentary contained in the inspired record, we have the explanation of it as an intervention of God, for the discipline of the nation.

Again : In the book of Daniel we have an account of Nebuchadnezzar's seven years' insanity —during which he was driven from his throne, " and from men," (either as it was in reality or as appeared to him,) " and did eat grass as the oxen ; and his body was wet with the dew of heaven, till his hairs were grown like eagles' feathers, and his nails like birds' claws." What would ordinary history do with this case, but merely put it down as a remarkable case of insanity, or talk learnedly about the predisposing and exciting causes of this great monarch's mental alienation ? Yet the inspired commentary teaches us it was a special intervention of the Most High—a judgment upon the king for the greatness of his pride—a moral discipline to teach him "that the Most High ruleth in the kingdom of men, and giveth it to whomsoever He will." And we are told that it had this effect,— that it humbled him, and led him to recognize, "to praise and honor Him that liveth forever, whose dominion is an everlasting dominion, and whose kingdom is from generation to generation—before Whom all the inhabitants of the earth are reputed as nothing—Whose works are truth, and Whose ways are judgment ; and Who is able to abase those that walk in pride." And so once more : take the case of Herod, recorded in the Acts of the Apostles. This haughty king was smitten with a loathsome disease, and died miserably from being filled and eaten up with worms. The shocking fact is all that mere human history could record, and some medical theory, some nosological disquisition concerning the nature and cause of the disease, are all that merely human philosophy could contribute in explanation of the fact. But the divine commentary teaches us that it was because of the pride with which he received godlike honors from men, and "gave not the glory to God," to whom alone it is due.

These are cases in which the inspired word discloses to us the Providence of God, interposing, with a special moral purpose, in events which to all outward appearance are the mere results of the ordinary laws of nature. We have taken them not because they are the most striking, but simply because they are cases that stand singly, and could be briefly stated.

But to see this truth—the providential intervention of God in the affairs of men, and the moral ' principle of it in all its fulness and impressiveness, we must not take such merely isolated cases, we must go attentively through the whole divine record of the history of the Jewish nation. There we see the Most High disclosed—constantly intervening—constantly working in and behind the visible procession of outward events—through all the alternations of their disasters and successes—their two captivities and restorations down to their final subjugation and extinction as a nation. There we have the history of a nation's rise and progress, decline and fall, such as no other document records. We have not only events—but their true explanation. We see that the Providence of God is the key to the story of their fates and fortunes as a nation ; and we see the *application* of that key to the explanation of all the significant events in the series. We see, too, that their national destiny is made dependent, under Providence, upon their national conduct.

And it is to be observed, too, that this people not only brought their various national calamities upon themselves, but all in the most ordinary and natural way. There was nothing miraculous, nothing even strange or out of the ordinary course of human causes and effects, in the way in which they were subjugated by their enemies, oppressed, carried captive, and finally extinguished as a nation. And if we had not these divine commentaries, we should not find, in the mere outward historical events of Jewish history, any more reason for referring the rise and progress, the decline and fall of this nation to the continual intervention and overruling Providence of God, than in the history of the Macedonian or the Roman empires. It is precisely and solely because we have the special light of divine revelation, that we see the Hand of the Most High in the historical records of the sacred books in a way in which we do not see it in the records of the history of the world at large.

And now the question that comes up is this: For what purpose is it that we have ·these divine commentaries? Is it merely to gratify our curiosity? Or, is it to teach us a great practical lesson? Is the truth which these divine commentaries disclose, a truth only with relation to the Jewish and other nations whose records we find in the sacred books? Or, is it a truth, which is true for all nations and all times? That is the question : and we say that the very purpose for which these historical details and these divine commentaries are handed down to us, is to teach impressively for all nations and for all times, this great truth : —*that the Providence of God is the Genius of human history*—that the hand of the Almighty Ruler of the universe is upon all the nations of the earth, and that He everywhere apportions national destiny according to national character. If we had divine commentaries on the world's whole history, such as we have on that portion of it contained in the sacred records, then the same truth, which is so impressively taught in those records, would appear with equal clearness on the face of all the history of the world. We should see the right hand of the Almighty in all the fates and fortunes of all the nations of the earth—in the revolutions of dynasties, the rise and fall of empires, the wars and conquests, battles and sieges, famines and pestilences,

9

negotiations and treaties, with which the pages of history are filled. We should see it in the reports that come to us weekly across the ocean, and fill the newspapers of our eventful day. We should see the Hand of the Almighty and the purpose of the Almighty throughout the momentous struggle that has begun in Europe. We should have not only the events, but their true historical character, their moral significance, their causes and consequences set before us in a way that would put to shame the wisdom of diplomatists and statesmen, and turn into empty and foolish pratings the commentaries of the public press.

But because we have not these divine commentaries on the whole of the world's history, shall we any the less believe the great truth which the sacred records teach ? Because the light of special inspiration does not make visible the hand of the Almighty moving in and behind the visible procession of events, shall we any the less believe His hand is there at work ? No : we are as much bound to believe this great truth is true for every nation on the earth as for the ancient nations, of whom it is expressly declared in the sacred books. We are as much bound in reason to believe it true in reference to the great drama of political history, that now seems opening on the earth, as though we saw it supernaturally written by the finger of the Almighty, in characters of fire, on the earth and on the sky, on the hills and on the clouds.

And finally, we are not to believe that this divine interposition is merely for the sake of interposition, nor merely in the way of retributive judgment on the nations. The Almighty presides over the fates and fortunes of the nations, each in their successive epochs, with a GREAT PURPOSE which connects each with each in the flow of the great ages ; with a comprehensive IDEA to be realized in the whole Historical Life of Humanity, and in the whole History of the Universe.

YOUNG AMERICA—THE TRUE IDEA OF PROGRESS.

YOUNG AMERICA—THE TRUE IDEA OF PROGRESS.

———◆◆◆———

THE phrase "Young America," has become one of frequent utterance among us. The wise will not regard it merely as a phrase,—merely as designating a certain number of ardent young men, or a certain number of persons, either old or young. It is a great deal more. It involves ideas, thoughts, sentiments, instincts, and practical tendencies of the gravest significance in the political and social sphere. It will not do either to ignore it or to scout it. It suggests something to be well considered by calm and thinking men. It imposes on them a duty which must not be neglected until too late. What is working obscurely, unreflectingly, in the mind and heart of the age, should be analyzed and made clear. What is right, noble, and salutary in it, should be accepted, greeted, entered into with hearty sympathy. What is superficial, mistaken, dangerous, should be signalized, rectified, guarded against. All honor to noble impulses, while we watch against every thing that may defeat or mar the great objects to which they prompt.

The Idea of a Perfect Social State is a necessity for the human reason. It is one that more or less obscurely possesses all minds ; but over all the nobler, more earnest and generous minds it exerts a powerful domination. Whether or not it is in the purposes of that Divine Providence, which is the Genius of Human History, that this idea shall ever be realized in the actual condition of the human race, we shall not undertake to determine. On the one hand, it is not absolutely necessary ; men may successfully solve the problem of their own individual destination in a very imperfect state of society. But, on the other hand, to believe in it, to desire it, to hope for it, is the impulse and necessity of all the better and loftier spirits among men. To work towards its accomplishment is the duty of every man. So far as Young America means the feeling of this idea, the stirring of this impulse, it is a noble and sacred thing. Herein lies the only ground for any thing respectable in another word much heard among us—the word

PROGRESS. Mere progress in itself, mere going forward, without regard to the end to be reached, is not any thing admirable. It may be something very terrible. Make any word a watchword, stirring with electric thrill the hearts of unreflecting masses, and rousing them to action, and you do a thing which in its nature and results should be well considered beforehand.

Young America is antagonistic. It opposes itself to what it calls " Old Fogyism." What is that ? Is it a dogged adherence to old abuses ? A dread and dislike of all changes ? An inability to see any remedy for present evils but in a return to the past ? Doubtless, as against such a spirit, Young America is in the right. It is the natural reaction against it. Old Fogyism forgets that the past can never be reproduced on the scene of the present. If it could be, its resurrection would be any thing but desirable. It would be out of place, out of keeping—not benignant.

But Young America needs guard itself, lest it go (as every reaction tends to go) too far. It must not be ignorant of the past, nor despise it, much less hate it. The spirit of true progress is an organizing, not a destroying spirit. It is a spirit of love, not of hatred. It is wise and reverent, not

9*

ignorant and arrogant. Only out of a profound knowledge of the past, and a deep sense of the wisdom of its lessons, can come the right guidance that shall safely conduct society onwards to a better future. Human history proceeds according to living, not mechanical laws. Political and social ameliorations can never be accomplished by destroying, by pulling down the old, even in order to the reconstruction of something new and better. It is not an affair of destruction and reconstruction. It is a growth. It is mainly an affair of unfolding—the result of the mutual counterworking of forces which are vital, not dead. The old historical life of humanity must not be regarded as standing in no relations, much less in relations purely hostile, to the life of the present. The life of the future must be the continuation of the life of the past—invigorated, purified, it is to be hoped, and unfolding itself in new and fresh forms. Young America, therefore, in a wise and right-hearted fealty to its mission, will not fall into the error of setting itself in hostility to the past, as if it were something to be hated, crushed, extinguished. It will not arrogantly claim, as its own exclusive creation, all the germs of true progress it discerns. It will remember that the great heart of humanity has beaten

the same in every age. Every age has had its side
of true and right, as well as its side of error and
wrong. No age has been all right, or all wrong.
Young America must not presume itself an exception to the universal law. It must not take for
granted that it is all right, and every thing else all
wrong. It must not imagine there is no truth anywhere in the universe but in its own possession ;
that there is no possibility of its falling into one-
sidedness, exaggeration, error—and that through
the very intensity with which it finds itself possessed by the great idea of the age, and the very
strength of the impulse which leads it to protest
against all that seems to stand in opposition to it.
It must learn to recognize the element of truth,
and the element of error, which, in their blending,
and in their mutual counteraction, go to constitute
the actual life—the inner spirit of every historical
epoch, no less of the present than of the past ; for
herein precisely lie the conditions of the true progress of humanity.

Young America must therefore beware of the
dangers incident to every noble attempt to give
reality to great political and social ideas. Questions of political and social amelioration are eminently practical ; and there is not one lesson which

history enforces with such tremendous emphasis as the peril of proceeding in ignorance or in disregard of this truth. Push an abstract idea out with reckless absoluteness into practical application; ally it (as in such a case it will most surely come to be allied) with the frantic fanaticism of human passions—and you may produce a Reign of Terror, but you will inaugurate no Age of Reason. "The eternal principle of Liberty made MAN, seeking to incarnate itself in the world by the Republic!"—this is what Young America proclaims itself to be. How much that is glorious in idea; how much that is also terrible in possibilities of evil, these words contain! Let Young America guard against the perversion of the idea of Liberty. Let it beware of Political Absolutism. Let it remember that no Absolutism, democratic any more than monarchic, is safe—that political liberty is not the absolute supremacy of mere *will*. The Almighty claims no such supremacy.

Let it be remembered that politics—the science of organizing and directing the powers of society for the greatest good of all, is eminently a *practical* science. It is a science of expediency. All its determinations rest on the practical consideration of consequences—provided always, of course, that they do not contradict the eternal principles of justice. That is best in politics (however it may look in the abstract) which actually works best; which best secures the true freedom, the just rights and the real well-being of a nation. To uproot what works well, merely to replace it with something more theoretically perfect, is far from being always wise.

There is another thing to be avoided. Questions of economical policy are not questions of political principle, and should never be confounded with them, still less should the passions and prejudices of the people be enlisted for or against them by any such misuse of words as puts them in the same category with the great and sacred principles of right and justice. For instance : the question of Free Trade is purely economical. It has no more to do with the question of political freedom, than the question of gas or oil in street-lighting ; and to argue it (because of the word " free ") as if it had, is absurd and mischievous. Free Trade may be a democratic policy in the sense of happening to be adopted by a political party styling itself the Democratic party. But that there is any thing which makes it either necessarily or exclusively democratic in principle is thoroughly absurd. The

English would laugh the pretension to scorn. Yet
Young America has talked in this foolish way.
We signalize it, not because of the question itself
of Free Trade, but as an instance illustrating the
wrong of confounding questions of economical policy with questions of political principle. What
our views are on the subject of Free Trade it is of
no consequence for our readers to know.

Finally, let Young America beware of becoming
the mere tool of profligate political managers, scram-
bling for the spoils of office, misusing and abusing
all the great ideas and sentiments, instincts and
impulses which are stirring in the great heart of
the people, into a miserable machinery for selfish
ends. If it sinks to this, our interest in it is gone.
Its respectability, its title to the sympathy of the
wise and good is lost. It will never guide the coming age in the path of true Progress. It will never
help inaugurate the era of Social Perfectionment.

THE HISTORICAL DESTINATION OF THE HUMAN RACE.

THE HISTORICAL DESTINATION OF THE HUMAN RACE.

----••----

GENTLEMEN OF THE NEW JERSEY HISTORICAL SOCIETY :—It would perhaps be most appropriate to this occasion and to the special objects of this Society, if I could contribute something to the illustration of the history of New Jersey. But this is a task I shall not presume to undertake. New Jersey has indeed a history of which her sons may well be proud—particularly of that portion of it embraced by the revolutionary struggle which accomplished the independence of the United States. She was the first to resolve on independence. She was the second to comply with the recommendation of the Continental Congress, and to establish for herself a government on the basis of a constitution of her own formation. She was one of the first to enter into the old confederation of the States, under which the war of Independence was conducted to a successful issue. She adopted promptly, and with remarkable unanimity, the present Constitution of the United States. During the war of the Revolution her patriotism was pre-eminent, and her contributions to the pecuniary expenditures of the contest greatly exceeded her own proportionable share. Her soil was long the theatre of contending armies, and her sufferings from this cause were very great. Within her bounds some of the most interesting operations of the war took place. At Monmouth and at Princeton the enemy were worsted; and here at Trenton, where we are now assembled, the tide of the war was undoubtedly turned.

But I will not impertinently take up your time with a rehearsal of what is probably more familiar to you than to myself. Nor will I attempt to cast any new light upon the history, or upon any particular portion of the history, of the State. The original sources of this history, as they exist either in public archives or in private collections, have not been within my reach; and if they had been, the pressure of many engagements since I had the honor of the invitation to appear before you, would have left me no time to go into such an investiga-

tion of them as alone could yield any results entitled to be presented here.

In the inability therefore to make any contribution of original value to the history, or materials
for the history of New Jersey, I propose to occupy
the hour with some considerations of a more general nature, bearing upon the great problem of the
History of Humanity at large, and the ultimate
Destination of the Human Race.

I am the more led to this because the idea of
the historical Progress of the Human Race, which
in itself, and at all times, presents a theme of the
deepest interest, has of late taken a strong hold of
many thoughtful minds, and been the subject of
much discussion, more or less profound ; and it is
a subject which, to be rightly treated, should be
considered not merely in its external aspects, whether
material or political, but from a higher, more comprehensive and rational point of view. The consideration of it may be said to belong to the Philosophy of Humanity, rather than to the History
of it. If we accept the distinction thus intended
to be made, then doubtless we must affirm that as
there is a History of Humanity—of the Human
Race as a whole during all time—so there must be
a Philosophy of it. But both are necessary, each

to the other; and only in the union of both can
our knowledge become true science.   In fact there
can be no true History of Humanity which is not
philosophical; and no true Philosophy of Humanity which is not historical.   The true History of
Humanity is something more than annals of outward events; the true Philosophy of it is something more than abstract speculations.

The problem of the Historical Life of the Human Race upon the earth is undoubtedly one of
the greatest problems with which human thought
can grapple.   But there is this peculiar difficulty
attending the attempt to solve it : that which we
would explain is yet incomplete, is but partially
before us.   The biography of the plant, of the animal, or of an individual man, may lie before our
eyes, written out in actual completeness from the
first germinal unfolding to the close of life.   Now
History in its large sense is to the Human Race
as a whole, what Biography is to individual man.
"Humanity is the Man of History."   But this is
a biography which cannot be written—neither now,
nor at any future period—until the world's historical life has reached its term.   That life is yet in
its flow; and we, who would calculate its course
and its end, pronounce upon its significance, and

sum up its character as one great whole, are in
the midst of it ourselves, flowing onward in the
stream of the ages. The Past is behind us ; the
Present is around us ; the Future lies undeveloped
before us.

Standing thus in the midst of the ages, how
can we explain the Past, comprehend the Present,
and forecast the Future ? Are we not like common soldiers on the battle-field, ignorant of the
commander's plan of action, and if we were not,
yet incapable from our position to get such a view
as would enable us to understand what has taken
place, what is going on, and what is likely to be
the issue of the fight ? This no doubt is partly
true. Yet we are not altogether like common soldiers on the battle-field. We are also spectators
of the course of events ; and in the necessary convictions of reason, in the light of some communications from the Highest source, and in the significance which the progress of events—both of itself
and through the light that is cast upon it from
above—has already begun to assume, we have some
grounds for a philosophical criticism of the History
of Humanity, of the Human Race as a whole, not
collectively at any one period, but in the successive
flow of generations and ages, throughout the whole

duration of the world's historical life. We must not indeed take our limited faculties as the organ of perfect insight. We must not erect our finite judgment into an absolute standard. But we may know enough to make us understand how that which seems confused and aimless may, in a higher and wider view, have clearness and purpose, that which seems stationary or retrograde may yet be in progress to its destined end. In short, we may reverently attempt to form a judgment that shall embrace the past, the present, and the future— that shall explain the historical destination of the human race.

The solution of the problem which would naturally suggest itself to our minds—if we consider the nature and capacities of man—is the Development of Humanity to its Ideal Perfection—which again can be rightly and worthily conceived only as the perfection of a true Rational Life—a life of Moral Freedom, of self-subjection to the law of duty—a life of goodness, of justice and love. In this, and in nothing else, according to the absolute determinations of reason, does the true perfection of nations as well as of individuals consist, and in the Advancement of Humanity towards this ideal is the only just and worthy conception of Human Progress.

This idea of a perfect social state is indeed only one form of that idea of perfection which gives the law to all human thinking and striving. Ever stirring in the soul of man, more or less consciously and clearly in proportion to the development of reason, is the conception of something more perfect than any thing we see or know—an ideal of which all that the world calls true, and beautiful, and good, are but inadequate expressions—an ideal which yet, by the necessity of his reason, man is incessantly prompted and impelled to express, to make real, both in the sphere of nature and of rational life. The philosopher, seeking to make knowledge science, by penetrating beneath the ever-fleeting phenomena to the substantial ground of absolute truth ; the artist, working, by forms, or colors, or tones, or winged words, to express the beautiful ; the saint, striving to realize in the moral sphere, in his own personal life, the ideal of goodness ; all evince the domination of this idea and this impulse. Hence it is not strange that the idea of a better, more perfect social state should announce itself in every age of the world—in the

traditions of the past, of a primeval age of innocence and bliss, and in the visions of a future reign
of righteousness and peace, to which the mind and
heart of humanity, dissatisfied with the imperfec-
tion of the actual state of things, has ever turned
for solace and for hope.

How profoundly this idea of a perfect commonwealth has stirred the best and noblest minds in
every age, from Plato to Milton and Harrington,
to Fenelon and St. Simon. It has inspired the
song of the poet, the thought of the sage, the
prayer of the devout, the hope of the believer, and
the labors of the philanthropist, of statesmen and
legislators, planters of colonies and founders of
states. In short, all human history reveals the
power of this idea and this impulse—and that in
spite of the follies and crimes with which the annals of the world are filled, often indeed precisely
in and through those follies and crimes, as mistakes
and perversions of the true idea, as blind workings
of the impulse. All history is the history of human strivings after a better, higher, more perfect
social state. Its actual realization in the world, in
individuals and in society, in nations and states,
and in their relations to each other, would be the
regeneration of human society, the fraternization

of the nations, and the pacification of the world. Wars and crimes would cease, and with the moral nearly all the physical evils of human life would disappear. It would be the inauguration of the Age of Reason, in the true and noble sense of those much abused words.

But is humanity destined ever to reach this perfection of the social state during the world's historical lifetime ? The Age of Reason—will it ever actually arrive ? The millennial reign of universal justice and love, brotherhood and peace, which every good heart that believes in a good God is so fain to cling to—will it ever be established on the earth ?

This is a great question. Let us venture to look it in the face. Let us see what and how much there is to justify the absolute unqualified affirmation it so often receives.

In the first place, the theoretical possibility of the development of humanity to a state of social perfection cannot be denied. It lies in the rational constitution of man. Reason in man is the germ of a rational human life, as in individuals, so in nations and in the community of nations. Whatever is possible may become actual. Whatever lies in germ may, under its proper conditions, be unfolded. It is a perfection which may not indeed be actually attainable to the full extent of the absolute ideal ; for the most perfect individual must still in this life at least be an imperfect creature, and the highest perfection of the social state can never rise higher than the highest perfection of the individuals that at any time compose the collective whole of the human race upon the earth. But as there are degrees of saintly excellence which may be realized by every individual within his sphere, and which are measurably realized by some in actual attainment, so there is a degree of social perfection which may properly be considered as a satisfactory proximate realization of the absolute ideal, and which must be admitted to be theoretically possible for humanity as a whole.

But what positive guaranty for its actual realization does this afford ? In the life of Nature not every thing possible becomes for that reason actual ——not every germ unfolds itself to the perfection of its normal life. On the contrary, observation shows us numberless cases of abortive attempt and failure. To this it is obvious to reply : that though multitudes of living germs in nature perish——in germ, and in every stage of development, yet these are individual cases, exceptions to the general rule ; that on the whole—in the large view of its orders, species, races—the life of Nature is not an abortion and a failure of its proper end.   Can we then suppose that the higher life of Humanity is not destined to attain its normal development ?   Must we not regard the capacity of man for social perfectionment as a guaranty for its actual attainment ?

This might be held conclusive, if the rational perfectionment of human society depended upon no conditions different in kind from those of the life of Nature ; and even notwithstanding the essential difference between *nature* and *free-will*, if humanity had no destination beyond this world, the analogy of the universe might lead us to expect that human society would in some way and some time here in this world reach its normal perfection ; although the problem of human existence would then in other and higher aspects become a dark insolvable enigma—of which I will hereafter more particularly speak.

But admit the idea of another world, and all sense of moral contradiction is removed, even though humanity never attain to a perfect social state on the earth.   Reason may then be regarded as the germ of a truly rational social state, which is destined to have its ultimate realization ; but that realization, as for individuals, so for humanity as a whole, may be accomplished in a supermundane eternal sphere ; and so from the capacity and theoretical possibility it is not necessary to infer its actual realization in this world.

In like manner, again, with respect to the universal prevalence of the idea of a perfect social state and of the impulse to realize it. It indicates undoubtedly the goal, it propounds the law of human endeavor, the end towards which humanity may and should indefinitely advance. But does this in itself prove that it will ever be actually reached in this world ? If both for individuals and for humanity as a whole, there be a destination to a life beyond the world—and this can never be disproved—then the earthly history of humanity enters into the history of humanity in another sphere ; and the highest destination of the human race may be realized there, and that end may be subserved by the very fact that the earthly history of human society is a history of perpetual unsatisfied strivings after a more perfect state ; and so it is not necessary, in order to a rational explanation of man's earthly destination, to suppose that the social perfection, for which he is by the law of his nature perpetually to strive, must be actually realized during the lifetime of humanity on the globe—however much, as to the rest, we may be naturally and reasonably led to hope or to expect that the history of the world will in a large and complete view disclose itself as an actual progress towards it.

Again : does the actual history of mankind thus far warrant any confident prediction that human society will ever reach its normal possible perfection during the lifetime of the world ? I exclude now all reference to whatever Divine ideas and interventions human history does or may hereafter disclose, or to any Divine purpose which may thereby be ultimately accomplished. I speak now only of the actual progress which the history of human efforts to perfect itself in society discloses. And I say that after four thousand years of human strivings, humanity, neither as a whole, nor in any single state or nation, presents the spectacle of society advanced to a true rational state, nor to any such degrees of it as measurably to satisfy the demands of reason or the wishes of the heart, or to contain the certain promise of a better future.

I will not go over the old story of four thousand years—the rise, the culmination, the decline, decay and dissolution of states and empires. I take my stand in the present time. I admit every thing that any one chooses to allege respecting the mighty difference between the present and the past—the changes, the progress, the improvement—and then I ask: what is the present state of the world? Human society is seen in its brightest aspects in Europe and in America. A high degree of what we call civilization prevails in most of the states and nations of these continents—and also in some of the colonies established by them in other parts of the world, chiefly by the English people. The rest of mankind is but partially civilized; some tribes and peoples are yet in the barbarous or in the savage state. Barbarism and savageism have, however, nearly disappeared; and at no very remote period will, in all probability, entirely disappear, through historical causes now at work, and whose force, direction and results we can pretty well estimate; so that in a century or two, (provided meanwhile no old civilization falls to pieces,) the whole world may be civilized. But what then? The highest civilization, in the proper ordinary meaning of the term—the highest civilization, so far from being a guaranty for continual progress, does not contain in itself the securities for its own conservation and continuance, but on the contrary carries in its own bosom the seeds of dissolution and decay. The practical demonstration of this truth lies in the history of the past. And apart from this, it is obvious in itself that the highest state of mere civilization neither constitutes nor implies that true rational state of society, in which alone the perfection of the social state consists. A true rational society—a society in which the spirit of rational freedom or self-subjection to the law of duty, the spirit of justice and love, prevails—may be and will be a highly and truly civilized society; but a highly civilized society, in the ordinary sense of the word, is not necessarily a rational society.

Consider this point. There is, I humbly think, a great liability to delusion, in much that is said nowadays about the marvellous progress of the age, and the glories of its civilization. Look at it, then, in its highest forms. Take London. Take Paris. Take our own New York. It is precisely to such places, and nowhere else, that you are to look, if you would see what the highest actual civilization is, and how much it has accomplished towards perfecting the social state. Look sharply, then, at the spectacle which this civilization presents. What do you there see ? You see there the greatest concentration and the freest, most diversified play of human energies and activities of every kind. There the greatest wealth—the greatest abundance of the means of physical ease and comfort. There, too, the greatest social polish and the highest culture. There flourish philosophy, science, art, letters, industries. There noble virtues and much of the beautiful happiness of a pure and right life. Undoubtedly. But there, also, the greatest proportionable prevalence of vice and crime, and the misery of an evil life. There the greatest refinement of luxurious enjoyment, side by side with the greatest proportionable amount of want and destitution. There gorgeous equipages, with glittering appointments, soft rolling side by side with shivering, ill-clad beggars, whom civilized language, noticeably enough, terms *mendicants.* There gilded palaces, purple and fine linen and sumptuous fare, soft music, mirth and elegant revelry—and, not far off, starvation in rags, sunk and crowded down into damp cellars, or stowed and packed up under sharp-roofed garrets.

Here is civilization in its highest actual state. Here you see all and the utmost that the civilization of the age has done to perfect the social state. Look at the picture then. Does it present the type of humanity advanced to the perfection of the social state? Does it satisfy the demands of reason, or the wishes of the good heart? Is it a rational state of society? No, I answer. No. It is a thousand million miles away from it. And if such a civilization were spread all over the globe, the spectacle would be very far from satisfying the wise and good man, either in the contemplation of the present or in the prospect of the future. On the contrary, *the progressive development of such a civilization in the same line, would be the intensification of all the irrational aspects it now presents* —wealth more and more regarded as the great good and the limits to its desire and pursuit more and more extended, with a corresponding increase in the strength of the temptations to frauds, dishonesties and other wrongs and crimes peculiarly incident to such a state of society—and, with the increase of wealth, a greater and greater increase in the number, variety and ingenious refinements of luxurious enjoyment and gratifications of vanity and worldly pride—and, by the inevitable laws of such a civilization, all this tending, not to equalize among the laboring masses the conditions of comfort and wel-

10*

fare, but to make the poor poorer, and more poorly
off in physical comforts, in the leisure and means
for rational development and true domestic life,
and so to increase the causes of degradation and
the temptations to vice and crime.

Besides: the perfection of human society on the
earth implies not only the advancement of individuals and communities, but also of nations and the
community of nations, to a true rational life.   It
implies the pacification of the world, the union of
the nations in a true brotherhood of justice, love
and peace.   But if mere civilization does not and
cannot make individual men in society live together
as brethren, how is it to effect the pacification of
the world ?   The widest extension of commercial
relations is no certain guaranty for the universal
reign of peace, though it tends that way.   But as
in the past, so in the future, there is no security
against collisions of interest ; and ambition, pride
and passion may still be stronger than the dictates
of prudence and enlightened self-love.   With all
its progress, all its superiority, the civilization of
our century—which flatters itself, as Carlyle says,
that it is the nineteenth—has not protected the
fairest, the most civilized portions of the world from
the scourge of bloody and desolating wars spring-

ing from oppositions of material interests or the mad ambition of sovereigns. During the early years of this period what scenes of carnage and devastation, what millions of human lives sacrificed on the battle field, what orphanage and heartbreaking sorrow in millions of homes—all to gratify the boundless selfishness of the most heartless egotist the world ever saw !*

Nor did the downfall of that great disturber of the world bring permanent peace. Europe has since then been repeatedly the theatre of bloody battles ; while the late Mexican war has proved that the civilization of the nineteenth century has been no more a security for peace on this than on the other side of the Ocean. And we have no reason to suppose it will be on either side a security in the future more than in the past.† I am not saying whether or not these recent wars are just and necessary according to the common way of judging.

---

* In the preface to Abbott's Life of Napoleon, we are told "the writer admires Napoleon because *he abhorred war !*" What to think of the man, pretending to be an historian, who could say that? What to think of him—an American, too—who could call Napoleon "the WASHINGTON of France?" At any rate it is blasphemy of the "Father of his country."

† With the recollection of *Magenta* and *Solferino* still fresh in mind, it is unnecessary now, in 1860, to remind the reader how soon what was written in 1855 found its justification.

I am only urging the undeniable fact that civilization in itself is no guaranty for the abolition of the custom of war, no security against the perpetual recurrence of the spectacle of human beings coming together by thousands, and hundreds of thousands, to butcher each other—a spectacle which I say is a million miles away from being a rational spectacle, or a spectacle compatible with the idea of human society even measurably advanced to a truly rational state. Not until wars cease will humanity have advanced to the perfection of its social life. Not until then the Age of Reason. Not until then the Millennium. This no world-wide spread of our present nineteenth century European and American civilization, and no intensification of its present elements and powers in the future, can ever accomplish.

But the progress of Civil Liberty and the establishment of Free Institutions, is much relied on as a ground of hope for the regeneration of society. It must be admitted that ideas of popular rights, and the disposition to demand free institutions, are gaining prevalence in many parts of the old world. It may be that the despotic governments of Europe are destined, at no distant day, to fall shattered to pieces, in the shock of ideas coming face to face, or to be gradually replaced by freer forms, through the transforming force of prevailing opinion. One thing, however, is certain : free governments can never get themselves permanently established by being *put upon* the people even by the people themselves, but only by *springing up* from within, from the inner life of the people. Europe is not prepared for self-government. Italy not yet fully. Nor France. Other countries still less. But it may be that democratic ideas will spread and take root more and more in the heart of the coming age, and it may be they are destined to realize themselves in the governments of Europe, and ultimately of the rest of the world, through the immense and every day increasing influence of Europe and of the United States.

But what then ? Suppose this accomplished—the preliminary conditions fulfilled, the requisite training gone through with, and the same degrees also of civilization attained as we have reached—and all the nations of the earth to be in the enjoyment of free governments, civil and political institutions modelled after the pattern of our own. What then ? Would the moral evils peculiarly incident to a high artificial civilization, would the

physical evils resulting from the inevitable working
of its economical laws, be done away ?   No: no
more then, than in our own country now.   Would
the world present the spectacle of humanity advanced to a true rational life ?   Would it contain
the guaranties for the continual progress of humanity in the line of rational development ?   Would
it even contain the securities for its own conservation ?   No : no more in the world at large, than in
our own country now.

Besides : the tendency of democratic, as of all
other power, is to absolutism.   We see it in our
land.   But democratic absolutism is not necessarily
any more rational or beneficent in its workings than
monarchic or oligarchic absolutism.   If not in-
formed and actuated by wisdom and virtue, it is
more dangerous and disastrous—of which truth
history gives us more than one impressive demonstration.   Let the spirit of a people become an exaggerated sense of rights without a corresponding
sense of duties ; let it challenge for mere will—the
present will of self-willed majorities that legitimate
supremacy which belongs to absolute right alone—
and what are constitutions and compacts if they
stand in the way ?   Paper and words to men who
will neither read nor hear—especially in any con-

flict of ideas or interests, any struggle of parties or passions. That such is the tendency of democratic absolutism, of the supremacy of self-willed majorities, to override the checks of constitutions and compacts, of reason and moral right—it is impossible to deny. It may take long years before it becomes developed in any destructive way; but that in its unchecked working it leads on to anarchic convulsion, the subversion of rational freedom and the dissolution of the social bonds—it is equally impossible to deny.

And what are the checks that are to restrain the dangerous tendencies of democratic absolutism? Without enumerating those which may be conceived to lie in the modes in which, from the necessity of circumstances, the public will may be obliged to express and realize itself, I will say that there is one without which all other checks are inadequate, and that is the prevalence among the people of the spirit of unselfish patriotism, of justice and of love. This affords the only adequate conservative principle, the only certain guaranty for the beneficent working and permanent continuance of democratic institutions.

But does it lie in democratic institutions to create this spirit? Or to unfold it? Or to foster

it ?   Or even to give it fair play in public life ?
No.   History answers, no.   How is it with us ?
Politics a war ; " wo to the vanquished," the war
cry.   Politics a grand game, played by political
demagogues—the people the pawns—office and the
emoluments of office the stakes to be won.   Swarms
of greedy office-seekers eager to get into office, and
rival swarms of greedy office-holders eager to keep
in ; and so President-making nearly the supreme
political business of the nation—the question being
not about the best man, but the most available
man for party ends ; and the people kept in the
turmoil of this selfish struggle from four years' end
to four years' end.

Is this an edifying spectacle ?   Are these influences wholesome in their working, either for the
private or the public morals of the nation ?   Is it
to be wondered at that all the worst elements of
society come up into disgusting prominence in the
primary assemblies of the people during the heat
of elections ?   Can we wonder at the brutal scenes,
the ruffianly assaults, the trickeries and frauds,
false swearing and illegal voting enacted at the
polls ?   And—like people like rulers—can we wonder that the halls of the supreme legislative body
of the nation are disgraced by scenes of vulgar vio-

lence, personal encounters, and deadly weapons raised—to say nothing of minor violations of propriety and decorum unbecoming such a place ?

If it be permitted to the spirits of the departed patriots who sat in Congress in the days of the Revolution and of Washington's administration, to witness the conduct of their successors, what must they think of the men that now fill the places they once filled, and of the people that send them and sustain them there ?   Let me read you a passage from a letter I received in 1837, from a true gentleman of the olden time, an eminent man now gone, who, in his youth, lived in intimate relations with Washington and the public men of Washington's day :

" In the years 1794, '95, '96, I often saw the House and Senate of that day.   In the month of May last I went to Washington solely to see a House and Senate of forty years later.   What a contrast !   If the majority of our nation be now fairly represented, we are the lowest and most vulgar of all the Caucasian race."

This was twenty years ago.   The House of Representatives had but just begun to be the bear garden it has since become, and the Senate was still a comparatively dignified and decorous body—

no scenes of personal encounter and brutal outrage (I believe) had then been enacted within the walls of its chamber. What would the writer of this letter have said if he had beheld what has since been seen there ?

Now if the picture of political corruption and violence—which I have rather referred to than sketched—be to any extent a true picture—and you know it is—I ask again : does it lie in the mere working of democratic institutions to create, or to cherish, or even to give fair play to the spirit of unselfish patriotism, justice, and love ? And again I answer no. And if the evils we deplore have been greatly increasing for the last twenty-five years—and that they have cannot be denied—what guaranty for the future progress of our nation in public and private virtue can democratic institutions give ? What guaranty can they give even for their own conservation and continuance ? And therefore, in fine, what guaranty could they give, if spread all over the earth, for the social perfection of the human race, for the advancement of humanity to a true rational life, for the cure of the moral and physical evils of society, for the fraternization of men and nations, the universal reign of justice and of peace ?*

* Since the above was written we have had, among the startling

But again : the advancement of Science and the diffusion of Knowledge, are much looked to as the promise of a better future. No one can think more highly of these than I do as conditions and elements of the highest social state ; but as they do not in themselves alone constitute it, so neither in their own efficacy nor in any efficacies which they necessarily imply, do they make it sure.

Much stress is laid upon the marvels of scientific discovery and their application to human uses, to which the last fifty years has given birth. The secrets of the Life of Nature are disclosed ; the wonderful processes, conditions and laws of the growth and nutrition of vegetable life are so ascertained, that agriculture—the great art on which the physical life of humanity mainly rests—is coming to be the most scientific of all arts, supplying

proofs of our progress on the road downwards, the established fact of the whole Legislative body of a Western State *bought up* in the interest of a profligate corporation. And the New York *Daily Times* of to-day (April 18, 1860), speaking of the passage of certain bills, sacrificing the public good to great moneyed monopolies, carried in the Legislature of New York against the Governor's veto, says : " It will not be possible to convince any considerable portion of the community that these votes were not *bought and paid for !* " I do not suppose there can be found a single person of any intelligence in the State, who does not believe that those votes were " bought " and sold, and probably not without security at least that they should be " paid for."

with the greatest certainty, exactitude, and economy, the conditions for the restoration of worn-out fertility, and the appropriate food and tillage for each several product, and thus multiplying a hundredfold the capabilities of human subsistence on the face of the earth, to which the earthly life of man is tied ; the sun is made to copy as no artistic human eye and hand can portray ; steam and lightning have annihilated space and time, and brought the ends of the world into contact—the world both of matter and of mind. These are indeed the marvels of the age. I stand in admiration, wonder, and awe, before them. And greater marvels still will doubtless be disclosed in the coming age.

But it should be remembered that all the dominion over nature which the human understanding gains should be subordinated to the control of reason, should be used for rational ends. Scientific discovery, and the subjugation of the tremendous forces of nature to man's uses, if it minister only to man's self-willed pride, destroying the filial reverence with which he should stand in the midst of Nature, as in the great temple built by the Almighty Father's hand ; if it be valued and employed only as a means of increasing and diversifying the sphere of physical enjoyment or selfish gratification, will neither make men wiser, better, or happier, nor society more rational, or better off in any element in which the true well-being of society consists. The tendency on the contrary—a tendency augmenting with every fresh conquest over the powers of nature—would be to such heights of selfish and ungodly civilization as, like the gigantic science and gigantic wickedness of the world before the Flood, must needs be swept from the earth, and humanity be made to begin again anew.

And as to the general diffusion of knowledge— it must be remembered that knowledge is a power for evil as well as for good. Light in the head is not necessarily goodness in the heart. Men instructed with knowledge may be the wiser and the better for it, or they may be merely more sharp and knowing in evil. Scientific discoveries, the most useful and beneficent in their proper application, can be turned to account as instruments of crime. Knaves and rogues have seized on photography and made counterfeit bank notes, which the bank officers, whose names they bore, could not distinguish from those they signed. Anæsthetic agents, designed to relieve human pain, are employed by thieves and burglars, to put to sleep, or to deepen the slumbers of those they would plunder. It may indeed be said that science will ever find out, and general instruction diffuse the knowledge of new methods for protecting society against such evil uses of scientific discoveries. What sort of a race is this ? Quite a forlorn hope for human progress —it seems to me.

It does not follow from this that ignorance is the parent of devotion—as the old saying goes— or of any thing else that is good. But we must beware of expecting from the mere diffusion of knowledge that regeneration of human society which can never come from that cause alone. Unless permeated and actuated by higher influences, the widest diffusion of knowledge will only make society less wise and less happily off in all that constitutes its rational perfection and true welfare.

We have now seen, I humbly presume to think, that neither the theoretical possibility of the social perfectionment of the human race ; nor the necessity and universality of the idea and of the impulse to realize it ; nor the actual progress of civilization ; nor the universal spread of civil liberty and free institutions ; nor any advancement of science, or widest diffusion of knowledge, contain in themselves—either separately or combined—any absolutely certain warrant that this ideal perfection of human society will ever be actually realized, or perpetually approached, in the lifetime of humanity on the globe. So far from it, in looking around upon the actual spectacle which the highest civilization of the world presents, and forward to its future progress in the same line of development, we are compelled to recognize elements of evil lying in the very bosom of that civilization—causes of disaster, perilous possibilities of defeat and overthrow to the dearest hopes of humanity. The fall of the unsupported tower is not more certain by the law of material gravitation, than in the moral sphere is the certainty that the historical causes which have wrought in the past, are causes which now and in the future will ever work the same results. Wealth, luxury, and corruption, as in the past they have been, so in the future they will ever be, the precursors of the decay, dissolution, and downfall of states and nations. This is inevitable unless prevented by adequate corrective and conservative powers—powers which the mere prevalence of democratic or of any other political institutions, the progress of science and the spread of knowledge, are not in themselves sufficient to call forth and put into action.

Unless, then, we give over in despair of a brighter future, where shall we turn to look for those corrective and saving powers? I know but one direction in which it remains to look. We have already looked everywhere else. Shall we then turn to CHRISTIANITY as the last hope for the social perfectionment of the human race? Shall we consider what and how much Christianity can effect—how and under what conditions—and what promise for the future is herein contained?

Here I see at once—as all must see—that the universal prevalence of Christianity as an *actuating principle* in the life of the world would be the advancement of the human race to the rational perfection of the social state. Let the life of humanity—of men and of nations, in their individual, social, and political relations, in their civilization, culture, science, and art—become permeated and actuated by the *moral spirit* of Christianity, and there would be nothing more for reason to demand or the heart to desire.

I see, too, that Christianity purports to embody the conditions and means of making its moral spirit a living principle in the life of humanity. In Christianity—not, indeed, considered merely as a body of doctrines and ethical precepts, and a visible institute of worship and moral discipline, but in Christianity considered as an historical organization of supernatural Divine powers—I see propounded the only adequate cure for the corruption of the human race.

I speak not now as a theologian, but as a philosopher, when I say, the corruption of the human race. For this corruption is simply a matter of fact, of which all history is the undeniable demonstration; a fact of universal observation; a fact testified in the inmost consciousness of every one of us—who know and feel that we are not, and of our own unaided power shall never become, what we know and feel we ought to be. It is this fact which contains the reason why the history of humanity has been ever a history of abortive strivings after a perfection never reached—the reason why the progress of civilization, why education, science, knowledge, and civil liberty afford in themselves no guaranty that this perfection ever will be reached. As a philosopher I see—what every genuine philosopher must see—that no creed, however sublime, no ethical teachings, however divine, no institutes of
11

worship and discipline, however pure and ennobling,
can work the regeneration of the human race ; because that is something which no merely moral influences can accomplish.   As a philosopher, too, I am
bound to look at Christianity in the character in
which it undeniably propounds itself to the world
—and that is not merely as a creed, a code, and a
worship, but also as the incorporation into the life
of humanity of Divine restoring powers, without
which all its moral teachings and influences would
be as ineffectual to cure the corruption of the human race as the Vedas and Shastras, the laws of
Lycurgus, or the institutes of Menu.

The peculiar pretension of Christianity is to
cure the corruption of the human race by supernatural powers, derived to humanity from the union
of the Divine and human nature, historically accomplished in the person of Christ, and through
the perpetual indwelling in man of the Eternal
Spirit of Divine Life.   As a philosopher I am unable to explain either the ground and reason of this
peculiar constitution of Divine powers—why it is
or needs must be so, or the mode and working of
these powers ; but I can quite clearly understand
that Christianity purports to be such a constitution ; and I recognize its immeasurable superiority

over any mere creed, or code, or institute, or any conceivable system of merely moral influences. Its eminent and peculiar pretension is to accomplish by Divine powers, in a supernatural way, what I know, as a philosopher, no merely moral influences can accomplish—the cure of the spiritual corruption and weakness of human nature, its restoration to spiritual freedom and the power of effectual goodness. If it fulfil this pretension, I see, as a philosopher, that it supplies also the requisite conditions for securing to the moral influences of Christianity their proper power, and for making the *moral spirit* of Christianity a living, actuating principle in the universal heart of humanity, and thereby, in the only possible way, making the universal spread of civilization, intelligence, and civil liberty, safe, salutary, and beneficent in the future progress of the human race.

That Christianity is destined to become the religion of the world, in the sense, for instance, that it is of our own country now, seems nearly certain, merely from the continued working of commercial, political, and other historical causes, which have already borne Christianity along with them, or opened the door for its entrance—as in China and Japan. But this does not of itself determine the question whether, through the universal spread of Christianity, the perfectionment of human society on the earth is destined to be ultimately accomplished. That depends upon the question whether, through man's concurrence with the working of the supernatural powers embodied in the constitution of Christianity, the moral spirit of Christianity is to become the actuating principle of the life of the world. And how can we, on historical grounds, decide that this will ever be the case ?

Christianity has been for eighteen hundred years incorporated into the historical life of the world. For five centuries it wrought in the bosom of the old corrupt Roman civilization, but could not save it. The Roman Empire crumbled to pieces at the touch of barbarian hands—less through the force of the shock than through its own rottenness and decay. Entering, along with the inheritance of Roman law, into the new fresh life from the North, Christianity, with its immense ideas, its ennobling influences, and its supernatural powers, has been working in the heart of modern civilization for fourteen hundred years. And what has it accomplished ? Much, doubtless, for numberless individuals ; much also for society, for nations, for the state—yet but little compared with what it must accomplish before it can effect the regeneration of society, the pacification of the world. Breathing peace and good-will, and proclaiming its mission to be the uniting of men and nations in a brotherhood of love, by the pervading bond of one and the same divine indwelling Spirit, Christianity, through man's corruption, has been itself the very occasion of some of the bloodiest wars, the blackest crimes, and the most heart-rending cruelties that the pages of human history record. That it has not yet taught states and nations to live in peace, or to settle questions of conflicting interest on principles of mutual justice, the late Mexican war, and the present state of Europe, are enough to prove. The moral spirit of Christianity is not in any tolerable degree the actuating principle of the life of any state or nation in Christendom. No Christian people presents the spectacle of human society advanced in any measurably satisfactory way to a true rational state.

But must we not believe that it lies within the resources of the wisdom and power of the Infinite Father of humanity to secure for Christianity its legitimate effect—to make its moral spirit a freely actuating principle in the life of men and nations throughout the world; and if so, is it consistent with our necessary convictions of His infinite goodness to doubt that the resources of infinite wisdom and power will be applied, through the providential government of the world, to the accomplishment of this end? Have we not herein, then, the sure guaranty for the final advancement of humanity to a true rational life on the earth? Must we not conceive this to be precisely the Divine plan and purpose in human history?

A stupendous question this! I freely admit the great ideas upon which it goes. The history of the world can no more be rationally conceived without the idea of the providence of God, than the existence of the world can be rationally conceived without the idea of the creative power of God. Doubtless there is a Divine plan and purpose, according to which the Most High conducts the history of the world. Human history is not, indeed, like the world of space, the mere product of the Almighty will; neither is it the product of human activity alone, whether of self-willed caprice, or of rational endeavor. There is a human element in it, and there is an element that is divine. An Infinite Mind presides over the busy activities of human freedom, through generations and ages—prepares the scene—calls the actors forth in their time and turn—and through their action carries forward, from age to age, the unfolding of His divine idea.

But I do not see that we are led, by any necessity of our conceptions of the infinite goodness of God, to believe that the conducting of humanity to the actual attainment of the highest possible perfection of the social state on earth is the special plan and purpose of His providential government of the world. For even if it be not, all objections on this score vanish by the supposition of a destination of the human race to a higher eternal sphere, and by the fact that meanwhile human beings, as individuals, may successfully solve the problem of their existence in a very imperfect state of society, and indeed precisely through the discipline which such a state implies—to doubt which would be to suppose the existence of every human being for six thousand years to be an utter failure of its proper end.

In venturing to pronounce concerning the Divine plan in the history of the world, we must remember that the earthly history of humanity enters into its history in a sphere beyond the world. The earthly history of the human race is not a complete drama in itself. It is but an act in the drama of the history of humanity. When the curtain drops at the end of the world, it drops but to rise again for another act on another and a vaster scene. The history of humanity, moreover, in its largest view, both in this world and in the world beyond, enters into yet another and a more comprehensive history still—the history of the universe. It is a part of that great history ; not only not a complete drama, but only an act—it may be not a whole act even, but a few scenes, or a single scene—in the grand Universe drama, that is to go on unfolding forever in the circling round of eternal ages.

Over this unfolding the Infinite Mind presides. Doubt not the grand drama has its plan. It does not roll at random through the ages, with a blind irrational flow. There is a Divine Idea underlying all—ever realizing itself—every scene, every act preparing for the next, and all carrying the great action onward to its grand development.

But how dare we, unless instructed by the Most High, pronounce what this all-comprehending, all-explaining Divine Idea is? How dare we pronounce what is the subordinate relation in which the earthly history of the human race stands to the history of the universe, and what is the *special* plan of God's providential government in the history of this world, through the accomplishment of which the grand plan of the universe is to be accomplished ?

There is, indeed, one comprehensive idea, which both reason and Divine instruction seem to warrant us to assume. EVIL exists in the universe—Moral Evil, not the product of God, but of finite self-will, through the abuse of that freedom, without which there could be no such beings as moral creatures. But Good and Evil, like light and darkness, stand in eternal opposition, mutually destructive of each other. They must ever be in conflict. It does not comport with the nature of the Infinite Father of the Universe, the absolute personal substance of Goodness, of Sanctity and Love, that he should, so to say, stand idly by, an indifferent spectator, or even as a watchful observer of the conflict between the finite powers of Good and Evil. He can take no neutral part, but must range Himself on the side of Good. *A grand and solemn struggle, therefore, between the powers of Good and of Evil, conducted by the Most High Himself—this we may believe to be the inmost sense of the history of the universe.* This is the comprehensive idea, which explains the plan of God's providential government over the

11*

universe.   As to the final issue, doubt not what it will be.

It is here that the history of humanity enters into the history of the universe.   Our world's history is also a struggle between the powers of good and of evil.   This idea explains the purport of God's intervention in the world.   Christianity is precisely the intervention of the Infinite Father of humanity, for the subjugation of the evil that is in the human race.   It is the incorporation of a divine principle into the corrupted life of the race, through the Incarnation of the Eternal Word, and the Indwelling of God in Man by the Eternal Spirit of Life.   *The union of God and Man in the person of Christ, is the central fact in the history of the world, and of the universe, too.*   It is the central principle of the unity of the human race, and of all rational creatures.   This truth the Infinite Father announces in these stupendous words : *" that in the dispensation of the fulness of time, He might gather together IN ONE all things in Christ, both which are in heaven and which are on earth, even in Him."*   What words can be more express and clear ?   You see that the ever-living Divine-human Person of Christ, is the centre of the unity of the human race, of its union with God, with it-self, and with the rational universe. Herein lies the divine principle for the pacification and perfec-tion of the world and of the universe, according to the wonderful words of the Son of God, the Divine Mediator between the Infinite Father and His finite creatures : *"that they all may be ONE ; as Thou, Father, art in me and I in Thee, that they also may be one in us . . . . I in them and Thou in me, that they may be made* PERFECT *in ONE !"* If this be so, how absurd to attempt a philosophy of human history upon any other basis. A philosophy of his-tory, ignoring its greatest fact, its central idea ! The height of absurd pretension can go no higher.

That this great all-comprehending idea of God's providence in human history will be ultimately re-alized—that humanity, united in Christ to itself, to the Infinite Father, and to the rational universe, will accomplish a glorious destination in an eternal sphere—of this let us never doubt. Let us never doubt the final triumph of good over evil in the empire of the Infinite Good God.

Subordinate this great end, the *disciplinary education* of the human race may safely be assumed as the special idea of God's providential government of this world. For since God does and needs must deal with His rational creatures as moral beings, free to improve or to abuse His gracious gifts, to concur with or to resist the Divine powers which Christianity imparts to the human race, it is evident that the disciplinary influences of His providential government are the great means He must needs employ in order to secure the concurrence of men with the supernatural efficacies of Christianity, and so to make its *moral spirit* a freely actuating principle in the life of humanity.

But this does not imply the rational perfectionment of human society upon the earth, unless it be necessary in order to the accomplishment of the all-comprehending eternal end of God, in regard to humanity and to the universe. Whether it is necessary or not, is something our thoughts cannot pretend to determine. If it be, then doubtless it will in some way be brought about, before the earthly history of the human race is closed—if ever it come to a close, and that it will is certainly the idea that Christianity goes upon.

But human society, states and nations exist,

not for their own sake, but for the sake of individuals, and individuals exist here in this world solely in order to a higher existence in another world, and it may be that God can conduct humanity to its great eternal destination in a higher sphere, though the pathway of the generations should, in the future, as in the past, lie through an imperfect and disordered world.

This much is certain : the idea of a merely temporary destiny for rational creatures—no matter how prosperous and prolonged—is one in which our minds can never rest. Men, indeed, suffer and die for their country—for the merely earthly welfare of those that are to come after them—and are honored and revered by those for whom they suffered and died ; but both the heroism and the reverence have their root in rational instincts and sentiments, that announce in man a higher than an earthly destination, and are inexplicable on any other ground. We are compelled, in fact, in every point of view, to hold this higher destination to be the great end of man's earthly existence. What is any merely temporal end worth in any right rational view ? Of how much importance is the certainty of a million millenniums of earthly comfort and enjoyment, or even of the highest degrees of rational welfare in store for future generations, if there be nothing beyond? It would neither satisfy the reason, nor console the heart. It is only in the full faith of a higher eternal destination, that the problem of man's earthly existence becomes clear; only in such a faith we find heart greatly to rejoice in the ever so sure prospect of an earthly millennium of righteousness and peace. Lighted by the radiance that streams down from the eternal sphere, the vision of an earthly millennium becomes indeed something beautiful and delightful, something to pray for and to work for; but apart from that there is nothing in it that gives us great heart to pray or to work. On the contrary, the problem of humanity becomes utterly dark and full of trouble to our thoughts; the long, long ages of delayed accomplishment—the slow progress, the little gain; and the long, long ages (it may be) yet to intervene before the consummate day—each previous generation existing only for the sake of the next, and all for the sake of those at the end of the series—and those favored generations reaching their goal only through the struggles and sufferings, the sweat, the tears, the blood of all that went before them! Of such a history of the world, rounded out and written up, how does the contemplation strike you ? Does the good luck of the favored generations console you for the hundred and sixty thousand millions (as I roughly compute it) of human beings that have already toiled and wept, and become extinct, and the million millions that may yet arise to toil and weep, and become extinct, for the advantage of the favored ones ? And what sort of advantage ? An earthly millennium—a temporary welfare, and nothing beyond ! How are you going to absolve God for such a history of humanity ? If He could do no better, better have done nothing ; so at least our reason and our hearts prompt us to feel. If He could do better, why has He not ? , Either way darkness and trouble to our thoughts. But granted a career of endless spiritual development, and

Doubt is dispelled and trouble chased away.

Whether the vision of an earthly millennium is to be realized or not, we no longer see thousands of generations existing for the sole advantage of others—and that a mere temporary advantage : on the contrary, we recognize each existing for all, and all for each—the last in the series as much for the first as the first for the last, and thereby the same great end for each and all.   God's purpose in the earthly discipline of the race may in either case get accomplished.   That purpose I regard as having a threefold object : the earthly profit of humanity in its successive generations, the profit of humanity (in individuals and as a whole) in a future world, and the profit of the rational universe.

If there is to come an earthly millennium for the human race, the education that conducts mankind to it will also be for the profit of each successive generation on its way to a higher sphere, as well as for the advantage of all in that sphere.   If an earthly millennium is not to come, the discipline of God's providence here is not made in vain. Mankind may learn something, if not all it might learn.   The world may become a better and a better world, even though it never become a perfect world.   And the lessons learned too late for this world, may not be too late for man's profit in another world.   And in either case, the great lessons which the history of the world may be intended to teach when that history is rounded and complete —and which cannot be learned till then—will be for the· profit both of humanity and of the whole rational universe in another sphere.

In the full faith, therefore, of a high eternal destination for the human race, we can look back upon the past without perplexity, and forward to the future with tranquil hope. We see, without dismay, that it took four thousand years to prepare for the historical incorporation of Christianity into the life of the world—four thousand years of disciplinary education of the human race, under the providence of God, in order to put into the world a grand historical demonstration of the radical corruption of the race, and its utter inability to raise, restore, and perfect itself; and so to prepare the way for the coming of the Great Restorer. We see, without dismay, the slow progress of Christianity, for the eighteen hundred years it has been in the world. We see that it has been ever struggling with the powers of darkness and evil. We see that wherever and in whatever degree it has failed to regenerate the social state, the failure is due to man's resistance of its proper power. We note, too, the victories it has gained—the lessons God has made humanity to learn, by sharp experience, of the consequences of its own self-willed pride and wickedness. And we may look with solemn awe for more such victories; for I see not how, but by bitter experience of the legitimate

fruits of overbearing and nullifying God's teachings and God's ordinances, the Gospel of Christ is,
in the coming age, to subvert the Gospel of Mammon, or the constitution of the State to maintain
itself against the spirit of self-willed democracy
setting up the exclusive, and therefore necessarily licentious and anarchical notion of mere Rights
as the standard of true Freedom, against the divine rational ideas of Duty and of Law.   But in
some way, through God's providence, I look forward
to future triumphs of Christianity over the evil yet
in the world—to future lessons learned, for the instruction of humanity, and for rational creatures in
other worlds.   And if I cannot give utterance here
to the ordinary strains of gratulation ; if I decline
to ring the customary changes in laudation of the
" spirit of the age "—which seems to me (much
and for many years deeply pondering the history of
the world) to be more a spirit of hard worldliness
and intense worldly pride, less heroic, less reverent,
less influenced by the enthusiasm of high spiritual
ideas and unselfish interests, than in any former
period of human history ; if I cannot draw bright
auguries for the future, from the mere progress of
material civilization, of knowledge and political
liberty—I can point you to better grounds for re-

pose and hope. *The destinies of humanity are safe
in the hands of God.* It may be that Divine predictions justify not only the belief in the universal
spread of Christianity, (which we have seen historical causes make nearly sure,) but also those
visions of a millennial perfection of society, with
which the heart of humanity solaces itself—when
darkness and evil shall be dispelled from the world,
when violence and wrong, and want and wo shall be
banished from the earth, and men and nations shall
dwell together in brotherhood and peace. Let no
man forbid the religious hope they inspire. Christianity *can* effect this. Nothing else can. It may
be God designs it shall. Let the heart of universal
humanity lift up the prayer the world's Restorer
taught the human heart to pour forth to the Infinite Father of Love : *Thy kingdom come—thy will
be done* ON EARTH *as in heaven.* And in the spirit
of this prayer let each one work through his work-
day on the earth. As to the rest, let us ever console ourselves with the fact that the destinies of
humanity are safe in the hands of God. Whatever be the future fortunes of our country, or of the
nations on the earth, the Infinite Father will gather
all things together in one in Christ—both which
are in heaven, and which are on earth. The final

subjugation of Evil in the empire of God is sure.
Evil will be destroyed by the all-converting, all-ab-
sorbing power of Eternal Love.   The destination
of humanity shall be gloriously accomplished in a
high eternal sphere.

REMARKS ON MR. BANCROFT'S ORATION ON HUMAN PROGRESS.

REMARKS ON MR. BANCROFT'S ORATION ON HUMAN PROGRESS.*

MR. BANCROFT'S discourse is, in many respects, a beautiful oratorical performance ; constructed with great artistic skill ; polished in style ; evincing a fine scholarlike culture of fancy and of taste ; embodying many just, many striking, many beautiful thoughts in the choicest forms of expression. But considered as a philosophical treatment of the great subject it propounds, it seems to us inadequate and insufficient. It does not strike one as the production of a great, clear, strong thinker, dealing in the might of his own original power with a problem which he thoroughly apprehends, knowing exactly what he ought to mean and say, and

* The Necessity, the Reality, and the Promise of the Progress of the Human Race. Oration before the New York Historical Society, Nov. 20, 1854.

marching with a firm tread on solid ground from a
well-defined starting point to a clear determinate
conclusion. There is a want of grasp and precis-
ion in the handling. There is a sort of vague hov-
ering around an object dimly perceived. It seems
like the work of a dealer in centos of striking
thought diligently collected, of a weaver of beautiful sentences, a culler of dainty phrases, one who
dallies fondly with words as if they were something
fine in themselves. The theme is proposed ; the
great divisions are marked off; the interspaces
are filled with choice utterances, many of them
true, but many of them, especially in the first division of the discourse, not very clearly to the purpose, either as argument to prove, or as considerations to elucidate or confirm, the point on which
they ought to bear ; exciting often your delight
and admiration, but leaving at last no clear perception of any thing you have reached except the
termination—a vague, fine, oratorical peroration.
You feel as if you had been floating in a cloudland
of shifting shapes and gorgeous hues, but where all
is unsubstantial ; or looking through a kaleidoscope
as from time to time it was turned round, disclos-
ing infinitely diversified combinations of form and
color, but without organic connection and signifi-

cance ; or contemplating an exquisite piece of Mosaic work wherein are wrought a multitude of separate figures, many of them individually beautiful, but having no unity, no expression as a whole.

This, we confess, is rather an exaggerated way of expressing our feeling, but it does express the nature of our feeling of disappointment and dissatisfaction. This elaborate performance is not such a contribution to historical philosophy as we had hoped to find it. Many profound truths are indeed enunciated or suggested, but the great problem it undertakes does not seem to us either adequately solved or even worthily conceived. We have read it again and again, and for the third and fourth time ; and each time the question has pressed on us—What does it all amount to ? What is its pith and substance ? How much and what is its clear significance and accomplishment ? And the answer we have been able to give comes to about this :

Mr. Bancroft proposes to discuss three topics—the Necessity, the Reality, and the Promise of the Progress of the Human Race. The nature of this progress is thus determined :—" The progress of man consists in this, that he himself arrives at the perception of truth."

12

The *necessity* of this progress is the first point.
And out of all that is said under this head—including many striking and beautiful utterances,
some of them true, some of them which we think
not true—the following is the substance of every
thing that has any bearing on the point, either in
the way of argument or of elucidation and confir-
mation : "The necessity of the progress of the
race follows from the fact, that the great Author
of all life has left truth in its immutability to be
observed, and has endowed man with the power of
observation and generalization." It follows also
from "contemplating society from the point of
view of the unity of the universe"—which, so far
as we can see his meaning and the nature of his
argument in what is added, amounts to this : that
the universe is God's creation, the reflection of His
perfections, subject to perpetual change, because
finite, and in its changes is governed by His providence according to universal and absolute laws—
the human race marching in accordance with the
Divine will, and therefore there must be a progress
of the race ; which progress, agreeably to what had
before been laid down as to its nature, should consist in arriving at the perception of truth ; though,
from what is said in this connection, that idea of

progress seems to be merged into a larger and more general notion not very precisely indicated.

Then, under the second great division, the *reality* of human progress is shown ; in the first place by referring to the immense advances in science which have been made, especially within the last fifty years—in mineralogy, physiology, astronomy, geology, chemistry ; in the next place, by reciting a number of the wonderful applications of the agencies of nature, steam, electricity, light ; the extension of commercial relations and means of intercourse ; social ameliorations.in regard particularly to the position of woman, the dignity of labor and the abolition of servitude ; and lastly, by referring to the recognition among men of the Triune God, the Incarnation and Indwelling of God in humanity, and the benign and ennobling effects that have flowed from the recognition of these great truths. Under the last division of the discourse— the *promise* of the future—the truth " that God has dwelt and dwells with humanity," is made " the perfect guarantee for its progress." And here the notion of progress is made to include not only the arriving at the perception of truth, but also all sorts of ameliorations, social and political, and the universal diffusion of them, especially the blessings of personal liberty and republican government—all which effects are to come from "the more complete recognition of the reciprocal relations of God and humanity," as constituting "the *unity* of the human race,"—although geographical science exploring the whole habitable globe, and colonization and commerce filling it with civilized men ; and the press ; and free schools ; are to have also a powerful influence—whether indirectly, in promoting the recognition of this principle of the unity and what he calls the universality of the human race, or directly, in promoting those ameliorations on distinct and independent grounds, or in both ways, does not clearly appear.

This is the substance of the discourse, as nearly and as fairly as we can make it out. This is its whole jointing and articulation. As to the filling up, we will not say that it is altogether destitute of organic relation to the framework ; but it does seem to us that there are many draperies of fine thought and beautiful expression thrown over it, which have little living connection with it.

But our chief dissatisfaction with this discourse is in regard to its most general spirit and purport. We give all honor to Mr. Bancroft, for his enunciation of the great truth that the Providence of God

is the presiding genius of human history, and of the
Incarnation of the Eternal Son of God, as the
great central fact in the history of the world and
of the universe ; and for the many profoundly true
and beautiful things he has said in this relation.
But notwithstanding its unspeakable superiority,
as in many other respects, so especially in this, to
most other performances of the class to which it
belongs, yet it does belong essentially to a class of
which we have more than enough : whose chief effect is to minister to the. pride and vanity of the
present age, inflating men with a self-complacent
sense of the wonders they have achieved, and making them feel that there can be no more glorious
future for the world than in its being just what the
world now is—only increasingly a great deal more
so, by the intensification of the spirit of the present age, and by the enlargement of the sphere of
its activities, discoveries, conquests, in the same
direction in which it has been going on so magnifi-
cently for the last fifty years. Seeing thus, in the
future, nothing but the colossal reflection of its
own image, the present age finds the contemplation
as gratifying to its vainglorious conceit as the contrast between the present and the past.

The question concerning Human Progress, as it

seems to us, can have no value or importance in a
philosophical view, and there can be no sound and
salutary thinking in regard to it, unless the nature
of that progress, in any desirable view of it, be
rightly and worthily conceived ; unless man be regarded in the highest attributes of his spiritual nature, and his development to the normal perfection
of that nature be assumed as the great end for
which he exists.   Regarded in this point of view,
the question concerning the progress of the human
race, is the question whether, and how far it has
advanced and will advance to a truly rational life,
in individuals, in society, in states and nations, and
in the community of nations.   All other developments of his faculties ; all other advancements,
whether in civilization, wealth, science, knowledge ;
all improvements in polity and social institutions,
are subordinate to this end, and are of worth and
importance as they conspire to this end.

In this point of view, it must become apparent
that the great aspects of human society—in communities, in states and nations, and in the brotherhood of nations—presents a picture in the highest
degree irrational.   Progress in civilization, in science and knowledge, in the subjugation of the tremendous forces of nature to man's earthly uses, has

not been a proportionable progress of humanity in true rational, moral and spiritual development. On the contrary, it has intensified some of the worst physical, social and moral evils which the aspect of society presents.. The greater the development of civilization, the worse the moral aspects at the extremities of the social scale ; the greater luxury and corruption at one end, and the greater misery and degradation at the other end : and throughout the whole scale the tendency to hard worldliness in place of true spiritual development. And by consequence, no highest intensification and world-wide spread of such a civilization in the future will carry humanity onward to a better state, to a nearer approach to its true spiritual perfection. Equally evident is it, from the aspects of the present, that a more hopeful promise for the future is not to be found in the mere spread of intelligence ; nor in improved civil and political institutions ; nor even in Christianity itself considered as a creed, a code, and a worship. It is only in proportion as the *moral spirit* of Christianity becomes the *actuating principle* in the heart of humanity—in the historical life of the world, in men and nations, in the state, and in the relations of states—that there can be any true progress of the human race in the line of its proper development. And this is what no mere *moral influences* can accomplish—not the moral influences of Christianity itself, however powerful and ennobling they are. Because moral influences are not an adequate cure for the corruption of the human race. Only in Christianity, as a historical constitution embodying *supernatural*, divine efficacies, is this cure to be found, and a basis thus created for making its moral spirit a living principle in the heart of humanity.

And here we touch upon a defect in Mr. Bancroft's discourse which we greatly regret. He has left it too much to be inferred that the guaranty for the true progress of the human race is to be found in the mere moral effect of the recognition of the Incarnation as the mediation between God and man, and as the centre of the unity of the race. We are sure he ought not to mean this, from the way in which he speaks of the "indwelling of God in man." He speaks of it not merely as a supernatural fact accomplished in the historical person of Christ, but as a perpetual fact in the human race, through the abiding of the PARACLETE and COMFORTER. Still he has not made clear the immense distinction between the moral influence of the doctrine of which he speaks, on the one hand,

and the supernatural, regenerating powers which that doctrine discloses, on the other.

Whether or not, under the Providence and disciplinary government of God, through the working of its supernatural efficacies and man's concurrence therewith, the moral spirit of Christianity is ever to become the paramount actuating principle in the life of the world ; and thus humanity to attain here in this world its proper development in society, is a point which we have not room now to consider at that length without which we should not wish to speak at all.

We cannot conclude without quoting one or two passages which we feel bound to subject to special criticism. The first is as follows :

" The life of an individual is but a breath ; it comes forth like a flower, and fleeth like a shadow. Were no other progress, therefore, possible than that of the individual, one age would have little advantage over another. But as every man partakes of the same faculties, and is consubstantial with all, it follows that the race also has an existence of its own ; and this existence becomes richer, more varied, free and complete, as time advances. Common Sense *implies by its very name, that each individual is to contribute some share towards the general intelligence. The many are wiser than the few ; the multitude than the philosopher ; the race than the individual ; and each successive age than its predecessor.*" (P. 10.)

12*

It is to the last two sentences, which we have distinguished by printing them in italics, that we wish to call attention. We have, in the first, a most uncommon use of the term common sense. Common sense is commonly understood to refer to truths needing no proof or analysis, but immediately evident to all men, because all men's minds are so constituted as, under certain conditions, to be affected in the same way. But who ever heard before of common sense as implying a mass of cognitions or convictions, brought together by an intellectual *pic-nic* process—one individual contributing one thing, and another another, each according to his several capacity and power, some discerning and contributing truths not discerned by the others! This is a violation of the usage of language, both popular and philosophical, and a perversion of psychological fact. No individual *can* contribute any thing to the common sense of mankind ; and so far as there are truths, facts, doctrines, now generally accepted among men, which are not in themselves immediately evident to all alike, but which have been discovered and contributed by individuals, and received into the general belief, on grounds of evidence proper to each, they can in no just usage of language be spoken of as the common sense, or as objects of the common sense of mankind. This is indeed merely a verbal matter, but still we think it best that the term in question should be used in the meaning it has always borne in general usage.

But our special concern is with the next sentence : " The many are wiser than the few ; the multitude than the philosopher." This, we take leave to say, is, in any pertinent and reasonable view of the import of the language, sheer absurdity and untruth. It is one of that sort of utterances that always move our spleen—smart sayings, with a certain ringing tone in them, but as empty of truth as " the sounding brass and tinkling cymbal," are of " charity "—fine sentences, which when grasped and subjected to a searching inquest are obliged to collapse into drivelling platitudes, in order to save even the smallest fraction and semblance of meaning and truth. " The many wiser than the few ! " What does he mean ? Wisdom is a relative attribute when predicated of men. Some may have more of it, some less ; some a great deal, some very little, some possibly none at all, or so little as to be ranked as unwise or foolish men. Does Mr. Bancroft mean that the number of wise men is greater than the number of foolish men ? Perhaps it is. It is to be hoped it is. But that is not his meaning ; it would reduce his sharp saying to a pointless platitude. What does he mean then ? Who are "the few" that he has in his mind ? Are they the comparatively ignorant and uncultivated ? No. Are they the comparatively instructed and cultivated ? Yes. And who are "the many" ? Are they the more instructed ? No. Are they the less instructed ? Yes.

His utterance then resolves itself into the assertion that the ignorant many are wiser than the instructed few—which is either a flat contradiction or else a paradox. If taken as a contradiction, we need pursue the matter no further ; if taken as a paradoxical utterance of a truth, we deny that there is any truth in it. On what ground can the ignorance or unwisdom of the many be pronounced wiser than the wisdom of the few ? Is it that the less cultivated many are individually each wiser than any of the cultivated few ? No. Is it that the collective wisdom of the many is greater than the collective wisdom of the few ? That might be the case—provided, in the first place, that the decisions or conduct of a collective body could be wiser than the wisdom of the individuals composing it—a thing likely to be when the water of a stream can contrive to raise itself higher than its foun-

tain ; and provided, in the second place, that wisdom were any thing to be measured by bulk or
weight. Under these two conditions, but not oth
erwise, this and the other utterances of this sentence—"the multitude wiser than the philosopher ;
the race than the individual"—may come to have
some meaning and truth, instead of being, what
they now are, absurdly untrue.

It may be thought, perhaps, that we are spend-
ing too much time in harrying and worrying this
poor sentence. We do not think so. It is a
pointed utterance intended to pass for a striking
truth. In our view it is not only untrue, but mischievous ; and we feel bound to expose its untruth
and to counteract its pernicious practical tendency
and effect. It belongs to a class of utterances,
very frequent nowadays, which have no other effect
than to minister to men's vanity and self-love, pride
and lawless self-will. Coleridge has somewhere
said something like this—that a half-truth is often-
times the greatest of lies. We would say that lies
which either contain a portion of truth, or the perversion of a truth, or which are practically made to
pass for some great truth standing in their neighborhood, are the most pernicious of lies. Of this
sort is the celebrated saying : " The voice of the

people is the voice of God." True, it is so—whenever the voice of the people is the echo of God's voice in man. And only then. In other words, it is not a universal truth. But proclaim it as such, and you proclaim a falsehood; a most mischievous falsehood. Proclaim it without any qualification, on platforms, to excited crowds, and a thousand to one, it will be taken as an absolute truth, and as a perfect vindication for all that their excited passions may prompt them to do. And thus taken, it may be rightfully pleaded as a divine sanction for all the crimes that have ever been committed under the impulse of popular frenzy, from the beginning of the world to the Crucifixion of the Son of God, and from that day to this.

But Mr. Bancroft's assertion—that " the many are wiser than the few; the multitude than the philosopher"—contains no truth, either absolute or contingent; either universal or general; either in principle or in fact. Undoubtedly there is a truth standing over against it—but not to be confounded with it, nor made to sanction it—in the light of which indeed the untruth of his assertion may be more thoroughly discerned. Doubtless there is in the public mind an unreflected sense of want and an instinctive impulse towards what is expedient and wise in the social and political sphere. Doubtless, too, in the higher moral sphere, there are instinctive convictions and impulses in the heart and conscience of humanity, which—prejudice and passion apart—prompt a consentaneous cry of the human race in behalf of justice and of right, whenever the chords to which they vibrate are rightly struck. And in either case, so far as the great multitudinous cry utters itself wisely and rightly, it is because it is in accordance with necessary principles divinely implanted in the universal human mind and heart—in " the few " as well as in " the many ; " in " the philosopher " as well as in " the multitude ; " the only difference being that the former can interpret the principles which the latter only feel, and give clearer articulation to the cry which the latter less distinctly raise. It is an absurd and wicked thing to set the many and the few over against each other as naturally and always opposed. They may be opposed. And in any actual case of opposition, it is not to be absolutely assumed that the multitude are in the right and the few in the wrong, that the voice of the multitude is the utterance of the divinely implanted instincts of the race, the voice of the few a denial of them. It may be so ; but the odds are in favor of

the contrary presumption.   The philosopher is subject to the same instinctive impulses towards what
is right and good as the multitude ; with better
cultivated faculties of observation and reflection ;
knows all they know, and more too ; and is no more
subject to passion and prejudice than they.   It is
not absolutely certain he is in the right ; but there
is a fair presumption of it.

And this brings us out to the general conclusion
we have to propound in regard to Mr. Bancroft's
assertion.   If made as an absolute assertion, *we
contradict it as false ; we say, the many are not
wiser than the few ; the multitude than the philosopher.*   If made as one holding generally true, we
not only contradict it, but *we assert the contrary ;
the few are wiser than the many ; the philosopher
than the multitude.*   This is what should, in all
good reason, be the case.   It is the case.   And it
furnishes the needful condition for the progress of
the general mind, so far as progress in truth and
wisdom are the result of the working of the reflec-
tive faculties of man.   The researches of the disci-
plined and cultivated few become diffused as the
intelligence of the many ; the discoveries of the
philosopher as the enlightenment of the multitude.
Such is the ordination of Providence.   God has

appointed the few to be the guides of the many; the philosopher to be the teacher of the multitude. Guides and teachers men must have and will follow; and if they choose not to follow those of God's appointment, they will follow those of the Devil's ordaining.

We give another passage immediately following the one upon which we have so long dwelt :

" The social condition of a century, its faith, its institutions, are analogous to its acquisitions. Neither philosophy, nor government, nor political institutions, nor religious knowledge, can remain much behind, or go much in advance, of the totality of contemporary intelligence. The age furnishes to the master-builder the materials with which he builds. The outbreak of a revolution is the pulsation of the time, healthy or spasmodic according to its harmony with the civilization from which it springs. Each new philosophical system is the heliograph of an evanescent condition of public thought. *The state in which we are, is man's natural state at this moment;* but it neither should be nor can be his permanent state, for his existence is flowing on in eternal change, with nothing fixed but the certainty of change. *Now, by the necessity of the case, the movement of the human mind. taken collectively, is always towards something better.*"

Now this passage is an instance, among others we might cite, of what strikes us as a want of clear,

just, logically coherent thought. Amidst utterances plain and plainly true, are some we are compelled to pronounce untrue, or obscure and doubt-
ful. We have signalized, by our mode of printing,
those which dissatisfy us.

"*The state in which we are, is man's natural
state at this moment.*" Assuming that something
more is here intended than the identical proposition that the state in which we now are, is the
state in which we now are, what is intended to be
understood? What is meant by man's "natural"
state in this connection? Is it his normal state,
his proper state, the state in which he should be,
according to the idea of what is necessary or most
fit and suitable to his nature? Then we deny the
assertion, whether as a principle applicable to every
historical period, or as a fact alleged of the present.
Or, by "natural state," is it intended to mean the
state which is the *natural result* of foregoing causes?
If so, why not say so in unambiguous phrase?
We suppose this is probably what is meant, from
something elsewhere subsequently said, namely,
that "the present state of the world is accepted
by the wise and benevolent as the necessary and
natural result of all its antecedents." This is a
different proposition from the one in question. It

is clear enough in its meaning, and in a certain sense true enough. But to say that man's present state is his "natural state," is, in the first and most obvious meaning of the words, to say that it is the state necessary or most suitable to his nature —a proposition which, as we have before said, we deny.

Again : we are told that "*by the necessity of the case, the movement of the human mind, taken collectively, is always towards something better.*" We suppose that by " movement " is here intended, not any instinctive impulse acting *upon* the human mind, and which must therefore be perpetually one and the same in its nature and direction, but an actual progress of the mind. We suppose so from what immediately precedes, and because it is the obvious proper meaning of the words. Now we do not see the necessity here alleged. It is undoubtedly a necessity for every individual, and so for the human race taken collectively, that reason should conceive and conscience command them to become something better than they are in the moral and spiritual sphere. The desire for well-being in every sphere is also undoubtedly a necessary desire in human nature. But we do not see that this engenders any necessity that the actual movement of

the human mind should be always toward something better.   And we deny that such is always the
actual direction of human movement.   Individuals,
nations, the race, can go the road downward, as
well as the road upward ; and at various periods
have done so from age to age.   History demonstrates this.   For near two thousand years the
movement of the collective human mind was ever
towards something worse—such a progressive and
accelerating degeneracy that at last the great bulk
of the race—all but one family—had to be swept
from the earth, and humanity made to begin again
anew.   Then followed another long period of more
than two thousand years, during which humanity,
starting from its new cradle in the East, unfolded
itself again in manifold developments from its rude
patriarchal condition.   Families became tribes ;
tribes nations ;   states got organized ;   industries
became more diversified and improved by division
of labor, thus producing   interchange, commerce.
Then came culture—science, art—first displaying
itself in the infinite striving of the Oriental mind,
embodying itself in vast transcendental myths, in
huge, gigantic symbols ; then among the Greeks,
as the sense of unity, proportion and the purely
beautiful ; and lastly among the Romans, as the

most perfect organization of the ideas of right and
law. All these developments, manifold and great.
But what, after all—applying the highest rational
standard, the only true criterion by which to estimate the progress of man—what was the progress
of humanity during that long period ? It was a
progress downward. It was a continual degeneracy. In the first place, in the spiritual sphere, it
was the loss—the obscuration, corruption, and well-
nigh total extinction, of the traditional light of the
primitive revelation, the true knowledge of God.
The struggle between pure monotheism and the
idolatrous polytheistic corruption of it began almost
immediately in the new cradle of the human race
—resulting after eight hundred years in the complete victorious establishment of polytheism. The
existence of monotheism may indeed be discerned
for six hundred years more ; but from that time it
was utterly driven out from the faith of all the
great historical peoples of the earth, and survived
nowhere except in some remote wilds and mountains of Asia and Europe.—In the second place, in
the political and social sphere, it was the destruction of the primitive patriarchal state, and the establishment, in Asia, of the pure despotism that
has existed there ever since, and in Europe, of a

pure democracy, giving way in turn to oligarchy and then to military despotism.—And finally, in the moral sphere, in practical life, it was a deterioration greater than which cannot well be conceived. No public and little private virtue. At the close of this period, the very culminating point of the ancient civilization, when the central-ization of the world under the imperial dominion of Rome was perfected, the human race had become, more thoroughly corrupt than ever before—everywhere unprincipled profligacy, beastly sensuality, filthy vices, unutterable abominations of every kind; whereof St. Paul's description, at the opening of his Epistle to the Romans, is but a faint adumbra-tion compared with what may be gathered from the literature of that refined and polished age. Here was the progress of the human race, its spiritual, social, moral progress, for more than two thousand years! Starting from the pure knowledge of the true God, from the simple government, the rude morals but comparative innocence, of the patriarchal state; and ending in universal polytheistic idolatry, absolute despotism, and unparalleled social and moral degradation and vice. Yet we are told that "the movement of the human mind taken collect-ively, is always towards something better"!

It may indeed be said that during this period humanity was being prepared, under the providence of God, for that grand intervention for its restoration which at the end of it was historically accomplished in the Incarnation of the Son of God. No doubt it was so. Humanity had completely unfolded itself in all its natural faculties and powers, . in every sphere—in science, art, laws, life. It had showed itself in its highest and brightest, as well as in its lowest and darkest aspects. And it had demonstrated its insufficiency for itself. It had given a full historical demonstration, on a world-wide stage, of its radical corruption, of its entire inability to raise, restore, and perfect itself. Philosophers and lawgivers, sages and prophets, had risen, century after century, and labored in every way at the problem of elevating and perfecting the human race—and all in turn had failed. Then undoubtedly was "the fulness of time," the fitting occasion for the Divine intervention. But it cannot be said on this account, that "the movement of the human mind" during this period was "always towards something better." It would be an abuse of language to use it in this way. You might as well say a long career of crime, terminating at length in the State Prison, was always a movement of a bad individual towards something better, because the discipline of punishment turned out to his eventual reformation ; or that a course of profligate intemperance, inducing at length frightful disease, was a constant progress of the profligate towards something better, because the wholesome dread of death led to a return to temperate and healthful habits.

We have dwelt thus long and spoken thus strongly on this point, because we think the doctrine untrue and practically mischievous. For the same reason we would signalize the following passage, putting in italics the sentences we particularly question the truth of :

" The course of civilization flows on like a mighty river through a boundless valley, calling to the streams from every side to swell its current, *which is always growing wider and deeper, and clearer as it rolls along.* Let us trust ourselves upon its bosom without fear, nay, rather with confidence and joy.   Since the progress of the race appears to be the great purpose of Providence, it becomes us all to venerate the future.   We must be ready to sacrifice ourselves for the coming generation, as they in turn must live for their posterity.   We are not to be disheartened that the intimate connection of humanity renders it impossible for any one portion of the civilized world to be much in advance of all the rest, nor to grieve because an unalterable condition of perfection can never be attained. *Every thing is in movement, and for the better,* except only the fixed eternal law by which the necessity of change is established; or rather except only God, who includes in himself all being, all truth, and all law. The subject of man's thoughts remains the same, but the sum of his acquisitions ever grows with time, so that his *last system of philosophy is always the best,* for *it includes every one that went before. The last political state of the world likewise is ever more excellent than the old, for it presents in activity the entire inheritance of truth, fructified by the living and moving mind of a more enlightened generation.*" (P. 36.)

Now here, as before, are some things true, some things which we cannot admit as true ; and the general drift any thing but sound and salutary. We are almost tempted to call it pernicious rigmarole. It is calculated to make men " accept the present state of the world " in a way that we regard as very detrimental to true progress. True progress begins in a sense of the need of reformation. It begins in mankind, as in individuals, with repentance, and that begins in the sense of sinfulness and evil. And the promise of it is hopeful in proportion as the sense of sin is pervading and deep. It is a poor thing, in our judgment, to tell mankind at this age, that they are going gloriously onward in a perpetual movement towards some-

13

thing better; which something, after all, as it is sure to be generally understood, is only the increase and expansion of what they now are. It just makes men satisfied with some of the worst characteristics of the age.

We are probably in no danger of a return to the Atheistic materialism of the last century, still less to the Polytheistic idolatry of the Roman world. Christianity is likely to be the prevailing, the popular, the fashionable religion, so far as a theoretic adoption of its formulas and a deferential recognition of its practical claims goes—provided they do not become too troublesome. The present age, above all others that have ever preceded it, is the AGE OF THE UNDERSTANDING—the faculty of adapting means to ends in the sphere of time and sense. Never, in all former ages together, has the understanding achieved such stupendous triumphs as in the last fifty years. And the end which all these achievements—discoveries, inventions, conquests over nature—are made to serve: what are they? Mainly, wealth and the multiplication of the means and refinements of enjoyment or other material or worldly ends. The spirit of the present age is the spirit of the intensest worldliness and self-willed pride. It is not Atheistic like the spirit of the last age. It is not Polytheistic. It believes in two Deities : God and Mammon. And never was the imperial government of Rome more obstinately determined on making the thousand gods of its conquered provinces dwell peaceably together in the Pantheon, than the spirit of the present age is on reconciling the worship of God and Mammon. Mammon has the *heart* of the age ; and if God would be content with a temple (a fine one sometimes, when it gratifies the vanity of the builders,) with the bended knee, and with the service of the lip—on Sundays,—that would be an arrangement profoundly acceptable to the taste of the age ; provided also that God's temples may be torn down and the consecrated earth carted off to fill up lots with, whenever the age wishes to dig the deep foundations of some Mammon's temple on the sacred ground.

PRESIDENT MAKING AND NATIONAL CORRUPTION.
THREE LETTERS TO THE HON. JOSIAH QUINCY.

PRESIDENT MAKING AND NATIONAL COR-
RUPTION.

THREE LETTERS TO THE HON. JOSIAH QUINCY.

LETTER I.—DEPARTURE FROM THE CONSTITUTION.

———•••———

My Dear Sir : In concluding to print some reflections I had set down on the practical working
of our political system in the matter of filling the
office of President of the United States, it was
natural for me to cast about for some one through
whom I might address the public with better hope
of gaining·attention to my thoughts than my own
humble and unknown name could warrant. Among
all those whose names hold (and justly) an honored
place in the regards of intelligent and good men,
there is none stands higher than yours for pure
patriotism and unsullied integrity, for every public

and every private virtue, through a long life devoted in no inconsiderable degree to the public service.

In availing myself of your frank and cordial permission to address these letters to you, I not only gratify long-cherished sentiments of respect and admiration, inspired by the principles and course of your public life, and of personal regard linked with the recollections of my youthful days, when I enjoyed the pleasure of your society and the benefits of your wisdom ; but I please myself with thinking there is a special fitness in placing myself under the patronage of your venerable name in putting forth the considerations I am about to present.

I propose to point out evils and dangers which are in a great measure the result of departing from the provisions of the Constitution, and to consider whether any thing can be devised to remedy or to lessen them. You are one of the very few survivors, if not the last, among those statesmen whose youth was cradled and nurtured amid the men and principles and sentiments that presided at the foundation of our government.

You tell me, indeed, that "our country is apparently running a career in which Constitutional amendments, however wise, cannot be effected, and if effected would be of little avail." I agree with you in thinking there is little reason to expect desirable Constitutional amendments. I am quite clear the one I shall suggest runs very little chance of getting practically accomplished. That may be a sufficient reason for a wise statesman not undertaking to accomplish it, but no reason whatever for not entertaining the question, whether it would not be well to adopt it. As to the other part of your remark, I hope to satisfy you, when you come to look at it, that if the change I venture to suggest were adopted, it would be of very considerable avail. Meantime, I am sure the discussion will have interest enough to secure your attention, and I hope that of other candid and thoughtful persons, even if it be regarded merely in the light of a political speculation, a disquisition on the science of Constitutional government. Truth is truth, in the political as in every other sphere, and ought to command, at least, the homage of respectful acknowledgment. Let it get that, and it may possibly, in time, win more. Any honest attempt to set it forth is entitled at least to kindly indulgence.

But the great purport and main substance of

13*

my labor is to call attention to undeniable facts
which it is infinitely important for the welfare of
the nation should be brought home to the minds
and hearts of the great mass of the people. The
first condition of salvation is to understand and feel
the evils and dangers that environ us.   " To
enlighten and diffuse sound principles among the
multitude," you tell me is, in your judgment, " the
highest and most hopeful of benefit, of all the labors
of patriotism."   If " the *few* are lost to every thing
but their own ambition, or their own interests, the
many may be influenced."   I thank you for thinking I may in this way do some good.

I shall therefore proceed first to show how the
intention of the Constitution, so far as relates to
the mode of choosing the President of the United
States, is not only frustrated, but completely reversed—what its provisions were intended to secure
being done, is not done, and what they intended
to prevent being done, is constantly done. It would
be sufficient merely to advert to this if I were writing only for you, and those who, like you, are familiar
with the Constitution and its working. But there
are great numbers who have never given particular
attention to the matter.

The Constitution commits the choice of President neither to a popular vote, nor to the State Legislatures, nor to the Federal Legislature (except partially in a certain exigency), nor to any permanently existing body of functionaries ; but to a certain number of electors temporarily appointed for this sole purpose. These electors emerging on a given day from the mass of the people, meeting, not in one grand Electoral College, but, in separate Colleges in their respective States, on the same day throughout the Union, cast their votes by ballot. This done, and the record dispatched to the seat of Government, their function is ended, and they are left to return again into the mass of the people as suddenly as they emerged.

What is the object of these provisions ? Plainly this : on the one hand to avoid the evils and dangers of a popular election—the demoralizing influences, the excitement and tumult, corruption, and violence to be apprehended from the struggles of rival candidates, rival combinations of partisan leaders, and conflicting parties and factions among the masses of the people ; and on the other hand, to guard, as far as possible, against the liabilities to intrigue, bargain, and corruption, incident to committing the choice to a smaller body—and to do

this by securing the appointment of a considerable
number of independent electors intellectually and
morally competent to the high trust, and removed
by the circumstances under which they act from the
reach of temptations to abuse their trust. The
provision under which the electors are to cast their
votes not in one College, but in separate Colleges
in each of the States, and on the same day throughout the Union, is specially intended to prevent
intrigues and corrupt coalitions among the electors
themselves, and to render it difficult, if not impossible, for ambitious candidates to exercise an improper influence over them. And if we consider
the state of communication then existing, and, for
aught that was then known, likely to continue—
when steamers, railways, and electric telegraphs
were things undreamed of by the wildest dreamers
—it is not too much to say that the framers of our
Constitution looked upon it as a thing next to
impossible for ambitious aspirants to bring any organized and effective scheme of corrupt influence,
or influence of any kind, to bear upon the electors,
dispersed as they were throughout the country. It
is not too much to say that the purpose of these
provisions went even to the extent of preventing
the office of President from being a possible object

of *ambition,* in the old original sense of the word, by putting it out of the power of candidates to get at and so to *get around* (*ambire*) the persons upon whom the choice devolved.

It is undeniably the theory of our government that the people of the United States, in their sovereign capacity, delegate the choice of President to the discretion of the electors—that the electors are to be held as fit persons to be intrusted with this discretion ; and that in their several Colleges they are to exercise the function of a free and independent choice, subject only to the high moral responsibility of choosing the man they find best fitted for the office.

This is the theory of the Constitution, lying on the very face of its provisions.   That such was the intention of its framers, may be seen in the *Federalist* at large.   And such has been the interpretation of its provisions by all the commentators since its adoption.

" The theory of this mode of election," says Mr. BAYARD, "evidently is that the people should delegate their right of choice to a select body of men in whose *judgment* they could confide, and with whom it would rest to elect the persons in *their opinion* best qualified for the stations." *

* Bayard on the Constitution, p. 102.

"It was found expedient," says Mr. RAWLE,
"that the President should owe his election neither
directly to the people, nor to the Legislatures of
the States, yet that these Legislatures should create
a select body, to be drawn from the people, who, in
the most *independent and unbiassed* manner should
elect the President..... It was supposed that the
election would be committed to men not likely to
be swayed by party or personal bias, who would act
under no combination with others, and be subject
neither to intimidation nor corruption." *

To the same effect, Mr. Justice STORY, who
sums up the intentions of the framers of the Constitution and their arguments in favor of this mode of
election, as drawn from the writings of MADISON,
HAMILTON and JAY, in the *Federalist.* "It was
thought," he says , "that the immediate election
should be made by men the most capable of analyz-
ing the qualities adapted to the station, and acting
under circumstances favorable to *deliberation* and a
judicious combination of all the inducements which
ought to govern their choice. A small number of
persons, selected by their fellow-citizens from the
general mass for this special object, would be most
likely to possess the information and discernment,

* Rawle, 52, 57.

and *independence* essential to the proper discharge of the duty." *

It was thus intended that the President of the United States should owe his election to the free, unbiassed suffrages of the electors, acting as the trusted representatives of the people ; that, in the circumstances under which they vote, as well as in the characters of the men, the people of the United States should have the strongest possible guaranties that the electors would cast their ballots under a full sense of their high moral responsibility to choose the best man they could elect, but subject to no other responsibility, and governed by no other influence ; and also that in the person elected by the concurrent votes of such men, under such circumstances, the people would have the strongest possible guaranties for obtaining a President eminently qualified for the high office ; and finally, that by such a mode of election, the President, not owing his elevation to power to corrupt arts, would enter upon his duties, on the one hand, free from all temptations to a corrupt use of the patronage of his office—seeing he would have nobody to reward or punish for exertions for or against his election, and nobody to buy in order to secure his re-election ;

* Story, Comment. III. 315. Federalist, No. 68.

and, on the other hand, equally unbound by political pledges, and so left free to administer the government, not in the interests or passions of a party or a section, but as President of the whole nation.

Now, to those who are familiar with the actual working of our system, nothing more than this bare recital is necessary to show how entirely the intention of the Constitution in this matter is overborne and nullified. Its provisions are in effect completely reversed in every particular.

In point of fact, no discretion is allowed to the electors. " In no respect," says Mr. RAWLE, " have the enlarged and profound views of those who framed the Constitution, or the expectations of the people when they adopted it, been so completely frustrated as in the practical operation of the system so far as relates to the *independence* of the electors..... They do not assemble in their respective States for a free exercise of their own judgments, but for the purpose of electing the particular candidate who happens to be preferred by the predominant political party which has chosen the electors. In some instances, the principles on which they are chosen are so far forgotten that the electors publicly pledge themselves to vote for a particular individual, and thus the whole foundation of this elaborate system is destroyed."

So wrote Mr. RAWLE more than thirty years ago. What was the case then is more completely and universally the case now ; if there were any instances in which electors exercised an independent discretion then, there are none now ; and whether they give public pledges or not, it is understood on all hands, both by themselves and those who vote for them, that they are all pledged to vote for a particular candidate—otherwise they would never be chosen ; and so completely is the intention of the Constitution subverted that an independent exercise of discretion would be considered a dishonorable breach of trust ; and thus (to speak in Hibernian fashion) the only alternative the electors have is not to be elected, unless they are willing to be parties and agents in doing what the Constitution not only does not intend should be done, but what it positively intended should not be done. If they shrink from this, they cannot honorably permit themselves to be chosen electors. They must choose between a breach of trust to the Constitution and a breach of trust to their party ; and this is all the discretion left.

The electors are thus wholly divested of their

constitutional character and functions. They are no longer a body of independent electors, but a mere board of registry, giving formal authentication to a popular vote. For the people, in point of fact, choose the President while nominally voting only for electors ; and in this view of the case the intention of the Constitution is also completely frustrated. It was no more intended that there should be a popular vote designating to the electors an individual to be chosen by them, than that the President should be directly chosen by a popular vote. Such a designation is not, indeed, expressly forbidden in the Constitution, but it is palpably contrary to the whole spirit and most positive intention of its actual provisions ; and to suppose that any such designation, if made, would or should be of any binding force upon the electors, is to render the whole system of Electoral Colleges a needless device, a clumsy farce—making pretence of doing what was already in point of fact effectually done before, a farce which the sooner it were put an end to the better.

We thus see that what the Constitution intended should be done, is not done ; and what it intended should not be done, is constantly done. It intended the electors should choose the President, and they do not : it intended that the people should not choose him, and they do.

This is notorious and undeniable. Nobody thinks of denying it, and hardly anybody thinks it any thing to be troubled about. Nay, there are those who justify it, on the ground that such is the Will of the People, and that the people have a sovereign right to have their own will any way. Some say this because they do not know any better, and some in spite of knowing better. The former are weak dupes of words, whom the latter (sharp demagogues) make dupes of by the abuse of words. The former say it because they do not see—the latter in spite of seeing its futility and fallacy. For it is too clear to need be argued—it belongs to the very rudiments of the science of government—that the people may, if they choose, embody their sovereign will in a Constitution, and may delegate their sovereign right of choosing their Chief Magistrate to a body of independent electors if they see fit. The people of the United States have done so ; and so long as the Constitution stands, the sovereign will of the people is embodied there, out of the reach of the numerical majority of the people. The present will of a numerical majority is not the sovereign will of the people. So long as the Constitution stands, it is the sovereign will of the people that the people shall not choose their President by a popular vote. If the people do not like this, if they wish to choose their President by a popular vote, then in the exercise of their sovereign power they should alter the Constitution. They can then have what they want in a regular way, and far more perfectly than by the present system of perverting the Constitution, under which it may happen, and has happened, that the President is chosen neither by the suffrages of independent electors, as the Constitution intended, nor by the majority of the people, as these persons claim should be the case, but by a minority of them. But so long as the Constitution stands, its intentions should be carried out, not frustrated. There is no end of fervors of devotion to the Constitution, no end of loving jealousy for the preservation of its integrity, when sectional or party interests are to be secured by scrupulous adherence to it : it is then something altogether sacred and inviolable. But when the violation of it serves those interests, its plainest intentions may be violated, and the violation justified by fallacious phrases which delude nobody but the unreflecting masses whom demagogues hold are made to be their dupes.

I shall next consider the evils and dangers resulting from this departure from the Constitution.

PRESIDENT MAKING.

———•••———

My Dear Sir : The perversion of the intention
of the Constitution which we have considered might
be thought not to matter much in a practical view,
if only it worked well.   But it does not work well.
It works badly every way.

It has made President making the chief political business of the nation.   It has carried this business into Congress, into the State Legislatures,
into all State elections and all municipal elections,
converting all public offices and employments of
nearly every sort and kind into means and instruments for carrying this business on ; in short, it
has carried this business everywhere and into every
thing ; and with pernicious influence everywhere
and upon every thing—upon the legislative bodies
—National and State ; upon all public functiona-

ries ; upon political parties ; upon the press ; upon
the great mass of the people throughout the country ; upon the candidates they vote for ; upon the
man they choose, and upon the administration of
the Government he takes in hand.

An exact and complete analysis of the actual
working of our system in all these particulars would
put the truth of these assertions into clear and bold
relief. But it would take volumes. I must content myself with briefer indications.

Our system has called into existence a race of
men, the like of whom, on an equal scale, exists
nowhere on the face of the earth—the race of politicians, not in the old, better sense, the word by its
origin was meant to bear—men versed in the principles which constitute the polity of nations and
the science of right government ; nor men ambitious of the highest public trusts, because they are
conscious of abilities to serve their country and of
the impulse to do so, and whose motives, if not absolutely unselfish, have in them nothing sordid,
nothing lower than the natural and respectable desire for honorable distinction in a high public career ; but, politicians in the low sense they have
degraded the word to bear—political intriguers, sa-
gacious demagogues, clever in electioneering arts,

cunning in contriving and skillful in managing the complicated machinery by which the ballot-box may be made to serve their purposes. A most pernicious race. The great curse of the nation.

These men, acting on the well established understanding that they who help make the President shall share in the patronage of his office, have taken possession of the country for carrying on the business of President making in the interests of the great parties to which they attach themselves for the furtherance of their own ends.

Each of the great conflicting parties—always two, and sometimes more—puts forward its candidate for the Presidency, nominated by a general convention of the party composed of delegates from every State, chosen for the purpose under the guidance of these political managers, and in the choice of which, (as well as in the nomination of electors,) especially in the primary assemblies, the most respectable portion of the people have but little share and less influence.

The nominations made, then begins the campaign, as it is significantly termed. The whole country is converted into a battle-field for the conflict of rival parties contending in dual or in triangular warfare. The whole nation is involved in the

din and smoke of the hot contest. Nearly every
thing is drawn into it and made to turn upon it—
even to the filling of the pettiest municipal office
in the smallest hamlet in the land. If any man in
the United States wants a public office or employment of any sort, under the Federal, or any State, or
Municipal Government, he must enroll himself in
the ranks of one or the other of these great parties,
and make himself serviceable in proportion to the
prize he seeks. He must work hard, and not be
over scrupulous in his work. There is dirty work
to be done ; but since there are tens of thousands
whose ardent longings are fixed on offices or jobs,
and among them thousands of men who are by no
means of the most respectable sort, (or to say it
clearly out, a multitude of needy, greedy, unprincipled men,) so there is no lack of willing hands to
do the work which the upper leaders see needful to
be done but may not quite like to do themselves.

So the contest goes on—with most admirable
perfection of organization of every sort of influence
—managing committees everywhere, general, state,
county and town ; newspapers established, bought,
subsidized ; pamphlets, speeches, and documents
dispersed everywhere, printed paper enough to cover
three or four-fold thick every square foot of land

throughout the country—in short, the whole mighty enginery of the press organized and set in motion, teeming with appeals to the ignorance, and prejudices, and passions of the people, stirring them up to the height of partisan excitement ; while, to intensify the excitement in the breasts of the masses, more apt to be stirred by the living voice than by the printed word, rival hosts of demagogue orators and smart stipendiary lecturers spread themselves over the length and breadth of the country, haranguing the people in all sorts of assemblies, ward meetings, town meetings, county meetings and monster mass meetings where men are counted by acres and not by numbers. And probably there are more calculated lies (to say nothing of a considerable amount of perjury and false swearing) perpetrated in the United States to serve the ends of parties during a " Presidential Campaign," than in all the rest of the world for any political purpose in a dozen years.

Hundreds of thousands of dollars are moreover staked in bets upon the issue, putting into energetic activity thousands of unscrupulous agents moved by cupidity, or by the mere gambling spirit that seeks to win for the winning's sake.

Then, to get at the baser sorts, whom the inflammatory influence of the press or partisan speech-
14

making cannot make serviceable, a host of stipendiary tools, bought with money or with promises
of offices or jobs, are everywhere zealously at work
in all grog-shops and hells before the day, and at
the polls on the great day of choosing the Presidential electors—venal buyers of venal votes at a
dollar a head or more, as the case may be. Everybody knows, or has moral certainty of conviction,
that immense sums are thus spent in buying votes,
especially the votes of that admirable class of free
voters, our adopted and recently imported citizens.
An edifying spectacle of the working of democratic
institutions, and of the sacred right of universal
suffrage !

In the hot ferments of our Presidential elections
all the social froth and scum of the nation are
brought to the top of the seething cauldron. All
the worst elements, the most disreputable members
of society, the bankrupt in character and good name,
blacklegs and blackguards, loom up into loathsome
prominence and activity. Bullies and rowdies
throng the voting places, making them scenes of
drunken violence and vulgar brutalities, destroying
the propriety and obstructing the business of the
polls, disgusting the decent, and frightening the

feeble, the aged, and the timid, from the exercise of their rights and duties.*

In short, looking at this whole party-managing, people-managing, press-using, vote-buying system, it is scarcely possible to imagine any thing more powerful to corrupt the public and private morals of a nation, to eat out of the heart of a people all reverence for law and justice, truth and righteousness—all sense of the sacredness of any thing in heaven or on earth.

Meanwhile, as part and parcel, cause and effect of these processes of popular demoralization, the halls of Congress and of the State Legislatures are filled, not with the best, but with the most available men for party ends ; and we have caucus recommendations, resolutions offered and speeches made, with a view to affect the issue of the Presidential contest—all this tending to lower the tone, impair the dignity and corrupt the integrity of our legislators, and to interfere with the proper legislative business of the States and of the nation. If it were not for this business of President making, all the proper legislative business of the nation in Congress might be better done in half the time.

* See at the end of this volume the development of an organized system of violence and brutal outrage far surpassing any thing suggested above, brought to light since the above was written.

Then, too, the weight of Executive influence is generally thrown into the scale of one or the other of the great contending parties ; the whole vast army of official functionaries is put under the necessity, willingly or unwillingly, of giving their votes, their influence, and a tax on their salaries to secure the victory of the favored party ; and ordinarily the chances are ten to one in favor of the success of the party that can command the influence of the Executive, with the Treasury at his back. We say ordinarily, for it is only in great exigencies which reach the universal pocket of the nation, or in the rarer cases when the sense of public interest and the sense of public right conspire to arouse the great heart and conscience of the nation, and to break down all old party lines and party disciplines—it is only in such great emergencies that the odds are not almost sure to the party in power.

Meantime, what the influence of all this is upon the candidates for the Presidency it is easy to see. When the nominations for President were made in the great party conventions, the question was not about the best man for the office, but about the best man for party success. The candidate selected was obliged to stretch himself, or to contract him-

self upon the platform framed for him, and stands
—lies we should say—before the country the candidate of a party.

The successful candidate in entering upon office
has until lately found it proper to repudiate in decent formulas of phrase the notion of administering the government merely as the chief of a party.
It is not thought needful to make any such dis-
claimer now. But whether he does or not, he enters upon office bound to administer the government in the interests of his party—pledged to reward the party leaders who placed him in power,
and on whom he must depend for support, and so
with every temptation to a corrupt use of the power and patronage of his office. Claimants come
clamoring thick around him. The eagles, and all
obscene birds of prey—kites, hawks, and carrion
crows—gather to the sharing of the spoils. Persons whom no honest man would like to shake
hands with, or introduce to his wife and daughters,
are received at the White House, and go out rewarded with public places. Men, whom in the
neighborhood of their own homes nobody would
trust, are put in offices of public trust. The demands of political parties allow but little scope for
delicacies of private taste or scrupulous regards of
any sort.

But the worst effect of our system upon the relations of political parties to the administration of the Government remains to be noticed.

In the theory of the working of constitutional governments, political parties have an important place. They may and should have a wholesome influence, as a means of maintaining the intergrity of the Constitution, the independence of its coördinate powers, and in protecting the country against abuses of Executive power. But under our actual system, these legitimate, conservative influences are nearly lost, and almost nothing is left but the evils necessarily incident to the existence of parties ; indeed, political parties have become a source of the greatest possible danger, through the natural disposition of the great mass of the members of the dominant party throughout the country to acquiesce in, to approve and sustain whatever is done by the man whom they have placed at the head of the nation. In their eyes he stands there the chief of their party ; that party is the majority of the people ; it is all right, in their notion, that their will should prevail. The President is the reflection of their will. They have triumphed in his election ; he is the eminent proclamation and embodied representation of their triumph ; and so what he wills they are naturally predisposed to uphold—at all events, through the strictness of party discipline that has come to prevail and the interests of party managers and Government officials who share in the spoils of victory, the great body of the rank and file of the triumphant party may be generally led to approve and sustain the course of Executive will.

Thus supported by party majorities, with tremendous powers of corruption through the offices and jobs at his disposal, and thereby able to wield an immense influence in retaining and acquiring the support he may in any emergency need, what is to prevent his initiating and controlling the legislative business of the country, and so subverting the constitutional balance of power ? Is there no room to fear even for the integrity of the judicial functions ? And what have we then—with all the forms of the Republic—what have we in effect but an Executive despotism ? It matters not in what way, however indirect, the legislation of a country comes to be controlled by the Executive power. It matters not in what way the Judiciary is made subservient. After the Book of Judges comes the Book of Kings, said that eccentric man, but sharp-sighted political seer, John Randolph of Roanoke.

We have already seen significant tokens of the tendency in this direction. ". I am the State," said Louis XIV. " I am the People," said in effect an iron-willed President in the name of the Democracy of whose will he proclaimed himself the representative and embodied reflection. He shrank not from threatening the existence of the Senate as " a concession to the aristocratic principle," and an obstacle to the free course of the popular will ; and at that day the suggestion was even made to subvert the independence, and thereby the constitutional existence, of the Federal Judiciary, by rendering the Judges removable at Executive pleasure. No attempt was made, that I am aware of, to carry these suggestions out. Perhaps they were only the passionate utterance of thwarted self-will. Perhaps it was concluded that the means already existing might be made sufficient for securing the objects of predominant parties. I mention them only as significant of the impulse lying in the nature of victorious party spirit, and of the tendency to the absorption of the powers of the State into the Supreme Executive.

Since that time twenty years have passed away, and the tendency to the centralization of power has not diminished. It has gone on increasing.

The convenient words and phrases which mark the progress of things in this direction are familiar to all. There are some persons who profess a great contempt for words : they go for things. Right, undoubtedly, if only they do not fall into the mistake of converting a partial and conditional truth into a universal and absolute one. For words are also things—and sometimes tremendous things. And political words and phrases are a surer index to the direction in which a nation's destiny is moving than unthinking persons dream. When the celebrated phrase, "to the victors belong the spoils," was first announced in application to our politics, it was thought the inauguration of a monstrous doctrine, at variance with all constitutional principles of righteous administration. It has become now the settled doctrine and practice of all parties ; and thousands who shrank from defending it then, do not think it needs defending now.

We have all become familiar with a mode of speaking which has of late come more and more to prevail—by which the Executive, under the terms, the Government, the Administration, is put into prominence and distinction above the co-ordinate powers of the State. The policy, the plans, and even the personal wishes of the President in regard

14*

to legislative measures, are spoken of as something that ought to have a prevailing influence upon the legislation of the country. And we have at length come to see the Executive, not merely submitting to Congress such recommendations as the Constitution makes it his right and duty to offer, not merely asking for such legislation as the discharge of his proper Executive functions may, in any case, make specially needful, but virtually initiating and pressing great legislative measures which are properly and exclusively within the sphere of the independent action of Congress, and with which he has rightfully nothing to do except in the sequel of their action. And we hear of the obligation to sustain the President in such cases as the paramount obligation of the party in power. It is made the test of fealty to the party; and fealty to the party is made the sole obligation of legislators —not fealty to the great political principles or measures that may be adopted by a party, and to which a candidate for a seat in Congress may be honorably called on to avow his fealty beforehand, and to make good his profession afterward; but implicit, unqualified obedience to the behests of party discipline and to the mere will of party leaders and their chief on all questions and under all circumstances.

EVIL CONSEQUENCES.   323

" It will not do," says one of the organs of the present Administration (I do not say an authorized exponent of the mind of the Executive), " it will not do for a man to say, ' I differ from the President on this single point.' It will not do to differ on that single point." A hundred similar utterances of the press—pending the so-called Lecompton struggle—might be adduced. The official organ itself (as it is termed) was not less strong to the same effect. It poured out reprobation and threats upon all recusants. And what is worst of all, on the floor of Congress, from the representatives of the people, speaking in their places, we have heard the same obligation of implicit submission to the President's will openly proclaimed, and the presumption of legislators in claiming the right to distinguish between the President's right to recommend and his right to command, boldly denounced as " the language of rebellion ! "* Is not this atrocious ?. Is it easy to imagine a greater outrage on the independence and dignity of the National Legislature, or a more destructive blow at the integrity of the Constitution and the balance of its great co-ordinate powers, than is contained

* See report of debates in the House of Representatives, Friday, March 25, 1858.

in such an utterance ? It matters not to say it may have been a thoughtless exaggeration of phrase, not to be strictly construed as a deliberate assertion of the doctrine and duty of implicit subserviency to Executive dictation. It is any way an unqualified assertion of the doctrine. And when such a doctrine can be proclaimed in such a place, and the man that proclaims it, no matter how thoughtlessly, is not put down, or put out, by one immediate, spontaneous, simultaneous uprising of righteous displeasure—I have only to say it is to me a significant token of the centralized absolutism toward which we are tending. It marks off the measure of many a mile of national descent on the road downward since the days of WASHINGTON.

It is meantime matter of universal belief that some of the most important legislative acts that have been passed within the last few years, have been passed under the pressure of Executive influence. They have been urged as Administration measures, and it is a matter of common assertion, and of universal conviction, that the whole immense force of the Executive has been brought to bear upon their passage. Whether the charge of using the Executive patronage to corrupt the legislation of Congress be true or not ; whether it can be established by legal and technical proof or not, I do not undertake to say. It is asserted on all hands. It is universally believed to be true. I do not suppose there is a man of any intelligence throughout the country that entertains the slightest moral doubt on the matter. Pending the passage of the bill for the admission of Kansas into the Union under the Lecompton Constitution, the corrupt influence of the Executive was everywhere talked of—not only by the opponents of the measure, as a thing to be feared, but by those who favored it as the ground of their hopes; and the fact of its exertion was admitted on all hands.

And worst of all is the fact that so many seem to think this all a matter of course—that things, which in the days of WASHINGTON would have been looked upon with horror, are now regarded with comparative unconcern, not merely by the great host of unprincipled politicians, for they do not care at all, but by the great mass of the people throughout the country. This is the worst feature of the case. Nothing so decisively and shockingly marks our national degeneracy, and the depths to which we have sunk, as the almost universal apathy with which things that nobody seriously defends, which everybody admits to be corrupt, flagitious, and dangerous to the liberties of the country, are acquiesced in as things of course—things which may be lamented but cannot be prevented—things that must be let go on, each party making the most it can for itself in the corrupt scramble ; and, as for the country, why the country must not trouble itself too much about what cannot be helped. It is a great country. It will take a great deal of bad government to ruin it. It will last some time yet. Its pockets are not much meddled with—certainly not in a direct way—it does not feel the draft made upon them. And meantime it has a great "manifest destiny" to fulfil. It will not do to be too scrupulous and squeamish. All governments are corrupt, especially all free governments. Human nature is no better than it should be. What is the use of being always on the alarm? *Laissez aller :* let things go, and keep out of the way.

Well, if nine-tenths of the politicians, and of the people too, talk in this way, I do not know that there is much use in saying any thing ; only he who blows the warning blast has ease of conscience, whatever betides.

I have thus sketched what seem to me the pernicious influences of our system of President making upon the people, and upon all public functionaries, and its tendency to overthrow the Constitutional balance of power, and to consolidate a central absolutism supported by party majorities resting on a demoralized people—with all the forms of the republic serving only to hold the nation more inextricably entangled in the vast net-work of corrupt officials and political managers, spreading its infinite inevitable meshes outward from the centre all over the land. That such is the actual influence of our system, such the direction in which we are moving, and such the inevitable result of unchecked progress in this direction, is a truth to which, in my opinion, no wise statesman, no profound student of human nature and human history, can shut his eyes. And judging óf the future by the past (which, though not an absolute canon of political prophecy, is yet, to a certain extent, a sound one), and looking to the growth of the country, and the constantly augmenting patronage of the Executive, what else can be expected but a constant and rapid increase of these evils and dangers ? A certain stage of degeneracy reached, the road downward is trodden with accelerated speed.

I do not mean to maintain that our system of

President making has been the sole and only cause
of the corruption and degeneracy I have sketched.
It is doubtless effect as well as cause.   In all governments—and in free governments most of all—
the tendency to corruption is such that no mode
of constituting the Federal Executive could give
us absolute exemption from such or similar evils
and dangers.   But our actual mode of doing it has
furnished a special basis, supplied peculiar conditions, temptations, means and facilities for the
growth and action of corruption, such as would not
have existed if the intention of the Constitution
in this matter had been strictly adhered to.

Special causes may also have concurred to increase the corrupt working of our actual system.

Chief among these is the institution of slavery,
and the invincible determination of the slaveholding States to possess and control the Federal Government for the defence and aggrandizement of
that institution.   Subordinating every thing else to
this, and holding the balance between the great
Northern parties, the policy of the Southern States
has always been to make entire subserviency to the
interests of slavery the price of that alliance, without which no party could come into power, to secure
a President bound to do their will in the exercise

of his Executive functions, and through him to control also the action of Congress, always at least negatively through the veto power, by preventing any unsatisfactory legislation, and positively, also, so far as Executive influence can go to secure positive legislation in the interests of slavery. With such a policy, it is not wonderful the Southern States have had the sagacity to see and the skill to avail themselves of the peculiar advantages our actual system of President making affords for the furtherance of their paramount object.

PRESIDENT MAKING.

———•◦•———

My DEAR SIR : We have looked at the evils and dangers that environ us—where shall we look for remedies ? Upon what can we rely to check the progress of corruption and the downward course of national degeneracy ?

Is it the intelligence and virtue of the great honest masses which make up the heart and conscience of the country ?

There is enough of it, no doubt—particularly " off the pavements," as an eminent statesman is wont to say—there is enough of it, if only it could have scope and sway. But how to get it to have scope and sway ? It is unable now to withstand the bad working of our political system. It is not strong enough now to stem the tide of political corruption. This we see. And how to make it stronger ? It is now the dupe of party managers —all the more serviceable because it serves their ends with a good conscience. This is a point greatly to be observed. The intelligence and virtue of the country—whatever it be—serves the ends of party managers all the more serviceably in proportion as it is duped into thinking them all right. Its very heart and conscience thus become an element of strength in the hands of party leaders ; and so the intelligence and virtue of the great honest masses—which certainly is their own individual salvation—does not become the source of a controlling public virtue for the political salvation of the country. Besides, nothing in the world tends so powerfully to a constant deterioration of the public morals of a nation as the corrupt working of political institutions. How to turn the tide ?

The Press, is it said—the Free Press—the great palladium of a nation's liberties ? That is a fine formula. It has a grand sound. But I do not look for political regeneration from that quarter. The Press ! Why, how much of wholesome truth and sound doctrine do the people get from the party press—which is pretty nearly all the press there is, so far as the political education of the people is due to the press ?　It feeds them on falsehoods and fallacies, morning, noon, and night.　The only consolation is that the more intelligent of the people have come to understand this, and to believe little or nothing merely because it is said by the party press.　But these persons are an ineffectual minority.　As to the great masses, how is it ?　One half of the press is the tool of one party ; the other half, of the other party.　The great mass of one party scarcely read any thing said by the press of the other party, and believe nothing it says.　They read their own party half of the press, and believe all it says.　I look upon the political party press as it works with us, in spite of certain good uses it serves, as on the whole very injurious to the moral spirit of the nation.　On neither hand does it, as a general thing, state facts truly, or favor or oppose public men and measures fairly.　*But what is worse still, on neither hand does it preach those great lessons of political truth and political duty which ought to be preached to a free people, and which must in some way be effectually learned in order to prevent such a government as ours from becoming the worst and most dangerous of all forms of government.*　On the contrary, both sides of the party

press vie with each other in flattering and cajoling
the people with watchwords and phrases addressed
to their passions and prejudices, tending to beget
in them an exaggerated sense of rights and a feeble
sense of duties—to make them feel that the sovereignty of the people is rightfully a sovereignty of
mere will, that the right of the majority to have
its own will and way at all events and in any way,
is a sacred inviolable right which only aristocrats
and tyrants can call in question, and to question
which is a monstrous outrage on the principles of
eternal justice.

But an independent Press—it may be said—
not in the interest of parties, a press that shall
boldly and ably preach the principles of political
truth and righteousness, state facts truly, canvass
public men and measures fairly, and warn the people of the evils and dangers that surround us, and
of the direction in which the nation is drifting onward ?

Well, how is such a press to be had ? Who is
to establish it ? Who to sustain it ? And what
is to be its influence ? How is it to reach and disabuse the great masses of the people whose minds
are abused by the party press ? It would have so
many things to say unpalatable to the popular

taste. It would go hard for it to get the popular ear. It would have both sides of the party press against it. And as to the party in power, what would they care? They would laugh at its preachings and denunciations of political corruption; they would even like them. It is a safety-valve in the State machinery under their control. EDMUND BURKE tells us that when Rome was in its most servile state, the destruction of tyrants was the common theme of boys in the schools. The tyrants felt strong enough to let it go so.

But Christianity—the influence of its spirit and principles?

Undoubtedly, if only they could permeate and actuate the political life of the country. But the Christianity of our country—that body of convictions and sentiments, observances and practices, which passes for Christianity among us—is for the most part made to run on at a safe distance from the political course of things, rarely coming into contact with it. It is graciously permitted, indeed, to subserve the ends of politicians by proclaiming the great doctrine and duty of " rendering to Cæsar the things that are Cæsar's." But if in any unlucky moment it is moved to condemn and denounce the conduct of parties and the action of Government, it gets well snubbed for its pains, and is bidden to mind its own business and not to "meddle with politics"—above all, not to preach "sedition and rebellion ;" for law is law, and a very sacred thing it is ; and "the powers that be are ordained of God," and Christianity must be careful not to talk about any Higher Law than human law, and not to tell the people that there can be such a thing as an unjust law, or a corrupt judge, or an atrocious act of Government—at all events, it must be careful to say nothing of this sort in any case where the interests of slaveholding are in any way concerned.

I for one do not expect political salvation from any such Christianity as we have now, or, for aught I see, are likely to have for some time to come. Indeed, were it ten times more disposed than it is to grapple with the political corruption of the nation, I should have little hope of its effecting much. He who runs a race with the Evil One, we are told, must needs have long legs. We have no reason to expect any *miraculous* lengthening of our Christianity for such a race'; and its ordinary powers— what guaranty for their effectual competition in the future do we find in the past ?

Besides, the Christianity of every country is practically what it is taken to be ; and the Christianity of our country is singularly unfitted for the race in question, from the fact that in its relations to public evils it has two faces, two voices, looks two ways, has two sets of legs, which run, or strive to run, in contrary directions, producing a dead lock, which gives the Evil One a clear field and an easy triumph. A great "Revival of Religion," is said to have spread throughout the land. But, without intending any disrespect to it, I must say that I do not much expect it will make the religion of the country any more a Christianity with one face, and one voice, looking and running in one direction, or with any more powerful influence in arresting the progress of political corruption than heretofore.

To what, then, are we to look? If anywhere, we must, it seems to me, look mainly to political influences, to changes in the working of our political system—partly as they may be forced upon us by future exigencies in public affairs, and partly as they may result from social changes under the gradual operation of economical and other historical causes.

I say political influences, political changes—for no causes act more powerfully upon the political character of a nation than the working of its political institutions. A practical departure from the intention of the Constitution, in the way we have seen, has been the great cause of the evils and dangers I have sketched ; and these evils and dangers, in their most peculiar and worst aspects, would in a great measure disappear, could the provisions of the Constitution be truly and thoroughly established in practical operation throughout the country.   But it is idle to expect the choice of President will now ever come to be made in strict conformity with the original intention of the Constitution.   It may be thought equally idle to expect any determinate and very beneficial alterations in our system.   Still, it is possible to suggest changes which it would be wise and salutary to adopt.

Various suggestions have been made with a view to reduce the patronage of the President, and so, on the one hand, to diminish the means and temptations to a corrupt and dangerous use of official power, yet without taking from him those powers which must on all sound principles be vested in the Executive ; and, on the other hand, proportionably to diminish the demoralizing influences of the Presidential elections.

Of this sort is the election of Postmasters by

15

the people of the towns and districts where post-offices are established—the persons thus elected giving proper securities to the General Government, and held to proper responsibilities to it.

Even the abolition of the Post Office system, as a department of the General Government, has been proposed—thus leaving the transmission of letters and other mail matter to the general laws of business.

Either of these schemes is practicable ; the latter is the preferable one. There is little room to doubt that private enterprise could accomplish as well and more cheaply what the General Government accomplishes through the Post Office Department. This Department is not now a necessity either for the Government or for the country, as it was once. The electric telegraph has already superseded its functions to an immense extent. A vast proportion of the commercial and other intercourse of the country is carried on by this means. This will be more and more the case. And what the telegraph cannot convey, the express companies can carry as well and as cheaply as the General Government—more so, in the opinion of the best judges. I have the authority of a late high public functionary (one of the best authorities in the country on such matters) for saying that the material interests of the country would not suffer but be benefited by the abolition of the Post Office Department.

So, too, the suggestion has been made to do away with our whole revenue system—leaving foreign commerce free from all customs duties and imposts, and providing for the expenses of the Government by direct taxation. This also is a practicable scheme. The collection of the taxes might be committed to the United States Marshals, who might employ the agency of the collectors of State taxes in their several districts, both taxes being collected at the same time. In this way, the expense of collecting the revenue of the United States, which now amounts to *seven* per cent., would, in the opinion of the same eminent authority before referred to, be reduced to *one* per cent. ; this, whether so or not, is, however, a point of comparatively trifling importance.

Whether these changes are likely to be adopted is not the question now. One thing is certain, that if adopted they would greatly diminish the means of corruption in the hands of the Executive. It ought to be expected, too, that the people would look more closely after the expenditure of the public money—feeling it drawn directly from their pockets ; and that the appropriation of immense sums to be profligately wasted in extravagant payment for jobs and contracts given in reward of the services of political managers, would not be tolerated. This ought to be expected ; and would to a certain extent be the case, although the working of universal suffrage among the great masses who pay no taxes, suggests a doubt whether it would be so to the extent it ought to be. But at all events, a very large number of offices now in the President's gift—objects of greedy desire and strenuous scramble among the hordes of office-seekers—would cease to exist ; and the corrupting excitements of the Presidential elections would be correspondingly lessened.

Modifications of our political system, such as I have mentioned, may possibly be accomplished in the course of time, through the pressure of public exigencies in peculiar (perhaps disastrous) emergencies, or through the influence of economical and social changes, wrought out by the progress of science and the arts of life, and in their turn acting necessarily upon the administration of political affairs.

But there is one other suggestion still. Since it is precisely the popular election of the President which the Constitution was framed to prevent ; since the subversion of this intention is precisely the great and special source of national demoralization and danger—would it not be wise to adopt some method of filling the Executive office by which the intention of the Constitution in this respect shall be effectually accomplished ? I think so. I think a method may be devised perfectly practicable in itself, and wanting nothing but the will of the people to effect its accomplishment. This method may seem to run very little chance of ever getting practically accomplished through the will of the people : that may be a sufficient reason, as I have said, for a politic statesman not undertaking to accomplish it, but it is no reason whatever for sensible persons not entertaining the question whether it ought not to be accomplished, whether the people of the United States would not do well and wisely to adopt it.

In case of vacancy in the Executive, suppose, then, that from the list of Senators of the United States, who have served one or two terms of office, one be taken by lot, under the direction of the Chief Justice of the Supreme Court and his Asso-

ciates, in such public manner and with such forms
and modes of proceeding as may be fitly prescribed
to give proper guaranty and authentication to the
procedure.   Let the person thus designated become
President for four or for six years, upon taking the
prescribed oath in the usual way.

This mode of filling the office is simple, practicable and safe, and would, I am sure, work far better than our present mode.   Objections to it may
possibly be conceived : no human contrivance in the
matter of government but is liable to them ; although for myself I am free to avow my inability
to see any valid and sufficient objection, or indeed
any objection at all, except the single suggestion
that the person thus designated may possibly not
be the best man on the list for President.   But this
is an objection which, in substance, holds against
any possible or conceivable mode of filling the office ; while, on the other hand, the mode I have
suggested has many obvious and undeniable advantages above any other scheme.

In the first place, it would effectually accomplish the intention of the Constitution in the particular its framers had most at heart.   It would
prevent altogether what they especially designed to
prevent—the evils and dangers, the turmoil and

demoralizing influences of a popular election, the corrupt intrigues of ambitious aspirants and party managers. Whatever of excitement would remain possible would be divided and localized in the several States in the choice of Senators. The possibility that a man elected to the Senate might become President of the United States should, and doubtless would, be a reason, additional to those now operating, for choosing for Senators men of high character and eminent abilities for the public service ; while the chances of a Senator actually coming into the office of President—less than one in a hundred now, and diminished by every new admission of a State into the Union—would not be great enough, nor near enough, to supply much motive for corrupt practices and a dangerous excitement. The mischievous business of President-making, as it is now carried on, would be destroyed. The occupation of the President-making politicians would be gone. The whole pernicious race would become extinct—to the great comfort of honest men, and the great welfare of the country.

Then again : who can doubt we should be full as likely to get in general as good a man for President as we get now. I am quite clear the odds are in favor of getting a better man. The time for making our great men Presidents, under our present system, is gone by. No truly great and eminent public man, as things now are, runs much chance. There is almost always something in their position and past career to make them " unavailable "—that is the word—in the judgment of party managers. An available candidate is the one thing needful. And so it is found a necessary policy to nominate military heroes, successful generals, or even persons of small public mark and without positive qualities, rather than great statesmen. A more biting piece of ironical sarcasm on the actual working of our system can scarcely be conceived than is contained in the language in which the framers of the Constitution gave expression to their elevated hopes on this point. " This process of election," says the *Federalist,* " affords a moral certainty that the office of President will seldom fall to the lot of a man who is not in an eminent degree endowed with the requisite qualifications. Talents for low intrigue, and the little arts of popularity, may alone suffice to elevate a man to the first honors of a single State. But it will require other talents and a different kind of merit to establish him in the esteem and confidence of the whole Union, or of so considerable a portion of it as will be necessary to make him a successful candidate for the distinguished office of President of the United States."*. Shades of departed heroes, patriots and statesmen ! What a prophecy is this ! But then it is to be considered that MADISON, and HAMILTON, and JAY, when they indulged in this prophetic satisfaction, wrote under the delusive belief that the intention of the Constitution would be carried out, not frustrated ; that the President would be chosen by the concurrent votes of independent electors, casting their ballots under the sole responsibility of voting for the man they should find best fitted for the office, and that he would be a man commended to their choice by the sole fact of standing before the nation by general consent in the position of " pre-eminent ability and virtue."

I do not hesitate then to say that by the mode I have suggested, we should be likely to get at least as fit a man for President as we get now. He would be a man who had had experience of public affairs, had enjoyed the confidence of a sovereign State, and filled a position of the highest public dignity and trust ; and he would be quite as likely to be a man of " pre-eminent ability and virtue," as

* *Federalist*, No. 68.

any one we can ordinarily expect to have under our present system.

Then, too, he would have the advantage of coming into office unsullied by any complication with the corrupting processes of a popular election, exempt from all pledges or obligations to parties or persons, and from all such temptations to abuse his patronage, and free to administer the Government as President of the nation and not of a party. Abuse of power is still possible—power is never without temptations, and no man can be found not liable to fall. But it is certain he would be completely exempted from an immense amount of temptations to which the Executive is now subjected. And as to the still remaining possibilities of a corrupt use of his official powers during the term of his office for ends of personal ambition—if the suggestions already made in regard to diminishing the patronage of the office should be carried into effect, the means of corruption and the dangers of Executive interference with the constitutional balance of the powers of the State, would be still further reduced. But whether those suggestions, or either of them, were adopted, it would still be true to say —and a great thing to be able to say with truth— that he would be comparatively shielded from the

baser sort of motives, and environed by all the better and nobler motives of his position—the high behests of public duty, and the honorable ambition to
deserve the approbation of his country and the applauding verdict of impartial history.

Then, again, it is not a small advantage that
the legislative bodies of the nation would be protected from many of the evil influences of our present system.   They would have nothing to do with
the business of President making.   Its intense and
corrupting excitements could find no entrance to
warp the integrity, impair the dignity, and interfere with the proper functions of legislative assemblies.

And, finally, it seems to me an improvement
would be wrought in the character and working of
the great political parties.   Their differences and
conflicts would not be about President making—
they would be less about persons and more about
great public principles and measures.   Party spirit,
we might reasonably hope, would become less bitter, passionate and unscrupulous ; and the party
press would reflect this improved tone—would become less pernicious and more salutary in its influence on the public and private morals of the nation.
The action of parties, in their relations to the Gen-

eral Government and its administration, would be brought within its legitimate sphere, and would be more rational, conservative and beneficent upon the legislation of the country and upon the whole conduct of public affairs.

Such, it seems to me, would be the working of the plan suggested. It would be likely to give us a better government, a better administration of public affairs ; it would certainly prevent many of the worst evils and greatest dangers of our present system. " The mode of appointing the President," says Chancellor Kent, " presented one of the most difficult and momentous questions that could have occupied the deliberations of the assembly that framed the Constitution ; and if ever the tranquillity of this nation is to be disturbed, and its peace jeoparded by a struggle for power, it will be upon this very subject of the choice of President. This is the question that is to test the goodness and try the strength of the Constitution."*

So said this wise man many years ago. It is a warning of prophetic apprehension which every year's experience of the effects of subverting the Constitution in this matter, and of inaugurating, in

---

* Kent Comment. III., 253.

the worst form, the very system it was designed to prevent, serves only to enforce. And nothing appears so necessary as the adoption of some mode of effectually accomplishing the intention of the Constitution by putting an end to the constantly recurring party struggles for the election of the President of the United States.

If this could be done, what limits can be assigned to the safe and beneficent extension of the Union ? With a General Government truly Federal, and not consolidated—leaving to the States all State sovereignties and State rights, and the control of all State interests, and acting only as the agent of each and all in all matters of common concern ; thus giving to each member of the Union the strength of the whole at home, and the power, dignity and importance of the whole, as toward all the rest of the world—what is there to render unsafe the widest possible expansion of the Union ? With such means of intercommunication and living connection as steam and electricity now supply, what is there to prevent a Federal Union of sovereign States throughout this whole Western hemisphere ? If ever, indeed, the vision of a political millennium shall be realized, it seems to me the problem will be solved by three words : Free

Trade, State Rights, and a Federal Union of the World !

I conclude by again desiring it to be considered that the question is not whether the scheme suggested has any chance of getting practically realized, but whether it is not one that ought to be adopted ; one which the people of the United States would do well and wisely to adopt.

Under the operation of the causes that are now at work, we cannot stand where we are. The actual working of our political system is more demoralizing than that of any other government upon the face of the earth. I believe so, and therefore I say so. I think we have seen that it is so ; and there is reason why it should be so. It acts directly upon the great masses more than that of any other government. The imperial despotism of France, or of Russia, for instance, does not tend to corrupt the people like our system––for the reason that there are properly no politics there as with us ; the great officers of state may be corrupt and practice stupendous corruptions, but the great masses of the people have very little to do with the government, except to be governed by it. They are deprived of political rights ; they pay taxes which they have no voice in imposing. This is bad, no doubt. I do not advocate such a system ; but then it is undeniably clear that they are not exposed to the temptations to political corruption, not subjected to the demoralizing influences which the possession of such rights would subject them to. But our Government comes into perpetual contact with the masses, touches them at all points, and reaches every individual. The people act upon the Government and are acted upon by it ; and the mutual action, we have seen, is corrupting—precisely through the immense scope and the immense temptations to corruption inevitably connected with the actual working of our political system. And things are going on from bad to worse ; and so I say we cannot stand where we are. Historical causes work slowly, but they work inevitably. If we do not get on better, we shall get on worse. Under the influences that are now shaping our destiny, we may get on after a tolerable fashion for some time to come, but we shall not get on well. We are drifting toward the inevitable day of disaster upon the rocks of a lee shore. What will then be our fate ? Shall we then be able to wear off upon a safer tack, or shall the fragments of a shattered Union strew the shores of two oceans, a warning to the world never again to dream the fond dream of a great and permanent Republic, based upon democratic institutions and universal suffrage ? Who can unroll the Book of Destiny, and tell us what is written there ?

POLITICS AND THE PULPIT.

An immense outcry has of late been raised against what is called " clerical meddling with politics ; " and no end of exhortations addressed to the clergy about the duty of confining themselves to their proper work of " preaching Christ Crucified," " saving souls," and the like.

Much that is said on this matter is in itself unworthy of serious notice, and might be safely enough left to find its sufficient refutation in the good sense of the intelligent portion of the public. But experience proves what a power of pernicious influence lies in pious phrases constantly addressed to the religious feelings and prejudices of the less cultivated classes—especially when these phrases are adroitly framed to combine the twofold fallacy of begging the very question in issue, and of throwing odium upon all who do not immediately succumb to their fallacious application.

Besides, in these much-abused commonplaces, there is always a part of truth, to which the fallacy owes its delusive force, and which needs to be distinguished and accepted, in order to destroy the mischievous effect of their fallacious application. There is a right, and there is a wrong, in the matter, which are commonly confounded. Let us try to make the proper distinctions, and to get at the truth on this subject.

It will probably be conceded that clergymen, being men and citizens, as well as clergymen, have a right to feel an interest in all measures involving the welfare and right government of their country, and to give private expression to their views on all proper occasions and in all proper ways. The only question is as to their public conduct, whether personal or official.

On the one hand, it must be admitted, that by becoming a clergyman, a person is not divested of his rights, nor absolved from his duties as a citizen, any more than from those of his social and domestic relations.—On the other hand, it is equally clear, that the special obligations of his profession

—the proprieties of his calling, and the preservation of the peculiar influence of his office—impose limitations upon his public activity in political matters. ⸗Whatever personal part he may take in such matters, he must not forget his official character, and the duties it imposes.   There are a great many things not improper in a layman which would be unbecoming in a clergyman. ⸗So every one feels. And it is for every clergyman a question of charity —and so of duty—as well as of prudence, in what way and to what extent he may allow himself to take part in political affairs, without violating the obligations or impairing the just influence of his office.   To hold political office, or to put himself forward as a candidate for it, to take an active share in the business of organizing and managing parties, in the tactics by which the objects of individual ambition or the triumph of a party may be secured—in short, to " turn politician," in the just and ordinary meaning of the phrase, is as much at variance with the proper functions of the clerical office, as to turn stockjobber or innkeeper.   If a clergyman's taste inclines this way, he must renounce his sacred calling, before engaging in these purely secular activities.

But the important question is not so much

about the personal as about the official conduct of
the clergy in regard to public affairs. It is on the
relation of Politics and the Pulpit. It is what is
called " Political Preaching," that is most commonly and vehemently denounced as an unseemly
" clerical meddling with politics."

On this matter there is likewise a very prevalent confusion of right and wrong. No universal
proposition on the subject holds good. Not every
thing which may be denounced as political preaching is to be justified, and not every thing so denounced is to be surrendered to condemnation.

There may, undoubtedly, be a wrong sort of political preaching, at variance with the proper functions of the pulpit. Matters simply and purely
political or economical—questions on the organization of the public powers ; on points of constitutional law ; on trade, finance and revenue ; on the
policy of protective duties or internal improvements, and the parties and party conflicts that may
grow out of them—these, and such like matters,
lying wholly within the domain of political expediency, have no proper place in the sacred desk.
Preaching about such matters is political preaching in a justly reprehensible sense. We feel no
call to defend it, or to apologize for it. We sur-

render it to all the odium any one may choose to heap upon it.

But on the other hand, there is such a thing as political preaching—what is often so called—that ought not to be abandoned to the invidious application of the phrase. It is not political preaching in any justly odious sense. It is preaching Christianity in its relations to the political life of the nation. It is enforcing the spirit and principles of the Christian religion in their necessary application to the duties of citizens and the conduct of public affairs. It does not meddle with political questions which are purely and wholly such, and to which the principles and precepts of Christianity stand in no relation and have no application. It deals only with political questions which are at the same time religious and moral in themselves, or in their consequences, or to which, in themselves, or in the manner of their practical determination, the principles of religion and morals have a necessary application, and it treats all such questions only from the point of view of the Christian religion.

This sort of " political preaching "—if men will so call it—is not to be surrendered to condemnation. It is not at variance with the proper functions of the pulpit. It belongs to them. We justify it. We vindicate its legitimate rights.

Yet this is precisely the sort of preaching politicians have raised the outcry against. The other and really indefensible sort—the discussion of purely secular topics in a purely secular spirit—is, in point of fact, a merely imaginary thing; at least, we never heard of it as actually preached in any pulpit. Be this as it may, it is not this that corrupt politicians stigmatize. It is the application of the principles of Christianity to the criticism of public affairs, it is the enforcement of men's Christian duties as citizens, that they wish to repress. They have spared no pains therefore to render it odious—by raising a hue and cry against it—a clamor of watchwords, some addressed to the pious sentiments of the religious, and some to the prejudices and passions of the profane.

In this way a false and pernicious opinion has come quite widely to prevail, which the clergy themselves too generally give in to—some, because they are imposed upon by the fallacies it rests on; some, from scruples about impairing their power to do good, by going counter to the current of opinion, even when they know it to be false; some, from fear of incurring odium, or displeasing the laity in

whose pockets their livelihood lies ; and some, simply because it is their nature to imbibe, without
reflection, the opinions that pass current around
them, according to what old Jeremy Taylor says :
" It is the iniquity of men that they suck in opinion as the wild asses do the wind, without distinguishing the wholesome from the corrupted air,
and then live upon it at a venture."

We say false and pernicious opinion ; for nothing in the world can be less grounded in reason, or
more mischievous in its influence, than the opinion
which makes it odious for the Christian minister to
preach the sort of political preaching we have signalized as belonging to the functions of the pulpit,
and which alone we are concerned to justify.

What principle does this opinion go upon ? At
bottom it can have no conceivable ground in reason,
except this : that Christianity has absolutely nothing whatever in any way to do with politics—that
the two things stand in no relations to each other.
But is this doctrine true ? It is—provided there
is nothing in the political action of men and governments which falls within the sphere of morals :
otherwise, not. To hear some men talk, one would
imagine they believed politics and morals to be entirely out of each other's sphere, heterogenous even,

16

and falling within no common sphere ; and consequently that it is as absurd to apply the moral
judgments of Christianity to the maxims and practices of politicians and parties, and to the conduct
of governments, as it would be to apply them to
the quarrels of cats and dogs, the turnings and
doublings of the fox, or the predatory forays of a
commonwealth of ants into the enclosures of *aphides*
belonging to a neighboring commonwealth.

But talk as men may, they cannot look such a
doctrine in the face, and stand up to the affirmation of it.   Politics do fall within the sphere of
morals, not wholly, indeed—for there are matters
in politics which are morally indifferent—but to a
great extent and in a multitude of particulars : and
morality is ever the same in essence, its principles
are identical in every variety of application.   You
cannot have two standards of morality—one for
public and political, and another for private and
social life.

Now we take for granted not only that the principles and precepts of Christianity embody an ethical code of the purest rational order, but that for
the people of this country they are the supreme
law of moral conduct, the paramount standard of
moral judgment ; and therefore they have a legiti-

mate application to every particular of political action of which the ideas of right and wrong are predicable.

This application it is the business and duty of the Christian clergy to make. It belongs to the very idea of their calling, that they should preach Christianity in its integrity and completeness. What else is their function? For what else do they exist as a body of official persons? They are bound to preach, in due proportion, all the principles and precepts of Christianity in all their applications—to the public no less than to the private conduct of the people, to the action of government no less than to that of individuals.

Besides, in every free government, and in proportion as it is free, the welfare of the nation demands this enforcement of Christianity upon the people at large. In other governments it may be enough for the rulers to understand and feel the obligations Christianity imposes upon them as rulers; the popular teachings of the pulpit may be safely enough limited to instructions in piety and private morals. But where democratic institutions and universal suffrage prevail, the people are the rulers. They have political rights; and it is all-important they should understand and feel that these rights are at the same time sacred duties, for the virtuous and faithful discharge of which they are responsible to their country and their God. The supreme power is in their hands, and it is infinitely important they should have a profound practical conviction that the destiny of the nation depends on the way they exercise that power. A sovereign people may be the worst of all sovereigns. History has put on record at least one demonstration of this truth, never through all time to be effaced. It is so trite a saying, that one is almost ashamed to repeat it—but it is so trite because it is so true—that the success of a popular government depends on the intelligence and virtue of the people. Coleridge would perhaps have tried to give emphatic point to it, by adding that it must be a virtuous intelligence and an intelligent virtue. But a mere unreflecting admission of this truth, in a bare theoretical way, is of no use. There are great moral lessons of political right and righteousness, which must be practically learned by the people, to be any effectual guaranty for the happiness of society, the success, safety, or permanent continuance of a free government.

It is infinitely important, therefore, in our country, that the whole people should be instructed and enlightened in all that regards the just exercise of their political rights. It is infinitely important that the sacred duties, and the immense responsibilities, inseparable from the possession of those rights, should be taught and practically enforced, from the highest moral and Christian point of view.

Now how are the people to get this instruction ?

It will not do to leave them to political demagogues. Where the people are the sovereign, demagogues will be the courtiers, and like all courtiers, will flatter and cajole, in order to lead and control. They will never preach to the people the limitations which moral duty imposes upon their sovereignty. Like Richelieu they will make the sovereign absolute—and with the same end in view.

Nor will it do to leave the people to the influence of the popular press. The Press—that which especially so calls itself—is mostly a party press ; but whether so or not, it never has so pressed, and never will so press upon the people, the high motives of Christian obligation which ought to govern them in the exercise of their political· rights and duties, as to leave nothing needful and important for the pulpit to do in this respect.

We do not mean in any sweeping way to disparage or undervalue the press. It may always be relied upon to expose and denounce political fraud and corruption in the conduct of the party it opposes. It has also, irrespective of party relations, often lifted up its voice against public injustice, wrong and crime, in such a right honest, earnest, true moral and Christian way, as to shame the silence or feeble voice of the pulpit.

But it too often happens that the press is not on the side of moral right. It too often goes for the wrong, excusing or defending it, concealing or denying the truth and facts of the case, or perverting and distorting them—covering up the real issues and making false ones—corrupting or perplexing the moral sense by special pleadings, and so deluding and misleading the people. But apart from any such direct and positive corrupting influence, the press is too apt to preach to the people of their rights, without a corresponding enforcement of the duties that go ever inseparably with them, and thus to nurse the people in an exaggerated sense of rights and a feeble sense of duties— than which nothing can in the long run be more pernicious and dangerous.

But it is needless to urge this point further. It is enough to say that if the press contributed a great deal more than it does to the right moral guidance of the people, the duty of the Christian clergy in the matter would not on that account be diminished ; while on the other hand, the undeniably defective and often pernicious influence of the press, renders the faithful discharge of their duty all the more important.

And so there can be but one answer to the question, where should we look first and mainly for the people to get that instruction and admonition in political righteousness, which it is indispensably necessary they should have, in order to the safe working of democratic institutions. It is to the pulpit, whose very function it is to enforce morality, the morality of the Christian religion—the highest and purest morality—in all its length and breadth and strictness.

Besides, the opinion which would prohibit the pulpit from applying the principles and precepts of Christianity to politics, goes to the entire separation of the political life of a nation from its moral and religious life—in any nation, that is, where the supreme power is in the body of the people—and the unity of a nation's life cannot, any more than that of an individual person, be thus divided without harm. This is not saying that civil governments have their foundation, or their origin, in the

principles of religion or morals.   We hold no such
doctrine.   We might admit even what Macaulay
says, that " there is no sense in which religion can
be said to be the basis of government, in which it
is not also the basis of the practices of eating,
drinking, and lighting fires in cold weather."   This
may be quite true.   The inconveniences of anarchy,
and the necessity of social order, may be a sufficient basis for government and for the maintenance
of jural relations, quite distinct from the principles
of religion, or even of morals.   But what then ?
Would it follow that the action of government—
and in a democratic government, the political conduct of the people—should not be regulated and
controlled by religious or moral principles, in order
to secure the very ends of expediency and advantage for which governments exist ?   Not at all.
The practices of eating, drinking, and lighting fires
in cold weather—and a thousand other practices,
alike morally indifferent in themselves—must be
thus regulated and controlled, or the gravest mis-
chiefs will ensue.   Divide the unity of our national life ; cut off its politics from the permeating
and actuating power of a pure moral and religious
spirit ; and what is the consequence ?   It is just a
surrendering of the political life of the nation to

the Evil One ; and everybody knows what we mean, whether they believe in the existence of that personage or not.

Besides, in such a case, there cannot be, or will not long be, any true religious and moral life in the nation. To give up one-half of a nation's practical life to the Devil, and yet save the other half to God, is a problem of impossible accomplishment. The upshot of the attempt to serve God and Mammon is that Mammon becomes the only God that is served : the service of the True God becomes inevitably an hypocrisy and a sham.

And as to morals—there is nothing history more undeniably demonstrates, than that public corruption, in a country like ours, sooner or later, eats out the very heart of the private morals of a nation. How long will truth and honor, virtue and justice, prevail in the private relations of a people politically unprincipled, corrupt and vicious ? There may always be righteous men—more or fewer —even in Sodom ; but no pure moral law can long be the actuating principle of the private life of the great masses, who profligately disregard the principles of morality in their political conduct. A certain amount of thieves' law there may be—and must be, in order to hold society together—but no pure

16*

moral law in the heart of the nation. And a fine
spectacle of a people is that whose highest moral
spirit finds its expression in policemen and other
machineries for keeping rogues from damaging each
other in a certain number of too severely inconvenient ways !

So much in a general way. Let us now consider certain special objections.

And first, it is asked : what is this mingling of
religion and politics in the pulpit—this concession
to the clergy of the politico-ethical instruction of
the people—what is it but the union of Church
and State, which all history proves to be so pernicious and dangerous ?

Great is cant ! Wonderful is cant ! whether
infidel or pious !

There is, doubtless, such a thing as the union
of Church and State. And it is, or may be, a very
bad thing. In a monarchic, or oligarchic absolutism, where the State takes the Church into pay,
gives it powers and controls the exercise of them,
there Christianity may be corrupted into a tool of
despotism for the enslaving of the people. So, too,
in a government where the political power is vested
in the Church, or controlled by the Church, there

will be a theocratic or sacerdotal absolutism—as dangerous as any, and possibly more pernicious than any other sort of absolutism. In either of these cases there is room for talking of the union of Church and State.

But in the name of all that is sensible and to the purpose, what room is there for talking about Church and State, in a country where the Church is neither controlled by the State, nor possesses any of the powers of the State, nor any other power, except that of preaching—which it enjoys in common with the press, with political orators, with stump-speakers, lecturers, and all other public talkers? Would you take from the clergy the right of free speech, and leave it to all other public talkers? Why? May they not be as safely trusted as the other talkers? What power have they but to talk to such as choose to listen? They can compel nobody to listen. They can compel nobody to believe what they say, or to act as they say. They may convince and persuade such as choose to be convinced and persuaded. What then?

"Why, priestcraft." Cant again—and without a grain of truth besides. It is not priestcraft; it is nothing but influence—the legitimate influence of free public talk. It is speechcraft, if you

please ; and by what right would you repress the
speechcraft of the pulpit any more than that of the
press, the rostrum, the stump, or any other form
of free public speech ?   Is it an influence to be
dreaded any more than that of the other forms of
free speech ?   The clergy have no political offices,
honors or emoluments to gain, as most other public
talkers have.   It is utterly absurd, in a country
like this, to imagine any combination among them,
as a caste or order, to gain political power, or to
wield a corrupt influence, dangerous to the liberties
and welfare of the people.   It is possible error may,
in some individual instances, be preached—honestly
or corruptly ; but that is no reason for repressing
the free speech of the pulpit, any more than that of
the press, the rostrum, or the stump.   But on the
whole, if there is any class of men in the country,
likely to be disinterested preachers of salutary political truth and righteousness, it is the Christian
clergy.   The fair presumption is that standing in
the pulpit, with the responsibility of God's ministers upon them, they will honestly and rightly apply and enforce the obligations of patriotism, justice and love which Christianity imposes upon men's
conduct as citizens ; and there is not a decently
intelligent, honest and honorable infidel on the

globe, but will admit that so far as a people can be influenced to exercise their rights as citizens, under a true religious and Christian sense of those obligations, it is the best security in the world for the safe and happy working of democratic institutions.

Away then with this cant and nonsense about sacerdotal power in a country like this !

It is. time, indeed, that the mass of ignorant prejudices on the whole subject, in relation to the past, as well as to the present, should be exploded —that the whole people should learn what the learned already know well enough : that after all that is said and all that is true about priestly pandering to tyrannical power, there is another side of the story, and it still remains true, that the cause of freedom, human rights and true progress, owes more to the Christian clergy, all through the ages, than to any other single class.

In the first ages they alone proclaimed the equal rights of all—denounced the sin of holding the members of Christ's Body in bondage—preached manumission as the most sacred duty of charity— sold the holy vessels of the churches to redeem the bondman from his chains, and incited the rich to a like sacrifice of wealth.   During the stormy period of the Barbarian invasions, they were the pow·

erful and only protectors of the poor against the rude conquerors, who came seizing both the soil and its tillers as their property.—In the Feudal ages, they alone proclaimed the equality and equal rights of men, and opened, in the bosom of the Church, a career for the talents and abilities of the lowliest born. The monasteries were Christian democracies, and though subsequently corrupted, yet for several centuries, in spite of the faults necessarily incident to such institutions, they conferred immense benefits upon civilization—as places of hospitality to the poor, of refuge for the weak against the strong, around which flourished a rich agriculture, and within which were preserved all the light and knowledge that were preserved amidst the darkness of those rude and violent times.—At a later day the clergy began and carried forward the Reformation—translated the Bible for the people— combated the Papal power—and died at the stake for the cause of spiritual freedom. And from that day to this, throughout all Protestant Christendom, the cause of good learning and popular education has owed to them—we will not say more than to all other classes together, but undeniably more to them than to any other single class.—And in all time to come, we may be sure of this : that no democracy will be reasonable, safe or endurable, except a Christian democracy ; and for that there must be a free Christian ministry. " Without the priesthood," says one of the most sharp thinking and strong speaking writers of the day, " there can be no freedom for the people. . . . Statesmen, who would keep the people fettered, find it necessary to keep the priesthood fettered also."* In democratic governments profligate politicians (and none but such) have an interest to fetter the freedom of the pulpit ; and as they cannot do it by political or legal power (like the statesmen in despotic governments) they seek to do it by appealing to vulgar passion and prejudice, and stirring up popular odium ; and if the tyranny of false opinion is not enough, mobs and tar and feathers, or other less mild persuasives, are the not unfrequent resort.

But to turn to objections which take more the form of pious concern for religion, and the just influence of its ministers.

There is one we notice first, because it purports to go against the principle on which we rest the justification of " political preaching," so far as we have undertaken to justify it. The objection is

---

* Alton Locke, p. 362.

*that the principle goes too far, includes too much ; since, on the ground of it, " ministers must concern themselves, as ministers, in all the arts and employments of life, for there is nothing pertaining to humanity that has not more or less of a religious bearing."**

These terms are not an exact expression of the principle in question. It is not merely as having " more or less of a *religious* bearing," that we go for the right and duty of the preacher to preach about certain political matters. Our principle is a practical one, and one of degree, relating to questions of right and wrong, affecting the character and destiny of the nation ; and it is not true that " all the arts and employments of life " come equally or fairly within its application. But no matter. Suppose they do : what then ? No matter how far the principle goes—that is no valid objection to it, unless it goes to include the allowance of something confessedly objectionable. If a minister cannot rightly instruct his flock in their duties without " concerning himself, as a minister, in all the arts and employments of life "—why, then, in heaven's name, let him " concern himself" with them. That is what he is for. If he has a

---

* Church Review, Oct., 1856.

congregation of swill-milk vendors, or cat-meat sausage makers, and cannot make them comprehend the enormity of their traffic without going into a pulpit discussion of the whole science of milk, or meat, let him go into it. So with stock gambling, and the " tricks of trade," its immoral maxims and sharp practices—why should the preacher hesitate to go into a special exposition of those " arts and employments of life," if it be necessary in order to awaken the consciences of thriving and " respectable " Christians addicted to them, or to warn and caution others ? And in fine, as to all the " arts and employments of life," however honest and honorable, what possible good reason can there be why the Christian preacher should not, in due proportion, specially " concern himself " with them, if thereby he can best strengthen his flock to resist the temptations, or to discharge the duties specially pertaining to them ?

The principle we go upon is not then unsound. It does not go to justify any thing wrong or unfit. It does not, therefore, go too far.

But, they tell us, *the Founder of Christianity has clearly marked the separation between the spiritual and the temporal order, and the peculiar*

*province of His ministers, by His saying : " My
kingdom is not of this world."*

Rightly understood it is a weighty truth this
saying declares. But what has it to do with the
question in hand? Though not of the world,
Christ's kingdom is in the world, is set up precisely
to overthrow the kingdom of Evil in the world, to
make all the kingdoms of the earth the kingdoms
of God ; and a grand and solemn struggle between
the kingdom of God and the kingdom of Evil, is
the inmost sense of the world's whole history. The
Founder Himself of this kingdom has bid us pray
for its coming on the earth. To promote its triumph here is eminently the function of His ministers. A nice way of making it come, to surrender
one-half the world's life to the dominion of politicians and the devil ! Political sins, wrongs, crimes
—that is, sins perpetrated in the political sphere—
are as much spiritual evils, and therefore fall as
much within the province of the pulpit, as any
other sins, wrongs and crimes. They belong to the
kingdom of Evil, which the Christian preacher is
to combat and subdue.

*"Ah, but the weapons of his warfare are not
carnal but spiritual !"*

The soft ineptitude and irrelevancy of this pious platitude would be simply amusing, if it were not vexatious to think there are human beings, with brains in their heads, so foolish as to utter it, and other human beings so foolish as to look upon it as a respectable utterance, and so to make an answer needful.—Let us try then to answer them, " not according to their folly," though it may be logic thrown away.

Is it, then, O inept and irrelevant friends, a question about the sort of weapons, or about the use of them ? Granted that the Christian preacher's weapons are not the bowie-knife, revolver, Sharpe's rifle, howitzer, or any other form of " carnal weapons," but only " the sword of the Spirit, which is the Word of God,"—yet is not the question between us precisely this : what is he to strike at with that sword ? Is he to strike only at private and not at public sins ? Is he to hit away sharply at dancing, card playing, theatre and opera going, the Sunday fresh air recreations of poor artisans and their children, pent up all the week in unwholesome places—and never to aim a single stroke at political corruption, fraud, crime, oppression, cruelty ? To our poor notion, the preacher who, in a crisis of great national wickedness, when judgment and mercy are crushed beneath the iron foot of power, does not rush to the rescue with strong arm and clear ringing shout for " God and the Right," must be either too foolish a person to be trusted with the sword of the Spirit, or else a recreant coward or traitor to his Lord.

Or do you (perhaps) mean by " spiritual weapons," preaching against such sins as Sabbath-breaking and the like, and by " carnal weapons," preaching against political sins—that the same sword of the Spirit, the same word of God, when directed against " worldly amusements," for instance, is a " spiritual weapon," but when directed against political rascalities, national crimes, and the wickedness of the people who choose or sustain the public men that perpetrate such things, is a "carnal weapon ? " If this be your idea, then, O sharp and clear-seeing friends, the distinction is too fine for us to see it. We can talk no further with you.

But Christ has bid us " render unto Cæsar the things that are Cæsar's, and unto God the things that are God's."

Yes, and godly bishops of Christ's Church, when warning their clergy against " preaching politics," quote this text. There is not, perhaps, in

the whole Bible, a text that has been so excessively
ill-used. Our Lord evaded a direct answer to a
malicious ensnaring question ; and because the
question happened to have a political bearing,
therefore his ministers are never to open their
mouths to preach on any political subject—exhort,
rebuke, plead, warn, though humanity lies bleeding, and justice and mercy are perishing in the
streets, and every impulse of love to God and love
to man prompts them to lift up their voice ! A
precious and noble specimen of logic and of feeling,
of head and of heart !

Nor less remarkable is the perversion of our
Lord's language. The meaning lying on the face
of it is as clear as the sun. It embodies the simplest axiom of universal morals, old as the ages :
suum cuique ; yet it has been a thousand times
quoted to prove what it does not come within a
thousand miles of touching. Because our Lord
said Cæsar is to have his own things and God His
own things, does that prove that politics and religion are to be kept entirely separate—that politics
belong exclusively to Cæsar; and neither God nor
His ministers have a right to say a word about
them ? That is a long logical leap ! We need
not wonder that those who take it can jump fur-

ther still, and make the saying mean that Cæsar's
things are Cæsar's, and God's things are Cæsar's
too, if Cæsar choose to put his stamp upon them—
at least, that God's ministers, in such a case, must
not say they are not.

But to us it seems that there is a great deal in
politics which belongs to God, and if not rendered
to Him will be rendered to something worse than
Cæsar.   Political righteousness—justice, mercy and
truth in the administration of public affairs, are
God's things.   In a country like this, it is one of
the things above all others to be rendered to God,
that the people (who have the power) should put
into and sustain in office only such men as will rule
righteously.   And it is the sacred duty of the
Christian preacher to warn the people perpetually
that if they do otherwise, disaster and evil will
come upon them sooner or later—through the inevitable operation of the laws that govern human
history, and under which historical causes work out
the destiny of nations.

*But St. Paul said he "determined to know
nothing but Jesus Christ and Him crucified," and
he is the model for the Christian minister.*

To be sure St. Paul did say so : look at the

place, and you will see he was set against recognizing any of those sectarian divisions that had sprung up among the Christians to whom he was writing. This is what he meant. If he had intended to say, in literal strictness, that he preached about nothing but the crucifixion of Christ, even in the largest view of that subject taken by the objectors, he would have told an untruth. For he did preach about a hundred other things—special points of morals, order and decorum, the dress and behavior of men and women, financial and economical regulations, not forgetting also points of civil and political obligation. And in fine, if he had conducted according to the notion of those who quote him, he would have preached Christ without a Christianity. So much for St. Paul's testimony against political preaching.

But it is urged that *the doctrine we lay down, by giving allowance to preaching on questions that may be in issue between political parties, goes to convert the pulpit into a political arena, and the clergy into political partisans.*

We deny this. Our doctrine forbids the minister of religion to bring into the pulpit any political questions, except such as involve the sacred obligations of Christian duty; and it requires him to treat all such questions not as a politician, but as God's minister—setting forth God's undeniable truth on the matter, regardless whether it tell for or against this party or that party. If he does any thing else than this, he does something out of our rubric ; we are not responsible for him. If he does only what our doctrine allows and enjoins, and does it in a right honest, earnest, religious, and true Christian way—as he may do and should do—he just does what is right, fitting, and his duty to do ; and it is a falsehood and an abuse of language to call him a political partisan, merely because the matter he speaks of may be in issue between conflicting parties. He may be called so, by those who know better, because the truth is distasteful or inconvenient. That is no reason for not doing his duty. He may perhaps be honestly mistaken for one, because he may, in the discharge of his duty, be obliged to take sides, or to seem to take sides, between the conflicting parties. That is something that cannot be helped. Time may correct the misconception ; most likely it will, in the long run, give him a chance to prove his impartial fidelity to God's truth, as against all parties. But if otherwise, it is not his fault, but the fault of the facts of the case.

All he has to see to is to take the right side, to go for what is right and against what is wrong in the sight of the Most High.

But it may be said, *the preacher is liable to mistake the right side—blessing what God hath not blessed, and cursing what God hath not cursed.*

This is possible. But there is an end of all preaching of every sort, if you insist on having none but infallible preachers.

But the question of moral right and duty, it is suggested, may be far from clear : honest men may differ in opinion about it.

That is possible too. But would you have no preaching on any subject until all doubt is removed, and all honest men see alike ? Rather, on the contrary, the more reason for discussing any great question of right and wrong, if it be one about which honest men really differ. In all other matters this is held to be the best way to clear up doubt, and bring honest men to be of one mind.

But we are bid consider *what a conflict of ora-cles we inaugurate—pulpit against pulpit—preacher against preacher, one banning, another blessing, and both in the name of the Lord.*

17

Well, that is possible ; but it is a liability that must be accepted as incident to all progress of truth. The minister of religion has nothing for it but to stand up for the cause of righteousness, as he in his best conscience understands it. Better earnest controversy out of love for the right cause, than dead silence when the interests of eternal justice are at stake.

But we are told *the clergy themselves will be in constant danger of falling under the influence of party spirit and preaching as mere political partisans.*
Granted the possibility again : but they are not to turn aside from the path of duty because of temptations in it. They must resist the temptation. That is all. There is grace enough for every body to overcome temptation in the path of duty.

But this sort of preaching, it is rejoined, *tends to foment party animosity and strife among the people, to excite ill-will to the minister, to impair his influence, and imperil his position.*
To this we have only to reply, that if the minister of religion preaches only God's truth and in the right way (and if he does not, he is not the

man we are defending), such results, if they occur, are not any legitimate tendency of his preaching; and he is not responsible for any tendency in men —whether bad men or good men—to pervert what is good. The worst evils come from abuse of the best things. Christ himself said the Gospel of Peace would be a sword and a strife. At the same time, it is true to say that the legitimate tendency of the preaching we uphold is to allay party spirit, to lead men to act in politics, as in other things, from a conscientious regard to duty and right; and it is no more than a proper homage to truth and to God's ordination of things, to hope and to believe that it will, in the long run and in the large view, have its proper influence, rather than become the occasion of evil through perversion. But whether so or not, we are quite sure it makes no difference as to the Christian preacher's duty. He is God's minister, the prophet of God's truth; and not the mere stipendiary agent of the people, employed to conduct the ceremonial of public worship, with allowance to say in the pulpit only such things as suit the public taste. Those good people who are so bitter against what they call "preaching politics," may well be reminded of a text some of them are very fond of quoting in reference to the faithful preaching of doctrines, not agreeable to " the carnal heart," (as they phrase it,) namely, that the minister must "not shun to declare the whole counsel of God, whether men will hear, or whether they will forbear." Whether this text applies to the great *quinquaticular* "doctrines of grace" or not, we are very clear it rightfully applies to the duty of enforcing the principles of Christian morals, and testifying against public wickedness and crime ; and if the Gospel preacher does this in a right earnest, loving, true Christian way, he need not disturb himself about the consequences, least of all, consequences personal to himself—ill-will, loss of place, or whatever else. It is God's affair to take order about those things.

But why not let the minister limit himself to inculcating the principles and precepts of Christianity in a general way, without going into particular applications of them to the public questions of the day, about which men and parties are divided ?

To which question we reply by another : why should he do this ?

It is a crisis, we will say—a question of the triumph of right or wrong, of public righteousness, or public crime, of individual virtue or guilt, and of

national glory and welfare or disgrace and retribu-
tion. That is the hypothesis. We have a right
to make it. Let this be noted. It is the ground
we take stand upon.

Now in such a crisis, why should the Christian
preacher limit himself to such generalities of Christian inculcation? Is there any good reason for it?
For, otherwise, one would say every thing right-
headed and right-hearted in him, every respectable
impulse of human nature, would bid him lift up
his voice with most unmistakable specialty of application, and pour the red-hot God's word point-
blank at the thing he meant to hit.

Why, then, should he content himself with
firing off great vollies of soft generalities, aimed
nowhere in particular?

Is it to avoid the risk of occasioning increased
dissension, or of incurring odium and loss of influence, and the like? This is mostly what is urged.

We have already disposed of this. But we
have now further to say that such a proceeding is
as foolish as it is unworthy of God's prophet. The
people will either see and feel the special application and force of the general inculcation, or they
will not. If they do, nothing or next to nothing
of the advantage looked for will be gained; the ex-

citement and offence is likely to be quite as great.
If they do not, the preaching does no good, certainly not the intended good ; and can a more mean
and contemptible spectacle be presented to the imagination than God's prophet, in such a crisis,
preaching generalities so general that the people
cannot see and feel their point and force—cannot
see what he is driving at.   But whatever may be
thought of him, his trumpet must either blow a
blast of generalities too soft to arouse the slumber-
ers to any definite comprehension of his purpose,
and so be without effect, or else will be quite as
likely to cause angry disturbance in the camp, as
the most clear and piercing notes of alarm.

*But why then meddle at all with such subjects ?
Why not let them altogether alone ?   He will thus
avoid odium, preserve his official influence with men
of all parties, and thus be better able to save their
souls—which is his great business and proper work.*
This is very specious.   It has a soft unction of
piety about it.   But O soft-hearted friends, who
talk thus, let us understand one another about this
" saving of souls."   For we, for our part, think
there is scarcely any thing about which so much,
and such pernicious cant and falsehood **has been**

said and sung, as about this same matter of saving the soul.

What, then, do you mean by saving the soul? Is it merely to escape a certain hot intolerable place when one dies, and to get into comfortable quarters in the other world? This, we fear, is pretty nearly all that a great many understand by saving the soul.

We will not stop now to suggest what a mean conception of the chief end of a rational creature this is; nor further, that he who makes the saving of his soul his supreme end, will be sure to lose it; nor, in fine, that, in a right just view, the soul is well saved only so far as it thinks more of doing its duty than of any thing it is to get in the way of payment, either in this world or in the world to come—all which things are perhaps dark to you, O friends, who would have the minister let political topics alone, and stick to preaching the Gospel and saving souls.

But this much we must insist upon: that the soul needs saving in this world, in order to get well-saved in the world to come, and that this needful salvation consists in something more than orthodox notions or devotional fervors—in truth, honesty and fair dealing, for instance. " Clear views of the

vital truths of the Gospel," and "sweet communion with God "—as some phrase it—are not all that
is needful.   Think of it : what sort of a saved soul
is he who has "clear views of vital truth," and
believes that "all is fair in horse trade"—holds
"sweet communion with his Maker," and delights
to come over a "knowing one," or to take a "green-
horn" in ;—is regular at family prayers, and cheats
in weights and measures in his trade ;—carries
round the plate at church, and swears falsely at the
Custom House ?

But consider, O friends, is he a better saved
soul, however orthodox in the faith and devout in
prayers, who believes that "all is fair in politics "
—cheats at elections, stuffs ballot-boxes, and swears
to false returns, or *connives at such things, by supporting the men that do them ?*   Such a soul, it
seems to our poor judgment, cannot in any way be
well-saved, either for this world or the next, until
it leaves off such practices.   Will subscribing to
the Tract Society atone for subscribing to a corruption fund ?   Will sending the Gospel to the heathen
be taken as an offset to sending armed ruffians to
take possession of the polls, and keep honest voters
from their right ?

It seems to us the Gospel preacher should speak

plainly to his people about such things.   They may
be angry with him.   So a congregation of swill-
milk dealers, or cat-meat sausage makers, would
most likely be angry at hearing their traffic denounced ; but should the Christian preacher on
that account keep a hushed silence about their
callings, and work away at saving their souls ?
Why, he knows that God Himself cannot possibly
save them unless they quit the swill-milk traffic
or the cat-meat sausage line.   Is it not altogether
best for him plainly to tell them so ?

In like sort it seems to us utterly absurd for the
Christian preacher to keep silence about political
sins, in order the better to save the souls of political sinners.   And wrong, too : it ministers to a
terrible delusion.   He is bound to warn them that
unless they leave off practising, or supporting the
practice of political wickedness, neither God, nor
any thing else in the universe, can possibly save their
souls.

Besides, saved souls are needed in this world—
rightly saved souls, who make the precepts of the
Gospel the rule of their conduct in all the relations
of life—political as well as social—who love their
duty so well that they do not stop to think of payment in another world, in order to find a motive for
17*

doing it in this. God has many present uses for such souls besides going to church and sacrament, praying in their families and in their closets, subscribing to the Tract Society, and the like ; among which uses we reckon eminently the standing up for truth and righteousness against fraud and corruption, for justice and mercy against oppression and wrong in public conduct. And so, even supposing a man, who is recreant to Christian principles, may be a good enough Christian to escape uncomfortable quarters in another world, he will still be a very poor sort of Christian for some of the most important uses God has for Christians in this world.

In fine, therefore, we do not see but the Christian preacher, in order to " save souls " to any good purpose, either for this world or for the next must in due season and proportion, concern himself more or less directly with political matters, cannot let them altogether alone.

But, it is still insisted, that if *the minister preaches the Gospel, wins souls to Christ, makes men good Christians, there is no need of political preaching ; get the heart right and you have the sure cure for all political and social evils.*

These are very respectable platitudes of phrase ; there would not be a word to say against them, if they were not used to beg the question. They imply the assumption that in a free country, where the people have political powers, rights, duties— where there are political temptations, sins, evils— you *can* preach the Gospel, *can* win souls to Christ, *can* make men good Christians, without meddling in any special way with political subjects. Which is precisely what we deny. Besides, where does the principle go ? It precludes all other special preaching—makes it needless, if not improper, to preach particularly about any of the special temptations, sins, wrong practices, and evil customs of society ; and would make great placards of Christian generalities pasted on the walls of churches, or in other public places, answer all the ends of the Christian pulpit—at a great saving of expense !

But not to urge this—remember that to get the heart right, you must get at it. How are you going to get at it, if it is environed and entrenched in habits and customs, maxims and practices which • it does not see or feel to be wrong ? Even to reach the citadel, there are sometimes outworks which must first be carried.

But whether so or not, there is a great deal of

political preaching, or of the proper substance of it, that must in some way be got into men's hearts in this country, before their hearts can be got entirely right, before you can make thoroughly good Christians of them. "Converting the heart," in the sense our obscurantist friends use the phrase, is not always of itself enough to make men good citizens. Our "converted" brethren are not, in point of fact, remarkably better models of political holiness, than other men. Our churches are full of "converted" men, who seem utterly unconscious of the wickedness of political fraud and corruption, unconscious of the sin of upholding it, and of the enormities of public crime, of which they are the actual upholders. Such men need a great deal more conversion before they can become really good citizens, or thoroughly good Christians.

Men may be very good Christians in the main, and yet very bad Christians in particular points. Good old John Newton, at one time of his life, on the coast of Africa, used to devote eight hours a day to sleep and meals, eight to reading the Bible and praying, and eight to fettering and stowing away poor negroes, captured in bloody wars excited by barrels of rum, paid by him to barbarous chiefs, —and never then, nor for some time after, felt any

contradiction between his prayers and his trade !
To some men Christianity is like a dark lantern ;
it does not illuminate at once the whole sphere of
their conscience : you must sometimes turn its
flashing light right upon the object you would
make them see.

Besides : if ever so much "won to Christ,"
ever so well "converted," men need to be kept
from falling away—to be watched and strengthened
by perpetual reiteration of instruction and warning, as special as the ever-recurring temptations to
which they are exposed ; wherein lies one great
function of the Christian preacher.

And so we conclude the Gospel cannot, in this
country at least, be rightly preached, souls truly
won to Christ, and men made really good Christians, so as to accomplish the objects proposed by
our objectors, namely, to make men good citizens,
and so to put an end to political sins and evils—
without a certain amount of duly-timed and judicious, in one word, good "political preaching."
We beg it may be sharply noted that we go only
for that which is good ; for however earnestly we
defend the principle of political preaching, as a
matter of right and of duty, yet we are as little in
favor of foolish political as of any other foolish
preaching.

But enough for objections. There is not one but is worthless or insufficient.

We conclude by directing again a single moment's more particular attention to the doctrine that would exclude from the pulpit all questions that may be in issue between conflicting parties ; for it is with reference to this point that the objections to political preaching have the greatest show of reason and force.

Consider then the consequences of the doctrine. Where does it go ? It goes in principle to shut the mouths of the clergy on any, and so by consequence on every question of Christian morals, no matter how great or sacred. No matter what wicked ends are sought, nor by what wicked means, God's ministers must not say a word, if profligate politicians have made party questions of them. The African Slave Trade and Polygamy are as yet crimes in law as well as in morals, and no political party has taken them under patronage ; it is admitted that they may therefore be now denounced in the pulpit. But let the legalization of these practices be attempted by any party, (and it would not be strange if the former measure should at no distant day be forced into issue,) and the voice of the pulpit must be hushed. We should then have

Bishops charging their clergy to render to Cæsar the things that are Cæsar's, and to let political subjects alone !

But the mere theoretical reach of the principle apart, what is the necessary influence, on the popular mind, of putting into vogue this notion that nothing must be said in the pulpit that touches on the conduct of political parties ? It goes to imbue the great mass of the people with a feeling that politics is entitled to a certain immunity and exemption from moral criticism and moral responsibility—that crime ceases to be criminal, atrocities are no longer atrocious, if perpetrated in the interest of political parties. In short, the putting this notion into vogue is just one of the cunningest of all possible contrivances, to sell out and surrender the conscience of the nation to politicians and to the Devil. It has done more than almost any thing else to weaken and pervert the moral sense of the nation. The deteriorating process has been going on with prodigious rapidity within the last few years. One is astonished to look back over recent political conflicts, and observe the callous insensibility to moral considerations, the utter indifference to corruption, fraud, wrong, cruelty, and crime displayed by millions of the people—millions who think themselves, and are looked upon by others, as highly respectable, moral, and religious. This demoralization is likely to go on with increasing rapidity, unless some stronger influences can be brought to check its progress.

This is the reason we have taken the subject up. It is infinitely important to the salvation of the nation that the pulpit should be free, that its voice should be heard—one great strong voice—against all public wickedness. If the clergy would unitedly speak out, continually enforcing upon the great mass of the people the tremendous responsibility that rests upon them, more than upon any other people on the globe, for the character of the government and the destiny of the nation, they might have an immense influence for good. If they do not thus speak out, we are not sure but they will have to give way to something better, or to something worse.

APPENDIX.

APPENDIX.

———•◦•———

VIOLENCE AND ABUSE OF SUFFRAGE.

Lest the statements made in several places in the fore-going volume—and particularly on pages 225—229—respecting the corrupt working and demoralizing influence of our political system, should be thought overcharged, and my expressions too unmeasured, I subjoin some extracts from the New York Times. They are merely specimens. I could fill a volume with undeniable facts of a similar kind, occurring in other parts of the country, especially in New York and other great cities.

As the information may be needful for readers in other countries, I may mention that the distinctive object of the so-called " American " party, is the exclusion of all except native-born Americans from the exercise of suffrage, and from the holding of public office. Also : that none but " naturalized " foreigners have the legal right of voting.

This is the party in whose interest foreigners—and some of them unnaturalized—were captured, and caged, and beaten, and drugged, and driven to the polls by armed brutes and ruffians, as may be seen below! A spectacle not only of unblushing disregard of all moral principles, but also of their own fundamental and proclaimed political principles!

A Baltimore correspondent of the New York *Times*, Jan. 18, 1860, says:

A book, embracing nearly four hundred pages, in the form of testimony legally rendered and elicited, narrating incidents of fraud, violence, etc., at our recent State election in Baltimore, has just been published. It is designed to be offered to the State General Assembly as evidence, by Reformers contesting their seats in that body, and will tell strongly against Hon. HENRY WINTER DAVIS and Hon. J. MORRISON HARRIS, when called upon to defend the right to their seats in Congress. This is, perhaps, one of the richest productions of the present century. Never was more rascality and political knavery compressed within the same number of pages. It shows the election to have been a monstrous fraud, effected through instrumentalities which should cast a blush upon the cheek of Satan himself. I have never read its like before, and never expect to again. A full insight is given into the mystery of " cooping." These details are in *minutiæ*, and though blistering with shame, are so novel, so foul, so ridiculous withal, so funny, so graphic, that they would make a saint, however digni- fied and solemnized, burst into irresistible laughter. Munchausen sinks into insignificance compared with it. Circumstances are told and sworn to which would make the quills start from the fretful porcupine. After perusing this document, it is easy to account for the sway rowdyism has had in our metropolis.

From the volume above referred to, I give an extract or two, as taken from the *Times:*

ELECTION FRAUDS REDUCED TO A SYSTEM—VOTERS IN DURESS.

The testimony taken in the investigation of the recent election frauds in Baltimore was laid before the Legislature a few days since. It bears directly upon the case of the contested seats of members of the Legislature from Baltimore City, and develops a systematic plan of rascality. We copy from the Baltimore *American:*

TESTIMONY OF PETER FITZPATRICK.

This witness is an unnaturalized Irishman, who had lived 18 months in the city.

Question.—Did you vote at the election on November 2, 1859, and if so, in what ward?

Answer.—I was compelled to vote the American ticket in the Tenth ward.

Question.—How many nights previous to the election did you spend in the Tenth ward?

Answer.—I was cooped there four nights and three days.

Question.—Where and by whom were you cooped?

Answer.—It was between Baltimore and Fayette streets, on Holiday street, to the best of my knowledge, by this here party of "Ras Levy's" and "John English's" crowd; I don't know many of them, but I know a few of them.

Question.—State the circumstances of your being cooped and having voted?

Answer.—They took me on Saturday night before the election, dealt me two blows with a billy on the head and two on the knees, to make me drink liquor; and after they compelled me to drink, they made me take oath on the Holy Evangelists I wouldn't tell any thing I saw down there after they let me out; *then they put me down in a big cellar, and put me through a hole in the wall into the next dwelling*, which was unoccupied on the second story; when I got in there, there were about fifteen in there before me, and from fifteen, up to Wednesday, the number increased, until, to the best of my knowledge, they had about eighty or ninety: and, on Wednesday morning, they took us out six at a time, to vote the American ticket; I told them I wasn't entitled to a vote, and they said if I wouldn't vote I should die; there was a good many others that they served in the same way; knocked them down with billies and slung shots, and took their money and their watches; I am a good Reformer, and if I had not had a wife and two children, *I would rather have died than have voted their American ticket;* as soon as the polls were opened, they were looking out of the windows, and they fired on the Reformers, and after the firing was over, they came up and took us out six at a time to vote; after I had voted, and I was one of the first six that came out, one of them told me to go home—which I did; in the afternoon I was taken sick and had to go to bed, and stayed there until next day; I was wearied, and the kind of stuff they gave us to eat and drink would have sickened a horse; *they brought up liquor by the bucket full, and only gave us half enough to eat.*

A VICTIM OF THE "ROUGHSKINS."

The evidence of J. Justus Ritzmin shows that this witness was also " cooped " and compelled to vote. He testifies :

On Monday morning, about eight or nine o'clock, I was near the sugar-house, where I was at work, and had no work there to do; I therefore went to the State tobacco warehouse, and inquired of a German at work there whether I could get any work; he pointed to a young man in the warehouse, and told me to apply to him; consequently I went to him, and he engaged me to work there at $6 a week for the whole year; I went to work, and at about eleven o'clock he told me that work would be stopped at four o'clock, and that we would go to another warehouse on the Point; after a while he told me to come along with him, and that I might either put on my coat or leave it in the office ; three others and myself got into a boat, went over the dock, and then crossed over Union dock, and so went to the corner of Wilk and Caroline streets; he stood there with us awhile, took me by the arm, and then led me and the two others into a house there to a bar, where we were treated; while I was drinking, another man present in the house said to me, " As soon as the work here is done you can go back to the other warehouse; " after a while our conductor came and led us through the back of the house into a court-yard, and then, apparently through one or two yards, until we came in front of a crowd of men, about five or six, armed with clubs, and guns, and other weapons, standing at a sort of

entrance through the fence or partition between two
houses; immediately I was pushed from behind, and
caught by the arm by one of the crowd, and dragged
through the opening; at the same time another German,
not one who had accompanied us, was pushed through immediately behind me; the conductor and the two others
I saw no more; after we had been got through the opening into the next house, as I have stated, another man
came *and led us into a little dark room, where we were
kept a few minutes;* while we were there, the man with
me began to make a noise, trying to break the planks out,
etc.; immediately thereupon the door opened, and three
or four men appeared, one of whom struck the poor fel-
low on the head with a club, which felled him to the
ground; *a second one raised an axe and struck at him
through the doorway;* seeing the intention of the man, I
pushed the door to, so as to intercept the blow, which
fell upon the door, beat it back against my mouth, and
hurt my lips severely; the party then came in and searched
us thoroughly, taking every thing of any value from us;
I had only a small pocket-knife, which they took; my
companion they made strip, and as he drew off his shoe
his money fell out, a few quarters and some small money;
we were left locked in for a while; *then the captain of
the coop came, opened the door, and led us down stairs
to a small trap-door, which led to the cellar;* we were
put down there, and as we were going down, I in front,
my companion was pushed down violently, and falling
against me, we both tumbled down into the cellar; *here
we found ourselves in a dark hole, full of all sorts of
men, with one solitary candle to give us light; there I
was kept until Tuesday afternoon,* when the captain
came down and selected the oldest of us; I was called by

name, and led up stairs to the second story, and put into a large room, which was also full of persons who were similarly cooped; there I was kept until Wednesday morning, the day of the last election; on Wednesday morning, after nine o'clock, we were brought out by threes and fours, and had tickets put into our hands; *I examined the tickets which were given me, and know they were " American " tickets ;* I recognized them by the names of the candidates, the black stripe down their length, the head of Washington at the top, and the extreme narrowness of the ticket; three others and myself were brought out, and led by the rowdies holding us by the arm, up to the window of the Second Ward polls, and voted; we four then were put into a carriage, and driven around through the town, through streets which I did not know, *to various polls, and we were voted five or six times ;* we were then driven to the Holiday street polls, voted again, and then shut up in the coop there next to the polls, in the cellar; we were then brought up into a room, and ordered by the captain of the coop to change clothes with some seven or eight other cooped individuals, which most of us did, but I retained my own clothes; the captain changed clothes with a German, taking a nice hat and black overcoat, in exchange for his cap and coat, which were of little value; *we were then voted again at these polls*, and then we were led on foot to Baltimore street, where an omnibus awaited us, and we were packed in till it was full, and driven down to the coop-house at the Second ward again; *arrived there we voted again at the Second ward*, and then we were driven around in the omnibus to various polls *and voted some six times*, until we came to a poll the other side of Ensor street, where there was a great crowd, hustling and pushing, screaming, etc., in spite of

18

which we were led up by the arm, by the rowdies, through the crowd and compelled to vote; I was let go for a moment, while the rowdies who had held me joined in the hustling and pushing, and seeing the chance I dodged into the crowd and escaped to my home; *I voted at least, in the various wards, sixteen times, compelled each time to give a different name;* none of the judges said any thing to me, or any of us, that I heard, except one judge at the polls near Ensor street, who asked me how long I had lived in the city; I told him two years; the rowdies behind me said to him, " All right! all right!" and the judge took the ticket without further question; the treatment of some of those in the coop was disgusting and horrible in the extreme; *men were beaten, kicked and stamped in the face with heavy boots;* in the cellar of the Second ward there were about seventy or eighty persons locked up, not allowed to be absent for a moment to satisfy the wants of nature, and in the upper room of which I have spoken, as many more; the three men who were with me voted, each of them, as often as I did.

Question.—Give the names of any of the parties on the tickets which you voted?

Answer.—I read Harris on some of them, and Davis on some of them, and the name of Colson; I do not remember precisely; and Whitney's name was also on them.

Patrick Finnigan testified as follows :

Question.—Where were you taken by the parties who cooped you?

Answer.—I could not say exactly, but it was in the neighborhood of Gay street.

Question.—What did they then do with you?

Answer.—They took me down along Gay street to

the double pump near Odd Fellows' Hall, and there I called out "Watch;" a policeman came, and then they let me go; I went round to the watch-house and told Captain Brashears all about it, and that the parties had pretended to arrest me for a murderer; he told me to come down the next morning and see if I could recognize them and make a charge against them; I then left the watch-house; when I got outside I met two men, one of whom I knew, and they insisted on my going along with them, and took me down to Holliday street, between Fayette and Baltimore streets, put me in a room in "Ras Levy's" house, and kept me there until the morning of election; in two rooms there were about sixty or seventy other persons cooped; *they beat me severely with billies and espantoons*, and I had the marks on my body for some two weeks; on the morning of election, they took me out, right after the firing, *and made me vote;* the man who held me did not want to let me go, but a gentleman came over, and insisted on my being let go, and so I was

Question.—While you were in the coop, did you see John Hinesly there?

Answer.—I did; I saw him there on Saturday night, when I was taken in; I then called to him by name, but he wouldn't say any thing to me, and then they beat me; he went out for a little while, and came back afterwards; I saw him in the coop afterwards; I think it was Tuesday, or it may have been on Monday; there were others cooped besides myself in the room when Hinesly was in there.

The New York TIMES of Jan. 19, 1860, has the following remarks upon the facts of which the foregoing are a sample:

THE BEAUTIES OF BALTIMORE VOTING.

The authorities of Baltimore are now edifying their
fellow-citizens and the world with an inquiry into the circumstances which attended the late election in that city.
The results already attained afford a curious commentary
upon the indignation to which certain of the Baltimore
partisan journals gave way on finding that the independent Press of the country had ventured to question the
propriety, decorum, and civilization, displayed by the Plug-
Uglies, Awl Clubs and other agreeable associations of
Baltimorean sovereigns, upon that occasion. The editor
of the Baltimore *Exchange*, as our readers will remember,
was forced to defend himself from the assaults of some of
these offended depositaries of political power, by a recourse
to the " last argument of Kings," simply and solely because
he had shown manliness in admitting, and good citizen-
ship in denouncing, the outrages perpetrated at the polls
upon unarmed voters. The NEW YORK TIMES was in a
like spirit set upon by some of its contemporaries for
calling attention to the shame and peril of such occur-
rences in a great American city. It now appears that
the system of intimidation by personal violence has become thoroughly organized in the Monumental City; and
that the excesses of Baltimore elections are not to be
treated as mere sporadic cases of popular ebullition. The
Jacobin Clubs of France were not more thoroughly
drilled in the art and mystery of harmonizing public opinion than are the so-called " Americans," of Baltimore.
Several days before the late election, these indefatigable
men were in the field. They scoured the city, as eagerly
bent upon finding " foreigners," as any Dublin oysterman
upon dredging for " natives." Irishmen, Germans, all

who fell in their way, were harpooned, carried off to sub-
terranean cells, locked up, compelled from time to time to
drink great quantities of whiskey—reduced, in short, to a
state of complete submission. When the day of election
came, these captives were paraded openly in the streets,
in custody of a guard with cocked revolvers, marched
from poll to poll, forced to vote five or six times over, re-
turned to their dungeons, beaten again, and finally released
when the great issue had been decided, and the "unbought
voice of freemen" had selected the officers by whom the
laws of an American community were to be administered
and its rights defended. All this took place in a wealthy
city, in open day, under the eyes of an organized City
Government, and in defiance of every functionary known
to the law.

Is it not time for thinking men to ask themselves
whether such things as these are the legitimate results of
popular institutions? We talk about the subjects of
Austrian despotism with a large commiseration; but the
peasant of the Tyrol or Steyermark is at least spared the
degradation of being whipped into outraging the institutions under which he lives. If an irresponsible empire
of sheer physical force is to be established in an American city, it is, at least, worth thinking of whether it would
not be better for all parties concerned that such an empire
should be confided to the most enlightened, instead of the
most brutal classes of the population. A man who is
driven through the streets by an arbitrary master, is
plainly a slave; but a slave who moves at the point of legitimate bayonets is surely more respectable, in his own
eyes, than a slave who is goaded onward by the sharpened
awls of a knot of vulgar desperadoes.

The only parallels which can be found in recent times

for such proceedings as these in Baltimore, must be looked for in some of the recent Parliamentary elections of England and Ireland. There, too, voters were seized in squads, drugged with beer, and driven in carriages, dumb and unresisting, to vote for whomsoever it pleased their captors to nominate. There, too, as in the case of Admiral WALTERS, at Cheltenham, voters suspected of independence were mobbed away from the polls, and the suffrages of freemen secured with the club and the horsewhip. But there is this special feature in the Baltimorean outrages, that they were committed on a great scale, openly, avowedly, with the air of a chronic institution. Nor is this all.

The inquiry which has brought these facts to light is, we believe, an inquiry simply into the legality of the election. It is not, so far as we know, proposed to base upon it any measures for the punishment or repression of these horrible disorders, unless a Metropolitan Police bill, in imitation of our own, may be so considered. But we think there can be no question in the mind of any man as to the necessity for some such action on the part of the Legislature as shall either deprive voting in Baltimore of its present sanguinary incidents—make it, in short, less terrible than actual service in the field against an invading army, or else relieve the poor, helpless, unoffending inhabitants from the duty of voting at all. It appears from the evidence before us, that a waiver of one's constitutional rights last fall did not furnish a peaceable Baltimorean with the least immunity from the horrors and dangers of election day. In vain he stayed at home and left politics to the rowdies and blackguards. The rowdies and blackguards would not permit him to abdicate, and knocked and cuffed, and stabbed and shot him into the repeated exercise of his privileges as a citizen. To those who went through this ordeal, the condition of a free negro, upon one day in the year at least, must seem positively enviable. What a caricature upon "the nature and tendency" of free institutions, might be composed in a sketch of disfranchised, despised Sambo, grinning in his morning lounge, at the spectacle of Anglo-Saxon sovereigns, dragged, battered, bruised, bleeding, in the custody of a gang of armed criminals to deposit their votes

—"Like snow-flakes on the silent sod,"

and thus perform one of those functions which Sambo is taught that nobody but a white man can fulfil with credit!

Baltimore furnishes the world with one more splendid example of the beauties of the "Municipal system." She is overrun by organized bands of ruffians and convicts of the worst kind; her elections are conducted under their auspices; her citizens hold their lives and property at their mercy; her streets are rendered dangerous night and day by their brawls; but to compensate her for these evils, for the conversion of society itself into a curse and a peril, she has her Municipal system intact, and her Mayor and Common Council appoint the police force.

THE END.